For

Bishop Ted Brown
with the blessings of

Bruce J White

March 11, 2010

CATHEDRAL
of
Our Lady of the Angels

by

Msgr. Francis J. Weber

CATHEDRAL
OF OUR LADY OF THE ANGELS

Containing a Message by
His Holiness
Pope John Paul II

Saint Francis Historical Society
Anno Domini 2004

The Archival Center gratefully acknowledges the dedicated interest of Sir Daniel Donohue, Richard Grant and the Dan Murphy Foundation for their generous support to the Archdiocese of Los Angeles in the publication of this book.

Copyright© 2004
The Archival Center
Mission Hills, California
Printed by BookMasters, Inc.
Ashland, Ohio

Jacket Design by Terry Ruscin

Library of Congress Cataloguing-in Publication Data
ISBN No. 0-9678477-6-1

The paper used in this publication meets the minimum requirements of American National Standard for Information Services—Permanence of Paper for Printed Library Materials

Table of Contents

CHAPTER TWELVE

CHAPTER THIRTEEN

APPENDICES

Preface

In ecclesial circles, the word cathedral derives from the Greek term *cathedra,* the chair from which the local bishop exercises his role as teacher, pastor and chief shepherd. In one of his more memorable apostolic constitutions, Pope Paul VI reminded Catholics that the cathedral

> . . . in the majesty of its building is a symbol of the spiritual temple that is built up in souls and is resplendent with the glory of divine grace. As Saint Paul says: 'We are the temple of the living God.' (2 Corinthians 6:16). The cathedral, furthermore, should be regarded as the express image of Christ's visible Church, praying, singing and worshipping on earth. The cathedral should be regarded as the image of Christ's Mystical Body, whose members are joined together in an organism of charity that is sustained by the outpouring of God's gifts[1].

Those conciliar thoughts were expanded by Roger Cardinal Mahony, early in 1995, in his own reflections of what a new cathedral would mean for the city bearing the patronage of Our Lady of the Angels.

> It is my dream and fondest hope that as people first catch a glimpse of our new cathedral they will be drawn and captivated by its beauty and symbolism. Viewing the cathedral from any direction should evoke sure recognition that this is the City of the Angels Catholic cathedral, while subtly luring the viewer by its sense of spiritual strength. As people draw nearer, the size, proportions and external beauty of the cathedral should cast an intangible sense of peacefulness and security upon all who behold it, while continuing to draw them closer–almost irresistibly. Their hearts and souls should experience soothing comfort in the vitality and the wonder of God's House in the midst of the human community. The cathedral should gently but clearly speak to the downtown hubs of government, business and the professional community, serving not only as a geographical point of reference, but truly linking the secular with

---

[1] Paul VI, Apostolic Constitution *Mirificus eventus,* declaring the jubilee of 1966, 7 December 1965: *Acta Apostolicae Sedis* 57 (1965), pp. 948–949.

the sacred: God's handiwork now in vital touch with our human handiwork.[2]

A study made in 1998 for the Center of Applied Research in the Apostolate reveals that the typical Catholic cathedral in the United States was dedicated in 1940 and last renovated in 1986, with seating for 800 people. Upwards of 82 percent of the cathedrals serve as parish churches, typically with more than 2,000 communicants attending Sunday Masses.

Ten percent of the cathedrals were built before 1850, 27 percent between 1851 and 1900, 42 percent between 1901 and 1950 and 21 percent since 1950. Only 43 percent of the cathedrals were originally built as cathedrals, while the rest were erected as parish churches. More than half of them are located in relatively poor inner-city residential or business districts. Typically many Sunday worshippers come from areas outside their parochial boundaries.

Just over half of the cathedrals have a seating capacity between 500 and 1,000; only one sixth can seat fewer than 500 and nearly one-third can comfortably accommodate more than 1,000. Architecturally, about 13 percent are modern; seven percent Spanish or mission style, one percent Byzantine, and 35 percent Classical or Romanesque and 44 percent Gothic or Neo-Gothic. Interestingly, about one sixth of the American cathedrals represent dioceses where there is a co-cathedral. Many of them are in areas with two major cities, such as St. Paul-Minneapolis or Fort Wayne-South Bend.[3]

Though not directed specifically to Our Lady of the Angels, the words of Pope John Paul II on May 30, 1999, while on a visit to the beautiful cathedral dedicated to Cyriacus, can be applied to the Mother Church for the Archdiocese of Los Angeles.

> Viewed from the outside, with this elevated position over the city, it symbolizes well the reassuring presence of the Trinitarian God, who from on high guides and protects the life of human beings. At the same time, the cathedral is a powerful reminder to look upwards, to rise above the routine of daily life and from everything that weighs down earthly values. It is, so to speak, the meeting-point of two movements: the descending

---

[2] Archives of the Archdiocese of Los Angeles (hereinafter referred to as AALA) Roger Cardinal Mahony, "Viewing our New Cathedral from the Outside," November 16, 1995.

[3] "The National Cathedral Profile Summary Report," (Georgetown, 1998). *The Tidings,* March 27, 1998.

movement of God's love for humanity and the ascending movement of the human longing for communion with God, the
source of joy and peace.[4]

This narrative about the background, erection and adornment of the
Cathedral of Our Lady of the Angels is based entirely upon the mountain
of correspondence, directives, internal memos, oral and written interviews, committee reports and newspaper and periodical essays that were
generated and bound into thirty-six loose leaf notebooks and several
boxes between 1997 and 2003 and are now on file in the Cathedral
Archives.
    Some *caveats* are in order about this book on the Cathedral of Our
Lady of the Angels. First of all, this is a narrative about what actually
happened, not what did not occur. For that reason, scant if any attention
is given to architects, contractors, artists or locations that did not make
the cut.
    Finally, while this book is anything but an in-house publication, the
author is grateful that four of those most intimately involved in the erection of the cathedral, Mr. Bill Close, Brother Hilarion O'Connor and Mon-
signors Terrence Fleming and Kevin Kostelnik, took the time to read the
manuscript and offer their suggestions.
    Compilation of this book was enormously assisted by a number of
people, surely too many to mention at this time. A few who loom more
prominently than others are Bill Close, Brother Hilarion O'Connor, O.S.F.
and Louis Stafford. Sister Mary Joanne Wittenburg, S.N.D. patiently
typed the final manuscript and Gladys Posakony read, re-read and cor-
rected the galleys and made copious very useful suggestions.

---

[4] Address by Pope John Paul II on a "Pastoral Visit to Ancona in Italy's Adri-
atic Coast" to celebrate the 1,000[th] anniversary of the archdiocesan cathedral.

Prologue

To My Venerable Brother
Cardinal Roger Michael Mahony
Archbishop of Los Angeles

With affection and joy in our Lord Jesus Christ I send greetings to you and your Auxiliary Bishops, to the Priests, Deacons, Religious and Lay Faithful of the Archdiocese of Los Angeles, and to all gathered for the dedication of the Cathedral of Our Lady of the Angels. Fifteen years ago, in 1987, I stood among you in your former Cathedral of Saint Vibiana. Today, in the year of our Lord 2002, I am with you once more, in the person of my Special Legate, Cardinal James Francis Stafford, President of the Pontifical Council for the Laity, as you dedicate your new Cathedral to Our Lady of the Angels. On this happy occasion, I make my own the words of Saint Paul, with a slight adaptation: "To all the beloved of God in Los Angeles, called to be holy, grace to you and peace from God our Father and the Lord Jesus Christ"

The Apostle reminds us that we are "called to be holy". This in fact is the clarion call of the Church in every age, and especially so at the beginning of the Third Christian Millennium. It is a call that must ring out loud and clear from this Cathedral: for it is here that the People of God will gather around the Altar of Sacrifice in fellowship and prayer to worship the Most Holy Trinity, Father, Son and Holy Spirit; it is here that they will be sustained and strengthened in their lives of faith through the celebration of the Sacraments, most especially the Sacraments of Reconciliation and of the Eucharist; it is here that they will continue to be built, "like living stones, . . . into a spiritual house to be a holy priesthood, to offer spiritual sacrifices acceptable to God through Jesus Christ."

The call to holiness is addressed not just to a select few, but to all. In striving to respond to this call to love God and to do His will, we embark upon "a journey totally sustained by grace, which nonetheless demands an intense spiritual commitment and is no stranger to painful purifications." On this journey, we have no greater Model and Advocate than our Lord's own beloved Mother, the Blessed Virgin Mary, who is specially honored in this Cathedral dedicated to her under the title "Our Lady of the Angels." Just as in heaven the myriad angels in their various orders all come together under the Queenship of one Woman, Mary, so in the "City of Our Lady of the Angels" the myriad peoples with the wonderful variety of their cultures and traditions all come together in the one Body of Christ and gather to praise God in the Mother Church of the Archdiocese

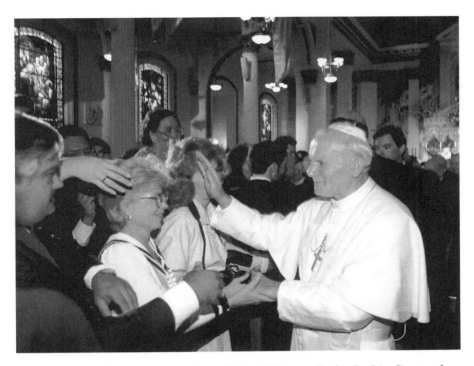

Pope John Paul II greets people at Saint Vibiana Cathedral in September 1987.

of Los Angeles, the Cathedral of Our Lady of the Angels. May this Cathedral always remain an eloquent symbol of communion and fraternity, of mutual respect and understanding; may it be an enduring monument to Christian faith, hope and love, to Christian holiness!

My fervent prayer, then, is that our Lady will be your sure guide, today and always, as you seek to "do what Jesus tells you." May those who enter this house of prayer reflect on Mary's example of holiness and treasure in their hearts the Mystery of Salvation and God's boundless love for all people. To those taking part in the various dedication activities, and to all the faithful of the Archdiocese, I willingly impart my Apostolic Blessing as a pledge of grace and peace in our Lord Jesus Christ.

Castel Gandolfo
August 5, 2002

John Paul II

CHAPTER I

Historical Background

The religious life of a diocese revolves about its chief shepherd and his primary church, the cathedral. Even in the 21st century, with its concentration on the parochial level of Catholic life, the cathedral continues to serve as the "Mother Church" of the faithful in a given ecclesial jurisdiction.[1]

Greatest among the New World's "Mother Churches" is Mexico City's Metropolitan Cathedral, the oldest religious edifice on the North American continent. Interestingly, the facade of its adjoining *sagrario,* begun in 1750, is reproduced over the entrance of the Edward Laurence Doheny Memorial Library at Camarillo, California.[2]

In the papal bull erecting the Diocese of Both Californias in 1840, Pope Gregory XVI directed that "the principal church in the said territory of San Diego be raised and elevated to the honor and dignity of a cathedral church."[3] The honor, then, of being the state's oldest cathedral belongs technically to *San Diego de Alcala* Mission, although there is no evidence that it ever functioned in that capacity.[4]

When Bishop Francisco Garcia Diego y Moreno (1840-1846) fixed his headquarters at Santa Barbara, the old mission there became the first real pro-Cathedral in California.[5] With the changing of the diocesan title in 1849, the episcopal residence was officially transferred to Monterey and the Royal Presidio Chapel served as Bishop Joseph Sadoc Alemany's cathedral.[6] With his removal to San Francisco in 1853, Alemany used old

---

[1] Traditionally the mother-church of an (arch)diocese is so named for the *cathedra* which it houses because that is the seat from which the (arch)bishop preaches.

[2] Francis J. Weber, *A Guide to Saint John's Seminary* (Los Angeles, 1966), p. 20.

[3] See Francis J. Weber, *Francisco Garcia Diego: California's Transition Bishop* (Los Angeles, 1972), p. 35.

[4] Francis J. Weber (Trans and ed), *The Writings of Francisco Garcia Diego y Moreno* (Los Angeles, 1976) p. 12.

[5] Francis J. Weber (comp), *Queen of the Missions. A Documentary History of Santa Barbara* (Los Angeles, 1979) p. 89.

[6] Francis J. Weber (comp), *El Caminito Real. A Documentary History of California's Presidio Chapels* (Hong Kong, 1988) p.100.

Metropolitan Cathedral in Mexico City.

Saint Francis Church temporarily as his pro-cathedral. Within a year after becoming the Metropolitan Archbishop of the new Province of San Francisco, Alemany dedicated the Cathedral of "Saint Mary, Ever Virgin and Conceived Without Sin," the first church in the world to be placed under the patronage of the Immaculate Conception.[7] The Bay City received its second cathedral dedicated to Mary in 1891, when Archbishop Patrick W. Riordan erected Saint Mary of the Assumption.[8] When the latter house-of-worship was destroyed by fire in 1962, it was replaced by the present structure which has become an architectural fixture on the Bay City's skyline.

In the southern jurisdiction, Bishop Thaddeus Amat of Monterey-Los Angeles used the *Asistencia de Nuestra Señora de los Angeles* for his pro-cathedral until 1876. It was a half-century after Garcia Diego's arrival in San Diego before work was begun on the Gothic brick church later to be known as Saint Joseph Cathedral. The handsome edifice was

---

[7] John B. McGloin, S.J., *California's First Archbishop* (New York, 1966), p. 161.

[8] James P. Gaffey, *Citizen of No Mean City. Archbishop Patrick W. Riordan of San Francisco* (New York, 1976), pp. 83–87.

San Diego de Alcala Mission, California's proto Cathedral. *Source: "Dick" Whittington Photography, Archives of the Archdiocese of Los Angeles*

dedicated by Bishop Francis Mora in 1894, and elevated to cathedral status in 1936.

Sacramento's Italian Renaissance Cathedral of the Blessed Sacrament owes its origin to Bishop Patrick Manogue, who had the seat of his diocese changed to that city from Marysville in 1886. When the cornerstone was laid on June 12, 1887, one local newspaper declared that "there is nothing that so beautifies a city as a handsome temple of God and the Catholics have shown a magnificent example."[9]

Saint John in Fresno has served the city as a parish since 1882. The present church was dedicated on June 7, 1903, by the Most Reverend

---

[9] William Breault, S.J., *The Miner was a Bishop* (Rancho Cordova, 1988), p. 128.

Bishop Francisco Garcia Diego y Moreno fixed his headquarters at Santa Barbara Mission which became the first pro-cathedral in Alta California. *Source: Archives of the Archdiocese of Los Angeles*

George T. Montgomery, Coadjutor Archbishop of San Francisco. When the Diocese of Monterey-Fresno was erected in 1922, Saint John became the "Cathedral in the Valley."[10]

Among the state's other cathedrals is Saint Eugene in the Diocese of Santa Rosa. Built in 1950, it achieved its designation in 1962, when the diocese was erected. Stockton's Saint Mary of the Annunciation antedates Saint Eugene by twenty years, while the Cathedral of Saint Francis de Sales in Oakland traced its origin back to 1886.[11] It was later destroyed by earthquake.

---

[10]See Francis X. Singleton, *Cathedral in the Valley, 1952–1982* (Fresno, 1952).

[11] Peter Thomas Conmy, *A Parochial and Institutional History of the History of the Diocese of Oakland 1962–1972 and Two Centuries of Background* (Mission Hills, 2000), p. 207 ff.

Bishop Joseph Sadoc Alemany established his residence at Monterey, thus making the Royal Presidio chapel his cathedral. *Source: Archives of the Archdiocese of Los Angeles*

Today, California has more Catholic cathedrals than many countries in the world. Each of the twelve ecclesial jurisdictions in the Golden State has or is building its own cathedral.

Fresno—Saint John
Los Angeles—Our Lady of the Angels
Monterey—San Carlos Borromeo
Oakland—Saint Mary, Immaculate Conception, Saint Francis de Sales
Orange—Holy Family
Sacramento—Blessed Sacrament
San Bernardino—Our Lady of the Rosary
San Diego—Saint Joseph

Vincentian Bishop Thaddeus Amat used the *Asistencia de Nuestra Señora de los Angeles* as his cathedral for the Diocese of Monterey-Los Angeles until 1876. *Source: Archives of the Archdiocese of Los Angeles*

San Francisco—Saint Mary of the Assumption
San Jose—Saint Joseph
Santa Rosa—Saint Eugene
Stockton—Annunciation

As early as 1856, reports began appearing in local newspapers about a proposed cathedral for the Diocese of Monterey. The Santa Barbara *Gazette* stated that "it is the intention of Bishop Thaddeus Amat to commence soon the erection of a cathedral in Santa Barbara, near the site of the present chapel . . ."[12] Whatever plans there might have been were postponed until the Holy See handed down its decision transferring the seat of the diocese to Los Angeles in 1859.

When Amat came back from Europe in January of 1868, he turned his attention to the long cherished project for which he had been setting aside funds for several years. Los Angeles was beginning its recovery from the protracted drought of 1862 and with a gradual increase in agricultural prosperity, it was hoped that a prosperous era would dawn for the

---

[12] Santa Barbara *Gazette,* May 22, 1856.

region. Amat appointed a committee to promote the project and a property was acquired on the west side of Main Street, a little north of Sixth, together with an adjacent lot fronting on Spring Street. The new cathedral would be dedicated, by express wish of Pope Pius IX,[13] to Saint Vibiana and would enshrine the maiden's relics which had been brought to Los Angeles from Santa Barbara in 1868 and placed temporarily in a chapel of Our Lady of the Angels.

By the end of 1868, the preliminary planning was completed. The following year was a noteworthy one in California annals for it saw the transcontinental railway in the north completed in May. Locally, a line was built from Los Angeles to Wilmington and the prospects of a southern roadbed were also promising. All these developments emphasized the need for the Catholic Church to have a fitting cathedral in the expanding southland. Sufficient water was available, a bank was in operation and, a smallpox scare notwithstanding, money was fairly plentiful. Speculation in land was rife and, for a short time, reached "boom" proportions. Interest in the proposed cathedral was obvious in all quarters. One paper spoke in terms more fanciful than true:

> The Catholics contemplate building a cathedral at a cost of about forty thousand dollars. Yesterday morning, a paper was circulated and about five thousand dollars was subscribed in a little time.[14]

The first official announcement of the bishop's plans was read in the churches of the diocese on Sunday, June 6, 1869. After stressing the necessity of better attendance of children at catechetical instructions, a formal declaration of the building project was made:

> We cannot close these lines without informing you of our initiatory steps toward commencing our Cathedral Church in honor of our Patroness, Saint Vibiana, whose sacred remains we received through the liberality of Our Holy Father, Pius IX, with the express understanding, not to say command, that they should be deposited within its walls. As there is question of the Mother Church of the diocese to be built in honor of the Patroness of the same, we can entertain no doubt that every one of our faithful children in Christ will hasten with generosity to assist us in bringing it to a speedy and perfect completion.[15]

---

[13] AALA, Rome, Rescript of September 1, 1856.
[14] Los Angeles *Republican,* April 15, 1869.
[15] Quoted in the *Alta California,* June 15, 1869.

Since Bishop Amat had planned to attend Vatican Council I, scheduled to convene in Rome on December 8,[16] it was decided to begin prepara-
tory work on the cathedral before his departure. Cornerstone ceremonies
were conducted on October 3, 1869, at four o'clock in the afternoon, on property donated by Mrs. Ozro W. Childs. Coins, newspapers and a formal
decree, together with other items of historic interest were sealed in a lead
box and deposited within the cavity of a Folsom granite stone. A large
crowd of people, estimated in excess of 3,000, braved the blistering heat to
participate in the historic function.[17] A long religious procession moved
down Main Street to the music of the United States Military Band from
Drum Barracks. First, in a carriage, was Bishop Amat accompanied by the
priests of the diocese. Then along the sidewalk came the Daughters of
Charity with their students and finally, in the rear, a huge line of the faithful and friends of the Church. When the procession had arrived at the proposed site, Pontifical Mass was celebrated. An episcopal blessing was
imparted to the area where the main altar would be erected.[18] A sermon in
English[19] was preached by Father James McGill, C.M., president of Saint
Vincent's College, followed by one in Spanish delivered by the bishop.

After Amat's departure for Rome, work on the cathedral lagged and
was soon suspended completely. Hard times had again overtaken the city
and the smallpox epidemic, while not overly serious, frightened investors
away. The hope of a silk-culture as a leading industry also grew slim. In
short, money became scarce and the entire project was discontinued.
There was also a rather prevalent opinion that the cathedral site was too
far out of town. The Catholic college with its private chapel was only two
blocks away and, although the Vincentians had agreed not to open their
chapel for public use, it seemed extravagant to build a massive cathedral
so close to existing facilities.

Upon Amat's return from Europe, a new site was selected further
north yet considerably south of the plaza. Amat had acquired property in
that area in August of 1858 from Amiel Cavallier.[20] It was an attractive
piece of land with a small stream flowing through the middle. The bishop
petitioned the city for a deed of quitclaim and received assurance that such
a request would be granted.[21] In May 1871, Amat gave his formal approval
and the work of clearing the ground began. The enterprise, like all others
of the time, was closely linked to the ups and downs of agricultural and

[16] AALA, "Libro Gobierno," p. 68.

[17] Los Angeles *Star,* October 7, 1869.

[18] Los Angeles *Daily News,* October 5, 1869.

[19] Quoted *verbatim* in the Los Angeles *Star,* October 7, 1869.

[20] AALA, Deed Book, Book IV, p. 204.

[21] The quitclaim granted by the City of Los Angeles to Thaddeus Amat was
dated December 14, 1877.

Right Reverend Thaddeus Amat, C.M., Bishop of Monterey-Los Angeles (1853–1878). *Source: Archives of the Archdiocese of Los Angeles*

sheep raising interests. The winters of 1868–1870 were exceptionally dry and, therefore, economically unfavorable. In order to adjust the original plans along more modest lines, a smaller church was designed by the local architect, E. F. Kyser, who in later days was assisted by W. J. Mathews with whom he formed a partnership. The general plan of the structure was suggested by that of the *Iglesia de Puerto de San Miguel*[22] in Barcelona and provided for a building eighty feet wide and 160 feet deep.

---

[22] The *Puerto de San Miguel* was damaged by a severe earthquake toward the close of the last century; hence a great deal of renovation on the historic church was necessary. Today there is a notable discrepancy in the stateliness of the exterior from the magnificent proportions of the interior.

The church of San Miguel del Puerto in Barcelona, Spain was the model for the Cathedral of Saint Vibiana erected in Los Angeles. *Source: Archives of the Archdiocese of Los Angeles*

Beyond clearing of the property, little work was done in 1871. The outer walls took form in 1872 and 1873 in a seemingly endless succession of delays. Bishop Amat went to Europe for his health the next year and during his absence, Coadjutor Bishop Francis Mora renewed efforts to complete the structure before Amat's return. Louis Mesmer took charge of the construction program in the winter of 1874-1875 and "inaugurated a renewal of the work by bringing to it an energy which never flagged until the structure was ready for divine services."[23]

By the end of June 1875, the building had been roofed. The giant bell of Mission San Juan Capistrano, cast in Massachusetts in 1828, was blessed on July 4th and, on the following day, a festival was held to raise funds for the continuance of the work. A group of ladies sponsored the gala affair within the bare brick walls[24] and it was estimated "that at least three thousand visitors were present during the day and partook of the elegant bounty."[25] On Sunday afternoon, January 2, 1876, the foundation stone of the high altar was blessed and set in place.[26] Later additions were no less newsworthy:

> The cupola of the new Church is, without exception, the most graceful specimen of architecture in California. It is a marvel of symmetrical beauty and comely shapeliness. The eye just naturally lingers on it, and never tires of admiring its elegance and handsome proportions. That beautiful tower will yet be sung in verse and commemorated in lasting prose.[27]

In the first months of 1876, the work of decorating the interior and exterior of the church was undertaken by Joaquin Amat, the bishop's nephew. The artistic stonework for the railing in front of the building was manufactured at an East Los Angeles firm, the artificial stone factory of Messrs. Bashard and Hamilton. Railings, fabricated from iron, products of Page and Gravel, formed a beautiful and suitable enclosure which lasted for many years. The two niches flanking the rose window received statues of SS. Peter and Paul, and, on the upper front wall of the transepts, images of the four evangelists were attached. Statues of SS. Patrick and Emigdius were installed at either side of the main altar.[28]

At last, on Palm Sunday, April 9, the first services were held within the cathedral walls. The palms were blessed at ten o'clock after which a

---

23 Los Angeles *Express,* April 10, 1875.
24 *Ibid.,* July 4, 1875.
25 *Ibid.,* July 6, 1875.
26 *Ibid.,* December 31, 1875.
27 *Ibid.,* February 11, 1876.
28 *Ibid.,* April 8, 1876.

Interior of San Miguel del Puerto in Barcelona. *Source: Archives of the Archdiocese of Los Angeles*

Early interior view of Saint Vibiana Cathedral. *Source: Archives of the Archdiocese of Los Angeles*

solemn pontifical Mass was celebrated in the presence of the city's leading dignitaries. The spacious new church easily accommodated the immense throng gathered for the joyous occasion. Immediately after the Mass, Bishop Amat imparted a special apostolic blessing and offered copious words of gratitude to his flock.

The colorful ceremonies of consecration were scheduled for the second Sunday after Easter, April 30. Archbishop Joseph Sadoc Alemany of San Francisco officiated and celebrated the Mass. The renowned Indian Jesuit priest, Father James Bouchard, gave an historical description of the symbolic ceremonies of which the only extant report says the

> . . . eloquent divine gave a graphic description of the ceremonies of consecration, and illustrated in a lucid manner all

View of Saint Vibiana Cathedral and the adjoining rectory from the earliest years. *Source: Archives of the Archdiocese of Los Angeles*

the symbols and mysteries of the magnificent spectacle. He spoke of the building of the Temple of Solomon, and compared the work of erecting a modern Tabernacle of God; he made a fervent appeal on behalf of religion and religious works, and adjured his hearers to turn from the sinful ways of the world and consecrate their souls to God.[29]

At the conclusion of the consecration rite, Bishop Amat hosted the archbishop and various civic officials at a banquet in the episcopal residence. Alemany delivered an interesting address outlining the historical background of the California apostolate, recalling some of the forgotten trials and tribulations that plagued the early missionaries. To these pioneers, Alemany gave the credit for planting the seed that had blossomed forth into Saint Vibiana Cathedral.

A solemn procession was scheduled for six o'clock[30] to translate the relics of Saint Vibiana from the Old Plaza Church to her permanent

---

[29] Quoted in John B. McGloin, S.J., *Eloquent Indian* (Berkeley, 1950), p. 292.
[30] Thomas Atwill Neal, *Saint Vibiana's Los Angeles Cathedral, 1876–1950*. (Los Angeles, 1950), p. 8.

Traditional artistic rendition of Saint Vibiana Cathedral.

shrine above the cathedral's main altar. Headed by the Mexican brass band, several of the city's societies, followed by more than 200 children, formed the honor guard. Father John Basso carried the metropolitan cross followed by sixteen priests chanting the litany of the saints. The shrine itself was borne by four priests, vested in alb and stole. Archbishop Alemany and Bishop Mora came behind the shrine and the aging Bishop Amat, exhausted by the long and tiring ceremonials, rode in a carriage. As soon as the procession reached the cathedral, the relics were deposited in the middle of the sanctuary and "a most eloquent and impressive sermon in Spanish was delivered by Archbishop Alemany." At the end of the archbishop's remarks, the clergy sang the *Te Deum* after which Father Joachim Adam delivered a short talk in English. The ceremony was ended with Benediction of the Blessed Sacrament. Early next morning, the crystal and gilt casket containing the relics of Saint Vibiana was raised to its place in a niche above the high altar, in the tower, where it remained for almost a century.

Among the earliest funerals conducted at Saint Vibiana Cathedral was that of Bishop Amat who succumbed after a short illness on May 12, 1878. Vested in full pontificals and placed in an artistically designed

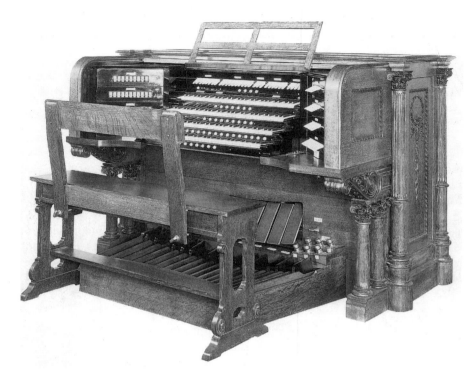

Earliest organ at Saint Vibiana Cathedral. *Source: Archives of the Archdiocese of Los Angeles*

metallic casket, the prelate was readied for interment in his cathedral which was generally thought to have been the greatest of his physical accomplishments.[31]

 With Archbishop Joseph Sadoc Alemany of San Francisco looking on, the casket was lowered into a vault beneath and behind the main altar where a brick outer casing was walled around the casket. The inscription read as follows:

   Illmus. ac Revmus. D. D. THADDEUS AMAT, C. M.

---

[31] For an account of the funeral and entombment, see Francis J. Weber *Past is Prologue 2* (Mission Hills, 2002), pp. 55–61.

Natus die 30 Dec. A.D., 1811. Consecratus Episcopus Montereyensis–Angelorum 12 Mart. 1854. Orbit 12 Maii, 1878, R.I.P.[32]

There the bishop's *restos* remained for the next eighty-four years until, at the direction of James Francis Cardinal McIntyre, they were disinterred and moved to the Episcopal Chapel at Calvary Mausoleum in East Los Angeles.

Bishop Francis Mora, who outlived his predecessor by twenty-seven years, spent his retirement in Sarria, just outside Barcelona, Spain, where he died on August 3, 1905. His remains were disinterred in 1962 and returned to Los Angeles where a pontifical Mass was celebrated in Saint Vibiana Cathedral on December 5, 1962.[33]

During the tenure of George Montgomery as Bishop of Monterey-Los Angeles (1896–1903) the historic house-of-worship was considered the most stately of the churches in Southern California. The prelate used that reputation to respond to a complaint made in the Los Angeles *Herald* for August 30, 1900 about the "excessive" ringing of the cathedral bells.

From time to time there has appeared in the press the expression of dissatisfaction on the part of some people with the ringing of church bells on the morning of Sunday, which is charged as useless if not a nuisance. I suppose the Catholic churches are the greatest offenders; and, as representing them, I beg leave to say a few words through your excellent paper in explanation and in defense of that custom.

I am sure that there is nobody in the city that desires less to be a nuisance to neighbors than do the Catholic people. The first bell rung in any of our churches on Sunday morning is at 5:30, except on Christmas. That first bell, as well as that of 12 noon and 6 p.m., is called the *"Angelus"* bell and the meaning of it is to remind our people in the first conscious moments of the morning and during the day of that great fundamental doctrine of the Christian religion known as the Incarnation when the Angel was sent by God to announce to the Blessed Virgin

---

[32] The plaque was removed from the wall of the cathedral after the bishop's remains were disinterred and has hung outside the chapel at Bishop Amat High School in La Puente, California since November of 1962.

[33] See Francis J. Weber, "In Search of a Bishop," *Southern California Quarterly* XLV (September, 1963), 235–243.

Father John B. McGloin, S.J., biographer of Archbishop Joseph Sadoc Alemany greets Bishop Thaddeus Amat's biographer at the latter's tomb in Saint Vibiana Cathedral. *Source: Archives of the Archdiocese of Los Angeles*

Mary that the Savior of man was to be born into the world, and that she was selected to be His mother.

There are prayers which Catholics recite at the ringing of that bell, nearly the whole of which are taken from the New Testament and bearing directly on that great mystery of Christian faith. There are many who honestly disbelieve in the divinity of Jesus Christ, but who at the same time believe that the human race owes more to Him than to any other person that ever lived on earth.

This *Angelus* bell is one of the ways in which we Catholic people make a profession of our Faith in Him and of our great gratitude to Him for what He has done for mankind.

I think that most people admit that religion is beneficial to society, and we all know that there are many agencies at

Bell from Saint Vibiana Cathedral that now rings at the Cathedral of Our Lady of the Angels. *Source: Archives of the Archdiocese of Los Angeles.*

work in human nature to weaken that influence; and I believe that fair-minded men will concede that whatever tends to preserve religious principles among men is a benefit. Therefore I believe it would be a great mistake to insist upon the suppression of the *Angelus* bell.

When rung at other times, it is to serve the purpose of notifying the people of the hour of service. Now we know that it is a great convenience to those who attend our churches. But about the inconvenience to others, I believe it is the experience of almost everyone that when we are accustomed to a regular ringing of church bells, or almost any other regular noise, it ceases to be the nuisance that some would like to make it. The street cars in this city and in most other cities run until

1 o'clock and, so accustomed do we become to the noise the cars
make, that I believe few people notice it.

I think that as noisy a place as is in this city from the
street cars is Second Street between Main and Los Angeles
and so accustomed have we become to the noise that I believe
if the cars should stop at 11 o'clock instead of 1 o'clock we
should notice the stopping more than the continuance of the
noise.[34]

The subsequent role of Saint Vibiana as the Mother Church of the
Diocese of Monterey-Los Angeles, Los Angeles-San Diego and the Archdiocese of Los Angeles, told in great detail in other places,[35] need not be
recalled in any detail in the context of this book.

On the other hand, over the years succeeding bishops and archbishops have made numerous attempts to better accommodate the historic
building to the growing needs of what eventually became the largest
metropolis in the world named for the Blessed Mother. The first major
interior change was made in 1893, with installation of a permanent high
altar of Parian and Carrara marble and Mexican onyx. The new altar was
consecrated on February 24, 1894.[36]

Lighting and other electrical facilities replaced the earlier gas
lamps in 1898. A circle of fifteen frosted globes was added around the arch
of the sanctuary to illuminate the sky-blue field of silver stars with a soft,
white light. Father Joachim Adam had a stained-glass window, with an
etched figure of a dove, placed atop the dome to represent the Holy Spirit.
According to one source, "the radiant rays coming from this dove upon the
relics in the shrine and down upon the altar, are of rare beauty and infuse
into the soul a happy thought of the world beyond the stars." The seating
capacity was considerably enlarged by replacing the antiquated benches
with freshly hewn, wooden pews. In place of the original fixed pulpit, a
portable lectern was rolled into the sanctuary in the late summer of
1898.[37]

Shortly after the turn of the century, the Catholic Church in the
United States passed through a cathedral-building era. So widespread
was the movement that by 1907, cathedral churches had been completed

---

[34] August 30, 1900.
[35] See Francis J. Weber, *Saint Vibiana's Cathedral* (Los Angeles, 1976).
[36] *The Tidings,* May 28, 1926.
[37] *Ibid.,* September 3, 1898.

Shrine of Saint Vibiana in the cathedral dedicated to her patronage.

or were under construction in twenty of the nation's ecclesiastical jurisdictions.[38] Southern California was not immune from this national trend as is evidenced by the following announcement, made only a few short months after the appointment of the Right Reverend Thomas J. Conaty as Bishop of Monterey-Los Angeles:

> Los Angeles is to have a magnificent cathedral church, a structure that will be a credit to the Catholics of the Diocese of Monterey-Los Angeles, and the pride of the city.[39]

The southland's newly installed prelate brought the matter before his diocesan advisors on January 26, 1904, and "after a thorough discussion it was the unanimous opinion of the counselors that the Right Rev.

---

[38] See Francis J. Weber, "The Cathedral That Never Was," *The Immaculate* XVI, (November, 1965), 11–12.

[39] *The Tidings,* August 22, 1903.

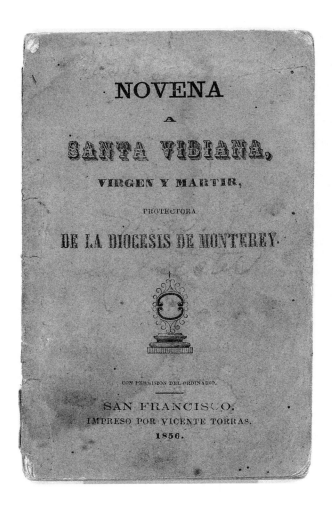

Ordinary petition the Eminent Cardinals of the Congregation *de Propaganda Fide* to be allowed to change the location of the present cathedral to a more suitable site and furthermore to be allowed to demolish the present one."[40]

A list of seven reasons supporting the proposal was drawn up and a formal petition dispatched to Rome. When the request was brought before Pope Pius X, on June 28, 1904, the pontiff granted permission "to remove

---

[40] AALA, "Acts of Council, 1892–1918," Statement of Reverend Polydore J. Stockman, January 26–27, 1904, p. 32.

the present cathedral in order to erect a larger church in a more suitable area of the town," provided "the location of the existing edifice not be put to bad use."[41]

Conaty's consulters urged him to build the new church "within the limits of the already existing parish in the center of that portion of the city inhabited by the most respectable and influential Catholics." A piece of property was selected in 1903 but actual clearance of title took until March of 1905.

In keeping with the advice of his council that the new cathedral of Our Lady of Guadalupe be "sufficiently large and entirely adequate to the needs of the parishioners," Bishop Conaty employed the nationally known architectural firm of Maginnis, Walsh and Sullivan of Boston, to draft plans for the proposed edifice. It was the bishop's ambition to see embodied in the cathedral all the sentiments and artistic feeling making up the soul of California's Catholic history.

The site was beautifully located on the north side of Ninth Street between Whittier and Green. It was planned to so place the church on the massive lot that its center entrance would directly face Valencia Street, thus forming a monumental approach from the southern part of the city. Some idea of the envisioned proportions of the structure can be grasped by considering the twin towers and central dome. Flanking the main entrance, the towers were to be set back sixty-four feet from Ninth Street and were to rise to a height of 198 feet. The great central dome, 164 feet high and 80 feet in diameter, was to have tiles in polychrome patterns of blue, yellow and green.

Conceived with the view of embracing the entire congregation within the piers of the nave, the organism of the structure was designed in such a fashion that the main altar would be visible from all points without obstruction. A considerable amount of national attention was given to the southland's proposed cathedral. The very first issue of *Christian Art,*[42] for example, gave the prominence of its front page along with some details of the building's design with strong words of praise for the architects. Approval of Bishop Conaty's plans was not at all universal, however. Archbishop Patrick W. Riordan of San Francisco, a strong dissenter, told his suffragan that he would "find the contemplated building to be very expensive and entirely too large."[43] The metropolitan wanted the whole

---

[41] AALA, *Propaganda Fide* to Thomas J. Conaty, Rome, n.d.

[42] Cf. I (April, 1907), 12–13.

[43] AALA, Patrick W. Riordan to Thomas J. Conaty, San Francisco, March 6, 1905.

Organ installed by Archbishop John J. Cantwell, parts of which still function in the new organ at the Cathedral of Our Lady of the Angels.

Exterior of Bishop Thomas J. Conaty's proposed cathedral to be located on the north side of Ninth Street near Green.

project delayed "for some time" believing that the envisioned church was at least a quarter of a century ahead of its time. Riordan advocated erecting "a temporary church on the site"[44] which could be used while construction on the cathedral was in progress.

The discouraging remarks of Riordan had little effect on the tireless Bishop Conaty who recalled that similar observations were made when his predecessor built the first cathedral in the 1870s.[45] In any case, as Conaty reminded his metropolitan, "I am in no hurry and do not intend to do anything until I know all the details."[46]

Originally, the bishop had hoped to put the cornerstone in place June 23, 1905, but delays in acquiring clearance of title along with Archbishop Riordan's absence in the east, caused postponement until after Conaty's proposed trip to Rome the following year. Planning went ahead

---

[44] AALA, Thomas J. Conaty to Charles Maginnis, Los Angeles, March 28, 1905.

[45] Cf. Francis J. Weber, "An Historical Sketch of Saint Vibiana's Cathedral, Los Angeles," *Southern California Quarterly* XLIV (March, 1962), 43–56.

[46] AALA, Thomas J. Conaty to Patrick W. Riordan, Los Angeles, March 19, 1905.

though and, in March of 1906, *The Tidings* told its readers that "the new cathedral, when completed, will perhaps typify better than any other public building the progress of the southland."[47]

The unforeseen financial depression of late 1907, however, brought to a grinding halt the entire cathedral project. Even this disappointment did not daunt the bishop for he noted that suspension of planning "gave us an opportunity to develop our charity work."[48] Realizing that the cathedral would be delayed for some years, Conaty decided to follow Archbishop Riordan's advice and erect a chapel on the projected site. On July 27, 1909, the Vicar General of the Diocese, Monsignor Patrick Harnett, blessed the new edifice and placed it under the spiritual patronage of our Lady of Guadalupe.[49]

Despite the manifold problems Conaty encountered, he never entirely abandoned the idea of his cathedral. In 1910, a prominent Los Angeles newspaper spoke in great detail about "Bishop Conaty's determination to proceed with the erection of the $1,000,000 cathedral in this city, whose plans have just been approved and accepted."[50]

Two years later, the bishop asked Joseph Mesmer to buy, if he could, the 6-1/2 acre A. H. Busch property at the southeast corner of Vermont and Wilshire for a possible cathedral site.[51] Even some years after the bishop's death, there was speculation about possibly building "Conaty's Cathedral" and, in 1923, sketches of the proposed edifice appeared in a national architectural publication.[52]

Though he was pre-occupied with the notion of a new cathedral, Bishop Conaty never neglected Saint Vibiana, probably because he revised his earlier plans of dismantling the cathedral in favor of keeping the earlier edifice as a functioning parochial church. It was just prior to the end of the century that the erection of a building to the south side necessitated installation of stained-glass windows to the vertical roof approaches. Fabricated by the Los Angeles Art Glass Company, each of the expressive panes had its own symbolic emblem.

Colorful dedicatory ceremonies were conducted on November 30, 1907, for the inauguration of a new organ. Following the solemn blessing, Bishop Thomas J. Conaty spoke at considerable length about music as

---

[47] March 30, 1906.

[48] AALA, "Address," n.d. (probably late in 1907).

[49] In later years, the title was changed to Immaculate Conception and in 1926 Conaty's nephew, Reverend Francis J. Conaty, built the present church.

[50] Los Angeles *Times,* November 20, 1910.

[51] *The Tidings,* September 4, 1931 (article by Joseph Mesmer).

[52] Cf. Sylvester Baxter, "A Selection from the Works of Maginnis and Walsh, Architects," *The Architectural Record* LIII (February, 1923), 108.

"the child of the Christian Church."[53] An elaborate Episcopal *sedes* or *cathedra,* along with a number of matching furnishings, was installed in the sanctuary in 1912. The throne, hand carved by Eugene Alker from native California woods, was used for the first time during the liturgy of Ash Wednesday.

Ironically, by the time of Conaty's premature demise in 1915, the venerable cathedral he wanted to replace was still referred to in the local newspaper as a "sacred edifice".[54] No mention was made in any funeral eulogy about Conaty's intention of replacing Saint Vibiana.

Soon after the appointment of John J. Cantwell to the Bishopric of Monterey-Los Angeles, the young Irish-born prelate received some sage advice from an old and respected friend, Father Peter C. Yorke of San Francisco. The legendary "priest of the working man" advised Cantwell:

> Don't start out by building a cathedral. . . . get the little ones to love Christ. . . . concentrate on Christian education of the youth and you will be a great success in the eyes of the Lord.[55]

Shortly after his installation as Bishop of Monterey-Los Angeles, John Cantwell expressed a desire to do something "in reference to a decent Cathedral Church in this city." He felt that "a good church always makes an appeal to the outsider" and he hoped one day "to see a respectable Catholic Church in this city." Anxious as he was to have a cathedral, Cantwell's concern about "building up the Kingdom of God in the fold of our young people"[56] forced him to settle for restoring the existing Saint Vibiana.

In April of 1922, the bishop authorized a complete renovation of the old cathedral. After almost a half-century service,[57] the historic church was badly in need of modernization and expansion. According to architect John C. Austin, the overall plan was "first to remove the present vestibule, the railings in the front of the building, and to reconstruct the building at

---

[53] *The Tidings,* December 4, 1907.

[54] *The Tidings,* September 24, 1915.

[55] Quoted in Francis J. Weber, *John Joseph Cantwell. His Excellency of Los Angeles,* (Hong Kong, 1971), p. 160.

[56] AALA, John J. Cantwell to Edward A. Scheller, Los Angeles, March 1, 1920.

[57] The Church of the *Puerto de San Miguel,* after which the cathedral was modeled, still serves the waterfront area of Barcelona, Spain. See Francis J. Weber, "An Historical Sketch of Saint Vibiana's Cathedral, Los Angeles," *Southern California Quarterly* XLIV (March, 1962), 50.

Right Reverend Thomas J. Conaty, Bishop of
Monterey-Los Angeles (1903–1915).

a point flush with the property line."[58] The fanciful new facade, fashioned
from Gray Bedford stone, closely resembled the traditional "Roman"
churches. In addition to renovating the cathedral proper, a gallery was
erected over the main entrance with accommodation for 250 people and a
gigantic organ.[59] Marble steps and railings were added to the considerably enlarged sanctuary. The walls were re-plastered and richly finished
in liturgical ornamentations. A new pulpit of white carrara, offset by colored marble columns and inlaid panels, was installed opposite the episcopal throne. The renovation process lasted almost two years, though it
never interfered with the normally scheduled divine services.

On February 3, 1924, Archbishop Pietro Fumasoni-Biondi, the Apostolic Delegate to the United States, celebrated a solemn pontifical Mass
marking the formal re-opening of the cathedral. In his sermon for the
occasion, Archbishop Edward J. Hanna of San Francisco likened "this

---

[58] Quoted in *The Tidings,* April 7, 1922.
[59] The organ was installed in November of 1929.

The Right Reverend John Joseph Cantwell, D.D.
joins the Clergy of the Cathedral
in cordially inviting you to attend
the celebration of the
Golden Jubilee
of the
Cathedral of St. Vibiana
on Sunday, May the twenty-third
nineteen hundred and twenty-six

Solemn Pontifical Mass at ten-thirty A.M.
  Celebrant:
    Right Reverend John J. Cantwell, D.D.
  Sermon by:
    Most Reverend Edward J. Hanna, D.D.
Exercises by the children, Procession,
  Conferring of the Sacrament of
  Confirmation at four P.M.
Solemn Pontifical Vespers at eight P.M.
  Sermon by:
    Reverend Thomas K. Gorman, D.D.

sacred place, wherein we gather to pay our vows unto the Most High" to that "greater Church which reached from sea to sea."[60]

Even with the added facilities at Saint Vibiana, Archbishop Cantwell did not abandon his dream of eventually erecting a magnificent new cathedral for Southern California. In 1943, he revealed his intention to build a new mother church for the city of Our Lady of the Angels. The archbishop pointed out to a friend that:

> There is not only the need of a cathedral, but the times
> are good now, and after the war I think we will be able to build

---

[60] Quoted in *The Tidings,* February 8, 1924.

Saint Vibiana Cathedral after its refurbishment by Archbishop John J. Cantwell.

economically. It is good to be ahead of time, so that when the opportune moment comes, we can launch a drive.

Cantwell apparently had no reservations about the financial burden of such an undertaking noting that "since the building of the seminary, I am not afraid but that my people will respond to the needed church in this city, one that will be worthy of its present and future."[61] A committee of advisors was organized to draw up plans. Almost from the outset, a traditional style of architecture was decided on for the new edifice. Several members of the committee believed that the modern approach lacked the basic elements of beauty and spirituality and was, in effect, a contributing factor to the materialism of the times. At first, the archbishop favored

---

[61] AALA, John J. Cantwell to Patrick Morrisroe, Los Angeles, October 20, 1943.

a Spanish Gothic design,[62] but later, persuaded that its cost would be prohibitive, he settled on a variation of the Basilica-type pattern.[63]

In August of 1945, the archbishop confided to his clergy that architects were already at work. He felt that "the time is now opportune," not indeed to build the church, but to make such collections as will make it possible, in a suitable time, to build a cathedral in honor of Our Lady of the Angels, the patroness of this city[64] and, at the same time, transfer the remains of Saint Vibiana to a shrine in the new church.[65] In his subsequent pastoral letter to the faithful of the archdiocese, Cantwell noted that,

> Mighty and far-reaching changes have come to Los Angeles since the building of St. Vibiana's. The little *Pueblo* is but a picturesque dream of the past, and the metropolis that it is today has taken its place among the great cities of the world, with a beautiful and suitable architecture of its own. As a people grow in material prosperity and in appreciation of all that is fine in art, their community should, and does, record their advance. Our Civic Center has done this. So, too, have the many fine Churches of the Archdiocese, and yet they are, as it were, but children. The cathedral is the Mother Church, and like an early mother has watched her brood grow into beautiful fulfillment; has felt a mother's pride, and with it a mother's peace, knowing that the spirit which she has enshrined is forever young, and is clothing itself again in new and glorious raiment to shine forth resplendent in the days to come. But it is unseemly that the children should longer allow their beloved Mother Church to remain in her worn-out garments, effaced by their splendor. They should not be satisfied until she has risen above them, clothed in the beauty that is a symbol of their love.
>
> To erect a great cathedral will not only be a spiritual satisfaction but a fulfilled obligation to this city and to the past; not to do so would be to break the long sequence of Catholic projects of which this noble edifice would be the next crowning addition. The soldiers of Spain brought conquest to the wilderness that was this fair land, but the Catholic Church, through

---

[62] Cantwell had a great fondness for the *Capilla Real* at Granada.

[63] AALA, John J. Cantwell to John J. Cawley, Los Angeles, January 5, 1944.

[64] See Francis J. Weber, *El Pueblo de Nuestra Señora de los Angeles* (Los Angeles, 1968), p. 12.

[65] AALA, Circular Letter, Los Angeles, July 11, 1945.

The plaques of this white carrara marble pulpit now adorn the wall of the crypt chapel in the Cathedral of Our Lady of the Angels. *Source: Archives of the Archdiocese of Los Angeles*

Study from the Northwest
Cathedral of Our Lady of the Angels
Los Angeles , California .
Philip Hubert Frohman, Architect , Washington, D. C.

Source: Archives of the Archdiocese of Los Angeles

its valiant Franciscan missionaries, brought civilization. The missions marked the heroic beginning. Through the zeal of many people who appreciated their significance, they have been restored to stand as monuments and historic shrines. But now that very civilization which was brought and nurtured by the Church, and grew into maturity under its protection, demands more than a pride in old achievement, however glorious. It rightly expects action in this, our day, and a flowering into the future. The missions fulfilled the past, but that is not enough. There must be a cathedral to give expression to the present and to form a link with tomorrow, that the branches may show forth the eternal life of the root.[66]

A few weeks after releasing his pastoral, the archbishop unveiled plans to locate the new cathedral on a block-long site along Wilshire

---

[66] Reprinted in *The Tidings,* August 31, 1945.

Boulevard,[67] extending from Hudson Avenue to Keniston and south to Eighth Street. No specific date was given for beginning the project since building restrictions had not yet been removed by the Federal Government. Nonetheless, in a letter to an old friend, the Southern California prelate said he was "looking forward, with the help of God, to laying the cornerstone of a new cathedral within a year or two."[68]

While no definitive figures are available, it was estimated that the cathedral shell, with seating for approximately 2,500, would have cost about $1,500,000. This figure excluded the rectory and other facilities which Cantwell wanted to locate at the site.[69] Plans submitted by Ross Montgomery of Los Angeles and Philip Hunnert Frohman of Washington, D.C., revealed that the lot on Wilshire Boulevard was too shallow to allow a church long enough in proportion to the length and width needed for the initially envisioned edifice. Subsequently, several alternate sets of plans were submitted embodying the necessary modifications.[70]

Cantwell's ambitious plans for a new cathedral in Los Angeles, like the even more elaborate ones of his predecessor, were never realized. With the gradual decline of his health, the archbishop lost much of the earlier enthusiasm, thus aborting the only one of the prelate's major programs not brought to completion.

In his eulogy for Cantwell's funeral, Auxiliary Bishop Joseph T. McGucken said that "up to the last (the archbishop) dreamed and planned a great temple, a cathedral dedicated to Our Lady of the Angels."[71] The final chapter in the saga begun by Cantwell for his cathedral of Our Lady of the Angels came in an insignificant article that appeared in the *Wilshire Press* for March 7, 1979. Therein it is noted that

> Farmers Insurance Company has purchased the three-square blocks known as the church property in the Park Mile area from the Catholic Archdiocese of Los Angeles, Harold Gingrich, Farmers vice president of real estate, told this newspaper last week.

---

[67] As early as November 6, 1925, Cantwell told his diocesan consulters of an "opportunity to purchase 4 acres on Wilshire Blvd. at $300,000." See AALA, Acts of Council . . . , p. 65.

[68] AALA, John J. Cantwell to Mother Cecilia, Los Angeles, September 29, 1945.

[69] AALA, Joseph T. McGucken to Michael McInerney, O.S.B., Los Angeles, September 15, 1944.

[70] AALA, Joseph T. McGucken to John J. Cawley, Los Angeles, October 26, 1944.

[71] *The Tidings,* November 7, 1947.

The 8-1/2 acres of land involved in the sale run from Rim-
pau Boulevard to Tremaine Avenue and from Wilshire Boulevard to Eighth Street. Most of the land presently is vacant or
improved only with parking lots, representing the largest
undeveloped parcel in the area.
    The land originally was purchased by the church in 1920
as the site for a cathedral.[72]

The only extant memorial to Cantwell's unrealized dream is the
magnificent Ezcaray Altar Piece that adorns the ambulatory leading into
the main section of the new cathedral. The ornately-executed Baroque
woodwork can be traced to 1687 when Domingo Angel, a wealthy silk
manufacturer from Burgos, had the reredos installed in the chapel
attached to the Congregation of Saint Philip Neri at Ezcaray, Spain.
When the chapel was dismantled in 1925, its contents were acquired by
Raymond Gould of Pasadena. After the new owner's death, a consortium
chaired by Edward T. Foley acquired the collection for use in Cantwell's
envisioned cathedral. The several hundred pieces were stored for many
years with part of them being installed in Queen of Angels Seminary and
the other in the chapel at San Fernando Mission.[73]
    When J. Francis A. McIntyre came to California in 1948, he found
detailed plans and a healthy financial nest egg set aside for a new cathedral which his predecessor had long wanted to build on Wilshire Boulevard. Though recognizing the need even then for a cathedral in the
southland, the newly installed Archbishop of Los Angeles felt uneasy
about the overall program, especially in view of what he considered more
pressing priorities. McIntyre met individually with his official consulters
and, in each case, he prefaced his remarks with a single query: "Would it
not be better to erect schools so that a future archbishop will have educated Catholics to worship in his new cathedral?[74]
    After determining the consensus of his advisers, McIntyre composed
a letter to the major donors whose contributions had already been

---

[72] Interestingly, the property for Cantwell's envisioned but never built
cathedral was purchased by the company founded in 1928 by Thomas E. Leavey
and John C. Tyler as the Farmers Automobile Inter-Insurance Exchange. In 1952,
one of the co-owners established the Thomas and Dorothy Leavey Foundation
which subsequently became one of the two lead donors for another Cathedral of
Our Lady of the Angels, this one dedicated in September of 2002. Archbishop John
J. Cantwell's dream then did have a quasi-fulfillment.
    [73] See Francis J. Weber, *Memories of An Old Mission* (Mission Hills, 1997),
pp. 135–139.
    [74] Francis J. Weber, *A Remarkable Legacy, The Story of Secondary Schools
in the Archdiocese of Los Angeles*, (Mission Hills, 2001), p. xiv.

received. He offered to either refund their offerings or to divert them to an education fund for Catholic school expansion. McIntyre later recalled that not a single one of the several thousand or so donors asked for the return of the money. From his own experience, McIntyre knew that the greatest "leakage" of young people from the Catholic Church occurred in the teenage years. For that reason, he directed the major portion of his concern towards increasing the number of archdiocesan secondary schools.

Though little attention was paid to the structural needs of the cathedral in the years after 1948, the edifice retained its esteem among the historical-minded. As late as 1940, one prominent writer still ranked Saint Vibiana cathedral as "one of the outstanding churches of Los Angeles."[75]

A fairly extensive modernization took place in 1953 when Msgr. Alden J. Bell installed the first heating system. It was on that occasion that the entire edifice was rewired and equipped with new internal lighting fixtures. The sacristies added in 1922-1924 were completely remodeled and the circular stairwell connecting the tower with the crypt was enclosed. An attractive vesting altar was installed over which were displayed a number of the relics acquired by Bishop Thaddeus Amat in 1850s.

The Cathedral was damaged by two conflagrations of incendiary origin early on the morning of March 14, 1956.[76] Fortunately, the fires, one in the vestibule and the other at the high altar, were discovered by the sexton before they had spread to the central portion of the building.

On November 30, 1962, the seals on the crypt were opened and the remains of Bishop Thaddeus Amat formally identified. The remarkably preserved prelate was removed from his metallic casket and transferred to Calvary Mausoleum for entombment with his episcopal successors.[77]

A number of minor sanctuary adjustments were made in the following years. During the summer of 1969, the high altar was separated and moved forward from its reredos, allowing for the newly prescribed liturgy *versus populi*. The episcopal throne was greatly simplified—and made over into a "Presidential Chair." The communion railing was deleted, and the whole sanctuary area was covered with carpeting. From that time onwards, the Blessed Sacrament was reserved on a side altar.

In the most recent renovation, made in preparation for the cathedral's centennial, the relics of Saint Vibiana were removed to a shrine on

[75] Joseph Seewerker, *Nuestra Pueblo: Los Angeles, City of Romance.* (Boston, 1940), p. 122.

[76] *The Tidings,* March 16, 1956.

[77] For further details, see Francis J. Weber, *California Catholicism* (Los Angeles, 1975), pp. 3–4.

the south side of the sanctuary. Placed directly over the high altar was a colorful Pattarino porcelain statue of Our Lady of the Angels, for whom the City and Archdiocese of Los Angeles are named.

During the extensive refurbishment, directed by Timothy Cardinal Manning for the nation's bicentennial in 1976, the historic bells were removed from the tower because of their weight. A number of mostly cosmetic changes were made and a massive, non-descript mural was painted on the sanctuary wall. The flooring of the sanctuary was reinforced. The cathedral had special meaning to Cardinal Manning who had been ordained priest, consecrated bishop, installed as archbishop and observed many jubilees there. In 1976, the cardinal wrote a "homily to Angelinos in 2076, in which he hauntingly said:

> To those who would be gathering for a possible celebration in the cathedral 100 years hence, the cardinal has a message from the grave. We reach out to join with you in professing the same unchanging faith, the faith of our forefathers. There will still be a one, holy, Catholic and apostolic Church, grounded on the apostles and ruled by a pope of Rome. Maybe a great heresy, like Arianism, will have swept across the Church

Most Reverend John J. Cantwell, Archbishop of Los Angeles (1936–1947).

of Christ, teaching, suffering, serving. To you, from our graves, we send our greetings and our love. The form of this world, like our mortal graves, will pass away. The everlasting only will remain. Pray for us who have gone before you, marked with the sign of faith and who sleep the sleep of peace. May the country which you serve still be a nation under God, dedicated to the protection of family life, the guarding of liberty and the pursuit of happiness. And may Our Lady of Angels, *Nuestra Señora de Los Angeles,* continue to look upon and love you all.[78]

Over the years, Saint Vibiana Cathedral withstood numerous earthquakes such as those in 1933, 1954, 1971 and 1987. Providentially and mercifully, the end came quickly and unexpectedly on January 17, 1994, when the devastating Northridge earthquake, described as the most costly of any natural disaster in United States history, delivered the death knell to the 119-year-old once-proud cathedral.

---

[78] Quoted in Francis J. Weber 's *Magnificat. The Life and Times of Timothy Cardinal Manning* (Mission Hills, 1999), p. 709.

Re-located Shrine of Saint Vibiana in the cathedral bearing her name. *Source: "Dick" Whittington Photography, Archives of the Archdiocese of Los Angeles.*

Chapter II

Renovate, Remove or Relocate

Like most antiquated buildings in Southern California, Saint Vibiana Cathedral had deteriorated visibly by the late 1980s. Fire and earthquake had taken their toll and the edifice had been structurally compromised by vibrations from the streetcars that had plied their way up and down Main Street for almost half a century. There was no steel in the century old building and its double-ply brick walls had not been effectively retrofitted. An old wag said that the cathedral was held in place by faith, hope and charity and those virtues had long been overly taxed. Even the several facelifts given to the cathedral during the Manning years were more cosmetic than structural. The most recent work on the cathedral had been done in 1987 when extensive preparations were made for the visit of Pope John Paul II. Numerous repairs made then, along with painting of the interior, had not addressed the building's structural integrity.

In a letter to his priests in 1991,[1] Archbishop Roger Mahony explained three phases of an improvement project envisioned for the cathedral. The first consisted in bringing the building up to the latest earthquake standards, the second involved a new organ to enhance the instrument installed in the 1920s and the third encompassed a comprehensive review and updating of the interior. Architect Robert Rambusch had been asked to chair a committee to study how best to bring the edifice into better compliance with current liturgical directives.

At that time the archbishop dismissed suggestions about a new cathedral for several reasons. He wanted Saint Vibiana to remain "at the heart and center of our city's past, present and future." He also noted that the downtown area was being re-developed and improved and finally, he felt that the existing funds were needed "to serve our poorer parishes in the archdiocese."

The architectural firm of O' Leary and Teresawa was engaged to prepare an outline of "Renovations and Additions to the Cathedral of Saint Vibiana." That report, submitted on March 3, 1992, called for an expenditure of $7,445,675 which would cover renovation of the entire building,

---

[1]AALA, Roger Cardinal Mahony to Priests, Los Angeles, January 2, 1991.

Tower at Saint Vibiana Cathedral after the
Northridge earthquake.

the opening of a "gathering space", the addition of a basement garage and
a garden area.[2]

Providentially at this point, local newspapers were reporting that
the "largest gift ever in the history of the University of Southern California" had been dedicated to the erection of a new "Dorothy Leavey
Library."[3] Known for her generosity, Mrs. Leavey was a prominent
Catholic attached to Saint Victor Parish in West Hollywood. Cardinal
Mahony boldly outlined a formal proposal about restoration of Saint Vibiana which would be memorialized in the "Thomas and Dorothy Leavey

---

[2]AALA, Rudolph V. DeChellis to Douglas Ferraro, Los Angeles, March 13,
1992.

[3]Los Angeles *Times,* May 30, 1992.

Kathleen McCarthy and her mother,
Dorothy Leavey. *Source: The Tidings*

Cathedral Pavilion." In his formal presentation, His Eminence noted that
to insure that "our cathedral may be updated with the latest liturgical
changes" and made structurally sound, it was imperative "that we plan
for an extensive renovation:"

SUMMARY

St. Vibiana Cathedral, the oldest building in continual
use in the City of Los Angeles, is in grave need of repair and
restoration.

The history of Los Angeles is closely interwoven with the
cathedral, just as the history of the Leavey family is closely
entwined with the Catholic Church.

The current plans are to restore the cathedral, to add a
new entrance and baptistry, to acquire adjacent property and
to enhance the beauty of the entire complex.

Annexed to the formal request was a "budget for the Cathedral
Restoration and Enhancement."

Preliminary Budget Estimate	$ 7,620,000
Architect, Engineers, Consultants	$ 1,650,000
Field Testing	
Disposal of Contaminated Materials	
Liturgical Furnishings	$ 980,000
Reredos Revision	

Acquisition & Development of Property $ 4,900,000
Renovation of Adjacent Buildings
Parking Structure
_____

TOTAL PROJECT $15,150,000[4]

    Several times in the subsequent months, the cardinal spoke with and wrote to Mrs. Leavey and her daughter and son-in-law, Kathleen and Thomas McCarthy. He explained more fully his earlier proposal, noting that it would include such items as new fire sprinklers, heating and air conditioning, updated lighting, a digital sound system along with a host of other sorely needed improvements. He was confidant that as the "Premier Catholic Family of Los Angeles" they would welcome the opportunity of insuring the future of the archdiocesan Mother Church.[5]

    It was in a subsequent letter that the cardinal spoke for the first time about "Cathedral Square" which would encompass the entire block bounded by Main and Los Angeles, Second and Third streets. He outlined plans for purchasing the property occupied by the Union Rescue Mission and emphasized that "the key to our own St. Vibiana Cathedral improvement is the Leavey Pavilion and the new formal entrance way, thus giving us immediate access to the new Cathedral Square development."[6]

    The cardinal was informed on July 28, 1993 that the Thomas and Dorothy Leavey Foundation would provide a grant of $10,000,000 to be paid over the next decade. The "funds from the pledge are to be used to renovate, repair and restore St. Vibiana Cathedral." The Leavey name would be "permanently and prominently displayed on the complex in accordance with the usual policy of the archdiocese regarding such matters."[7]

Northridge Earthquake

    The disastrous Northridge earthquake that rocked Southern California on Monday morning, January 17, 1994, effectively brought down the curtain on the long and distinguished career of Saint Vibiana Cathedral, the venerable Mother Church for the Archdiocese of Los Angeles.

_____

[4]AALA, Roger Cardinal Mahony to Dorothy Leavey, Los Angeles, November 1992.

    [5]AALA, Roger Cardinal Mahony to Kathleen McCarthy, Los Angeles, April 20, 1993.

    [6]AALA, Roger Cardinal Mahony to Kathleen McCarthy, Los Angeles, June 5, 1993.

    [7]AALA, Thomas McCarthy to Roger Cardinal Mahony, Los Angeles, July 28, 1993.

In a letter to his fellow bishops, Roger Cardinal Mahony reported that sixty people had died and another 8,000 had been injured in a temblor that measured a hefty 6.7 on the Richter scale. Damage was widespread: nine freeways snapped like twigs, an oil main and 250 major gas lines ruptured and fallen wires plunged 3.1 million people into total darkness. Mahony enumerated the damage to archdiocesan facilities:

126 locations affected—lesser to major damages.

One Catholic hospital closed; needs to be torn down.

One archdiocesan high school (1,600 students) condemned; will have to be torn down and replaced.

Four archdiocesan elementary schools most likely will have to be torn down and replaced.

Two churches are close to being declared lost; would have to be torn down and replaced.

Many churches cannot be used at this time pending final inspections and completion of repair work.

Innumerable locations have moderate to serious structural damage: churches, schools, rectories, parish halls, convents; estimates at replacement and repair costs at this time to the archdiocese: $50 to $100 million dollars.[8]

Though the cathedral was not immediately closed, it had been dealt a fatal blow that only became fully evident in the ensuing months: on January 31st, the firm of Wheeler and Gray issued its report of damage to the cathedral:

FINDINGS

Based on our visual observation, the building's structural elements functioned as intended during the earthquake. The tower's unreinforced brick masonry walls show considerable cracking. A vertical crack of considerable length is at the joint of the tower wall to the nave wall. Other cracking appears at openings adjacent to where the top section of the tower is anchored to the brick masonry. The anchorage (ties) of the nave roof to the tower wall and the anchorage of tower floor diaphragms to walls appear to have functioned well. Cracking on exterior tower walls

---

[8]AALA, Roger Cardinal Mahony to American Bishops, Los Angeles, January 26, 1994.

appears considerably more extensive than from visits to the site approximately one and one half years ago.

At the 1922 west addition to the building, there is considerable cracking in some of the hollow clay tile walls in both stairwells leading to the mezzanine. Some cracking may have occurred in the new concrete or block masonry walls. At the west end of nave above lower edge of choir loft (mezzanine), the high ceiling is quite severely damaged. This appears cosmetic in nature. As observed from the Main Street sidewalk, there appear to be some cornice pieces on north and south ends that have cracked at joints. These should be investigated from the roof level along with other roof features.

CONCLUSIONS AND RECOMMENDATIONS

Based on our investigation, for temporary continued use of the nave, we believe barricading should be provided around the tower, both inside and outside. We believe the tower is vulnerable to major aftershocks. In our opinion, the rest of the building can be occupied when all loose pieces of ceiling and soffit at west end are removed. The ceiling support system should be inspected by Illig Construction for adequacy. They should also inspect the roof area, including cornice pieces, and remove any loose pieces.

Two possible options for utilizing the space below the tower are:

1. Remove the tower down to nave roof and cover with new roof.
2. Inject all cracks in tower walls with a properly specified epoxy resin gel. This may require research regarding amount of void in the walls and volume and cost of epoxy.

The tower should be investigated and evaluated further as part of the proposed future modifications and additions program.

GENERAL

This report is based on a visual examination of the exposed areas of the structure. No tests, destructive or non-destructive, were made. Other than noted above, no drawings of the original construction were available and no precise measurements were obtained. The inspection was made solely to assist in evaluating the structural integrity of the building. Neither the investigation nor this report is intended to address mechanical, electrical, plumbing or architectural features.[9]

---

[9]AALA, Report of Earthquake Field Investigations, Los Angeles, January 31, 1994.

The architects felt that the cathedral could continue to be used, provided that a barricade be erected around the bell tower, that access to the sacristy and sanctuary be limited to the celebrant and that all loose plaster be removed.[10] In the months after the Northridge earthquake, engineers carefully examined the cathedral and noticed that the major damage to the bell tower and the front entrance had been further aggravated by after-shocks and several additional minor temblors. With the primary object of safety in mind, the consultants recommended that it would not be economically or structurally feasible to refit and otherwise upgrade the existing edifice to the levels demanded by the building codes. It was obvious that a wholly new building was in order. Though no announcement was made at the time, a staff writer for the Los Angeles *Times* told readers that several prominent donors had come forward with funds "contingent on construction of a new cathedral."[11]

Cardinal Mahony went public the following day confirming that the archdiocese "had accepted a number of multi-million dollar pledges which will be used to construct a new Cathedral Complex on the site of the present Cathedral of Saint Vibiana

> We accept with profound gratitude, and on behalf of the some four million Catholics in the Archdiocese, the generous grants from the Leavey and the Dan Murphy Foundations for the sole purpose of guaranteeing the building of a new Cathedral Complex here at Second and Main streets.
>
> While specifically designated for the new Cathedral Complex, these major grants complement the unprecedented and ongoing generosity of parishioners in the Archdiocese of Los Angeles.
>
> In a very real sense, the extraordinary generosity being announced here today is an answered prayer to our very serious concerns about the long-range future of the present cathedral as a functioning symbol of our faith and heritage.
>
> After very careful deliberation, and working closely with the leadership of our major archdiocesan consultative bodies, I have concluded that all the discernible data suggests that it is in the best future interest of the Archdiocese of Los Angeles to

---

[10]AALA, O'Leary and Teresawa Report, Los Angeles, January 17, 1994.
[11]Los Angeles *Times,* January 5, 1994.

Roger Cardinal Mahony announces that a new cathedral will be built to replace Saint Vibiana which had been critically damaged in the 1994 earthquake. *Source: The Tidings*

remove all the buildings on the present cathedral site, and to build on this same historic site a new complex, including a cathedral designed to meet the post-conciliar Catholic worship and liturgy norms and with double the present seating, adequate underground parking and meeting facilities, including a 800-seat meeting room, new parish offices, and a new rectory/archbishop's residence.

Additional details about what will be called Cathedral Square, scheduled for completion within the next five years and in time for the year 2000, will be announced over the next several months.

What is important to announce today is that the major bequests, $10 million from the Leavey Foundation in anticipation of our original refurbishing concerns, and $25 million from the Dan Murphy Foundation in direct response to the fresh realities of 1994—in addition to $10 million now being pledged from other Catholic families—assures the full financing of Cathedral Square. I want to stress that this Cathedral Square project will be completed without the need for any special fund raising projects in our parishes.

The cardinal addresses the press about the future of Saint Vibiana Cathedral. *Source: The Tidings*

Any future plans for the new Cathedral Square will include preservation of the more significant historical items from the present cathedral, such as the marble catafalque with the remains of St. Vibiana, the statue of Our Lady of the Angels, the stained glass windows, the main altar and pulpit, the organ, the bells and similar important historical objects.

It is our plan to bring the historical memory of the old cathedral into the new, and we intend to study the feasibility of preserving certain elements of the existing structure in order to do so. While some might suggest that we use the gifts to preserve the existing cathedral, the terms of the gifts do not permit us to use the money for that purpose.

There is a clear rationale for the cathedral to remain in the inner city core, near where Catholic Angelinos first worshipped at the Plaza Church in *El Pueblo de Nuestra Senora de Los Angeles de la Porciuncula.* A visible presence of the archdiocese in the historical center of Los Angeles must be maintained and our bonds with the business, civic and various ethnic communities must remain.

Cardinal Mahony completed his momentous announcement by noting that every great city in the world with a Catholic heritage has a dynamic and functional cathedral at the heart of its central core. Los Angeles would be no exception as the archdiocese plans ahead for a new millennium in the service of the people of God. "These generous grants and gifts insure that St. Vibiana Cathedral will serve as a vital spiritual center for millions of Catholics, as well as for the general community, for centuries to come."

Mahony looked "forward to this Cathedral Square project serving as a catalyst to hasten the fuller development of the entire historical core of our city, and to working closely with officials of the City of Los Angeles, the County of Los Angeles, the State of California and the Federal Government to bring new vitality to downtown Los Angeles. May our combined efforts now signal a wonderful renaissance for the City of Los Angeles!"[12]

Not surprisingly Mahony's announcement inflamed preservationists "who wanted to save one of the oldest landmarks in Los Angeles." The Los Angeles conservancy immediately appealed to a 1963 decision whereby the cathedral was designated the seventeenth structure in the city named as a Historical Cultural Monument.[13]

---

[12]AALA, Announcement, January 6, 1995.
[13]Los Angeles *Daily News,* January 6, 1995.

A few days later, the local press reported that "Saint Vibiana Cathedral will be razed and replaced with a new $45 million dollar cathedral and conference center that will better accommodate the pageantry of the nation's most populous Roman Catholic archdiocese and help revive its downtown Los Angeles neighborhood." Councilwoman Rita Walters praised the decision to keep the new cathedral "in the heart of the city's historic core" as "one of courage and vision which deserves strong commendation."[14]

In an interview on the grounds of the old cathedral, the cardinal outlined the new project: He envisioned a complex that would double seating capacity to 2,400 and would have an 800 seat conference center, an outdoor plaza and a residence for himself and the parish priests. He said that the planned building would be in "a classical California Spanish design"[15] which would incorporate many of the significant architectural and interior features from the old building. He pledged to meet with preservationists to address their concerns, but he emphasized that the Leavey Foundation, along with other donors, had made their offers on the understanding that they would be used for a new cathedral in an area that would be called "Cathedral Square." In the meantime the few parishioners remaining at Saint Vibiana were assured that services would continue to be held in a nearby building until the new facility was completed.[16]

There were, of course, those who wondered if a new cathedral was necessary, especially in view of the fact that the archdiocese already had a suitable facility in St. Vincent Church at Figueroa and Adams. A writer to the Los Angeles *Times* noted "we have St. Basil in the mid-Wilshire district that seems to qualify in all respects."[17]

The executive director for the Los Angeles Conservancy, Linda Dishman, announced a few days later that "her organization was committed to find a way to preserve the building." She wanted copies of the engineering reports to see if a cost-efficient way to maintain the structure was feasible. Another supporter of the Conservancy, William F. Delvak, contended that it would be a sin committed against our ancestors to erase one of our city's few remaining remnants of the nineteenth century. Delvak felt that "the fate of St. Vibiana will not turn on laws but on public opinion."[18] The preservationists appeared to have little support from City Hall. Officials there felt that the new cathedral complex would be the cor-

[14]Los Angeles *Times,* January 7, 1995.
[15]Los Angeles *Daily News,* January 7, 1995.
[16]Los Angeles *Times,* January 9, 1995.
[17]*Ibid.,* January 15, 1995.
[18]*Ibid.,* January 16, 1995.

nerstone of their efforts to revitalize a part of the downtown that was rid-
dled with abandoned buildings.[19]

It was then that the librarian for the State of California, Kevin
Starr, weighed into the controversy with an editorial in which he contended that "in its design and material fabric, St. Vibiana subsumes and
preserves the identity of the Catholic experience in Los Angeles, so central to the spiritual and cultural identity of the city." He noted that the
cathedral "creates a material link with Spain, which had brought European Civilization to California, in the same way that the Pilgrims had
brought it to Massachusetts on the Atlantic coast." To Starr Saint Vibiana
was "no mere cathedral, no mere landmark. It is one of the half dozen
structures through which Los Angeles knows itself. To amputate such a
structure, part of the living tissue of Los Angeles without dialogue, without entertaining alternatives . . . is too violent an act to contemplate."
Starr advocated incorporating the old cathedral into the larger complex
envisioned by the cardinal.[20]

The Starr essay was a blessing insofar as it gave the cardinal an
ideal forum for spelling out in greater detail the rationale for a new cathedral. Beyond suggesting that Starr misunderstood completely the role
and place of a cathedral in the life of the Catholic community, Cardinal
Mahony opened up the larger issue for public scrutiny.

> First, a cathedral church occupies a very special place in
> the life and soul of a Catholic archdiocese. It is the spiritual
> font as well as the source of identity and unity for the entire
> Catholic community. Its main purpose is to provide adequate
> worship space to carry out the various Catholic liturgies, and
> in a special way, those involving the archbishop of the local
> Church. Starr makes no mention of Catholic worship and
> liturgy in his article, thus missing the centrality of this vital
> mission of the cathedral.

---

[19]The Los Angeles Conservancy was established in 1978 as a movement to
preserve the Los Angeles Central Public Library from the wrecking ball. Their
fight took two years, but they won and today the city has a showcase bibliophilic
facility that both retains the old, serves the present and showcases the future.
There are approximately 6,000 members of the preservation group that provides
a $900,000 annual budget with a paid staff of seven, the largest historic preser-
vation agency on the west coast. Carol Bidwell, in an essay for the Los Angeles
Daily News, felt that "the group's track record speaks for itself; nearly three dozen
major preservation successes and more than 100 minor victories, a more than
90 percent win record."

[20]Los Angeles *Times,* April 30, 1995.

Several liturgical renewals have taken place in the Catholic Church since 1876—the year the old St. Vibiana was dedicated. Most important are the liturgical reforms of the Second Vatican Council. The council's extraordinary vision places all the emphasis upon the Church as the People of God, not upon a given pile of stones—regardless of their age.

The present cathedral was never built to accommodate today's Catholic liturgy, nor can its structure be reconfigured to accomplish this primary goal. Clearly missing from the old cathedral, but essential to the new one are:

• a main altar close to the people and with adequate space for deacons and priests to surround the archbishop in solemn Liturgy;
• the Blessed Sacrament Chapel;
• the new Reconciliation rooms;
• the Baptismal Font of Immersion;
• the Prominent Chapel of the Holy Oils.

The lack of these adequate spaces helps to explain why very few of the archdiocese's 4.5 million Catholics have ever been to St. Vibiana.

Starr dismisses out of hand the very real and serious seismic problems with the old cathedral. Originally, three buildings were constructed on this site: the cathedral, the bishop and priests' residence next to it and the original school. Both the residence and the school were so badly damaged by the 1933 Long Beach earthquake that both buildings had to be demolished. Successive earthquakes have taken their toll on the remaining cathedral to such an extent that today we permit only its very limited use.

The cathedral has been subject to several structural studies over the years, including one immediately following the January 17, 1994 earthquake. The cathedral is now undergoing an additional, more comprehensive structural study to determine its seismic stability and the dangers presented by recently discovered seismic faults. That final report is due in mid-June.

Four events in 1994 resulted in the final decision to remove all of the present buildings and to construct a new Catholic cathedral complex: the January 17th Northridge earthquake which seriously damaged the bell tower and the cathedral itself; the loss of the parking lot to the north to new development; the move of the Union Rescue Mission to a new and expanded site; and the lack of any commitment of funding to rebuild and renovate the old building.

As Archbishop of Los Angeles, I remain committed to fulfilling what I said at the January 6th press conference announcing the new cathedral complex: "Every great city in the world with a Catholic heritage has a dynamic and functional cathedral at the heart of its central core. Los Angeles will be no exception as the archdiocese plans ahead for a new millennium in the service to the people of God."[21]

On May 25, 1995, Cardinal Mahony closed the cathedral because, as he said, the Northridge earthquake had "left the landmark unsafe." In closing the 119-year-old edifice, Mahony cited the "potential for another temblor to collapse the 83-foot bell tower." Daily Masses and other services were moved temporarily to the former elementary school next door. The decision "was clinched by a report from the Peck/Jones Construction Company that found a temblor could topple the cathedral's bell tower through the wood roof and plaster ceiling over the sanctuary, threatening injury or death to the clergy and congregation below."[22]

A newspaper report noted that structural engineer Nabih Youssef, who was confronted with one of the most contentious architectural preservation squabbles in city history, had been hired by the archdiocese to make an unbiased study of the building. Youssef was highly regarded as "a competent, very sophisticated man" known to be "intellectually honest."

In order to tone down the rhetoric, Cardinal Mahony handed the reins of the project over to Ira Yellin, a developer with a track record in such successful projects as the Grand Central Market. The Yellin/Keller firm would take the Cathedral Square project from concept to construction, including the selection of architects, contractors and consultants. At that time Cathedral Square encompassed the block bordered by Third, Main, Second and Los Angeles streets. At a press conference Yellin said that the project would likely include "a very gracious plaza which will welcome the entire community outdoors for holy days and be a part of the city's regular life." Yellin pointed out that "when you look back to the history of civilization the building of cathedrals has usually defined what a city is all about. In Europe and elsewhere in the United States, the spaces around great cathedrals are some of the great spaces of urban civilization. We have the opportunity to model and create that here."[23]

Early in October of 1995, the study commissioned by the archdiocese was released in a 200-page report detailing the extent of the damage to

---

[21]Los Angeles *Times,* May 5, 1995.

[22]Los Angeles *Daily News,* May 26, 1995.

[23]Los Angeles *Times,* July 10, 1995. See also *Downtown News,* September 4, 1995.

the church that resulted from a series of earthquakes. Despite the fact that it experienced a relatively low level of ground shaking during the Northridge quake, "the cracking to unreinforced masonry walls is extensive and penetrates the entire wall thickness," the report concluded. In addition, those walls rest on "rubble with questionable support capacity." In addition to steel bracing and injected concrete, repairs would require new foundations and some new walls across the church's width.[24]

Although razing the structure would require an environmental impact study and city review, Mayor Richard Riordan supported the demolition, as did key financial backers of the new cathedral complex. Estimates were that without a $20 million seismic overhaul, the building could indeed collapse in another earthquake. Its precarious condition was aggravated by its resting atop an intense confluence of faults. The study was aimed at offering compromises between preservationists and those favoring demolition. The report strongly suggested that Saint Vibiana would emerge from seismic retrofitting more like a reconstructed replica than a restored original. Yellin noted that any final decision would center on how much money would be involved and whether the archdiocese was interested in saving the historic building or replicating it. Yellin's personal views were that he did not "believe in reproducing the past."

Whether all or part of the cathedral was preserved, the project would have the potential of transforming a section of Downtown Los Angeles that has long suffered the classic symptoms of urban decay—rising crime, homelessness, drug trafficking and deteriorating abandoned buildings. "The decision of the cardinal to build the permanent cathedral of the archdiocese in the old historic core is an extraordinarily important one," Yellin said. "In that one act, I believe he has done more to give a future to all the buildings in the historic core than all of us working all these years."[25]

Members of the Conservancy, on the other hand, argued that by incorporating the cathedral into a new complex of buildings, a less intrusive restoration might be feasible, perhaps one which would scale down the retrofitting to as low as $3 million. They argued that such a solution would keep Angelinos from losing their "oldest and grandest surviving structure from the founding era of the city."[26]

Early on the morning of June 1, 1996, a huge crane was rolled into place and before long the crowning cross and cupola from the cathedral's bell tower were removed in what preservationists complained was the

[24]AALA, Seismic Overall Report, Los Angeles, October 1995.
[25]Los Angeles *Times,* October 10, 1995.
[26]Los Angeles *Times,* December 5, 1995

Protestors "took control of the cathedral tower" and reclaimed it for the poor! *Source: The Tidings*

first step of demolishing the cathedral. The controversial action was halted abruptly when a hastily summoned city building inspector ruled that the archdiocese had not acquired the proper permits. Not so, argued archdiocesan officials who said they were following a city order issued the previous afternoon to "abate" the imminent danger that the earthquake damaged tower posed to public safety. Outraged preservationists engaged in an energetic duel waged with cellular telephone calls from the sidewalk next to the church. A local newspaper reported that "observers were provided with the spectacle of the wood-frame beige cupola, about twenty feet tall, being plucked into the sky like a decoration from an elaborate wedding cake and deposited in the parking lot behind the 120-year-old cathedral." O'Malley Miller, attorney for the archdiocese, said the demolition

A crane lowers the cupola from the tower to the
parking lot behind St. Vibiana. *Source: The
Tidings*

began in response to a Los Angeles Department of Building and Safety
order Friday to "abate" the seismic hazard within seventy-two hours.
Although that order did not mention the need for a permit, although the
archdiocese would apply for one.[27]

The skirmish of words continued with the Church's attorney arguing that had not the archdiocese taken action within seventy-two hours,
it could have been charged with a misdemeanor. The Conservancy was not
able to enlist wide support and even the prominent councilwoman, Rita

---

[27]*Ibid.,* June 2, 1996.

Walters, felt that the group "was overzealous in its attempt to protect the historic landmark" by obtaining a restraining order.[28]

Even the pundits admitted that the cardinal, who called a press conference over the matter, was "holding most of the cards." They recognized that should Mahony decide to move the cathedral elsewhere, it would be a "severe blow to city and state efforts to save the rundown and increasingly dangerous old section of downtown."[29] One writer,[30] commenting on the cardinal's performance at the press conference said, "It was a great show by a media master in a town where media and hype are powerful forces in politics." After being given a tour of the cathedral he concluded that "only fervent prayer has prevented the old church from collapsing."

An editorial in the *Daily News* said that if the Los Angeles Conservancy is "sincere about preserving the earthquake-battered Skid Row church, they should pass the collection plate among themselves and buy it." Otherwise "they should let the Archdiocese of Los Angeles exercise its First Amendment rights—freedom of religion—and decide where and how to worship, even if that involves demolition."[31] Mayor Richard Riordan complained that "unfortunately, a few conservationists threaten to trample the incredible effort of the archdiocese to build . . . a centerpiece for revitalization of the historic core of the city."[32]

Meanwhile officials of the archdiocese began the process of removing the stained glass windows, marble statues, furnishings and other significant items from the cathedral. Fearing that action foreshadowed the demolition of the building, preservationists complained that moving such historic items might violate city rules on a designated "historic cultural monument." The cardinal announced that all the items being removed, including the pulpit, lamps and candleholders would be "used in some way in the new and much larger cathedral planned for the same site."[33] An announcement was made that the relics of Saint Vibiana herself, "an enigmatic third century Italian martyr," would be housed temporarily at Calvary Cemetery.[34] Entrusted with relocating the artifacts was Carnivale and Lohr Inc. of Bell Gardens, the firm that earlier built the marble sarcophagus for Saint Vibiana's relics. The stained glass windows were crated and shipped to The Judson Studios.

Architectural opinions were all over the map. David Finnigan quoted a spokesman for the archdiocese to the effect that Saint Vibiana

---

[28]*Ibid.,* June 4, 1996.
[29]*Ibid.*
[30]Bill Boyarski.
[31]June 5, 1995.
[32]Los Angeles *Times,* June 4, 1996.
[33]*Ibid.,* May 18, 1996.
[34]Los Angeles *Daily News,* May 26, 1996.

Catafalque of Saint Vibiana is moved to its temporary resting place at Calvary Mausoleum.

Cathedral was "really an unremarkable replica of seventeenth century Baroque architecture . . . a pretty standard replication of an architecture that was already moribund."[35]

In any event, on June 4, 1996, after a brief inspection of the cathedral, the City of Los Angeles Department of Building and Safety "red-tagged" the entire building declaring it "a potential hazard to life and safety." The sidewalk along Main Street was closed as well as the parking lane next to the cathedral entrance.

The lead editorial in the next day's issue of the Los Angeles *Times* advocated that the "archdiocese should be allowed to go forward on rebuilding." It reported that Cardinal Mahony "was sufficiently provoked by the weekend's events to call a press conference to renew his threat to padlock the crumbling property and move . . . out of the downtown area." The editorial pointed out that "if Mahony does in fact walk away from the

---

[35]Los Angeles *Reader,* May 31, 1996.

Craftsmen from The Judson Studios remove the stained glass windows at the old cathedral. *Source: The Tidings*

property at Second and Main streets, as he threatens to do, there will be little new development left to energize a downtown revitalization."[36]

On June 10th the cardinal addressed a Civic Center rally for the new cathedral in which he agreed that "we are at a decisive and defining moment in the history of downtown Los Angeles." He pointed out that his role as archbishop forced him to reject what he described as efforts "to use legal maneuvers to thwart our efforts" at the free exercise of religion. Once again he repeated his decision that this was "the fundamental issue with which there can be no compromise." While stating that he and his advisors preferred to remain in the downtown area, he declared that "if we abandon this site, it will not be because we want to do so." Then speaking directly to members of the Los Angeles Conservancy, Mahony made the following observations:

- the old cathedral was never designed nor built to sustain the onslaught of earthquakes that have struck it repeatedly over the past 120 years, rendering it a dangerous building and an imminent threat to life and safety;

---

[36]Los Angeles *Times,* June 5, 1996.

- the archdiocese has absolutely no money to carry out any of the proposals to somehow save the ravaged structure, and the Conservancy has offered no money;
- the space available to us on Cathedral Square prohibits the inclusion of the old structure in our plans;

He concluded his remarks by inviting the Conservancy "to join with us in our efforts to build a fully new, free standing cathedral on this site, and to work with us and our architect to find ways to memorialize appropriately and meaningfully the old cathedral on our site."[37]

The feud with the Los Angeles Conservancy was insufferably long and costly to both sides and in the end, neither won. The cardinal charged that the Conservancy was making it "virtually impossible" to build the new cathedral on the present property. He went so far as to appoint a committee to begin considering alternate sites. The archdiocesan newspaper claimed that what Dishman and her board wanted was "capitulation not cooperation."[38] It decried the fact that Church officials had been forced to direct their resources towards those "whose sole interest is in preserving broken bones."[39] Despite it all in early June the Conservancy won a delay in the demolition. They even organized a vigil of supporters who prayed outside the venerable landmark in hopes of sparing it from the wrecking ball.[40]

Once again members of the Conservancy wanted to talk directly with Mahony. But it was too late and even Mayor Richard Riordan warned that "a few conservationists threaten to trample the incredible effort of the archdiocese to build a new cathedral."[41] Conservancy leaders were aware that the cardinal had bested them for TV air and newspaper space or, as one said, "he is a better poker player than they are." In an editorial for the Los Angeles *Times,* Harold Meyerson wrote that the cardinal's response to the Conservancy was "a terrifically theatrical press conference" wherein he had threatened to administer downtown the last rites."[42]

Meyerson was more right than he may have believed. Mahony announced that an eleven member Site Selection Committee had begun looking for alternative sites upon which to build a new Cathedral Square. That time was running out for the Conservancy was echoed by the influ-

---

[37]AALA, Statement, Los Angeles, June 10, 1996.
[38]*The Tidings,* June 7, 1996.
[39]Los Angeles *Times,* June 7, 1996.
[40]*Ibid.,* June 9, 1996.
[41]Los Angeles *Daily News,* June 10, 1996.
[42]Los Angeles *Times,* June 10, 1996.

ential and powerful Rita Walters who said that "if the Conservancy wins on this it is a Pyrrhic victory."[43] With a sad but determined gesture, the cardinal declared the fight over–the archdiocese would move on!

The mayor made no secret of his opinion about the cathedral. He was quoted as saying: "History matters, history informs, history challenges. But leaving St. Vibiana in her current state would be the reckless destruction of our future." He said the choice was clear: "Do we choose decay in our city's center or do we choose a centerpiece of renewal."[44] A more blunt viewpoint was expressed by Woodrow J. Hughes who described the Conservancy as "a gang that never paid a dime's worth of property tax. It is not elected by the people or appointed by the people we elect. Why are these nuts allowed to jump out of the woodwork shouting . . ."[45]

The next move was to have the Los Angeles City Council decertify the cathedral as an Historical Landmark. Linda Dishman of the Conservancy felt that would be "an extremely dangerous precedent for future preservation efforts in our city."[46] On the other hand the Cultural Heritage Commission's official guidelines provided that a building could be taken off the protected list if the evidence for its original designation is later found to be significantly wrong.

On June 18, 1996 the council voted to decertify, with only one abstention. The matter was then forwarded to the Cultural Affairs Commission,[47] but there were still obstacles. On June 17th, Judge Robert O'Brien called for further environmental studies. Effectively he felt that there was no emergency to take down the bell tower and proceed with the demolition.[48] The cardinal was furious and, in a private memorandum, he referred to the Conservancy as "urban terrorists." He worried that their action would unleash a litany of legal challenges, new suits, new TROs and the prospect of at least three years of legal expenses and enormous amounts of our time." He said "we must move to a new site that is cleared and that we can work with now."[49]

There were many others who shared his views. An example would be John Malloy, Administrator of the Community Redevelopment Agency, who admitted that "sometimes we must be prepared to lose some historic structures in order to obtain the new development we need to establish

[43]*Downtown News,* June 10, 1996.

[44]Los Angeles *Times,* June 10, 1996.

[45]Los Angeles *Daily News,* June 14, 1996.

[46]Los Angeles *Times,* June 14, 1996

[47]AALA, Terrance Fleming to Roger Cardinal Mahony, Los Angeles, June 18, 1996.

[48]Los Angeles *Times,* June 18, 1996.

[49]AALA, Roger Cardinal Mahony to Terrance Fleming, Rome, June 19, 1996.

the economic environment necessary to sustain the larger historical interest. Here in Los Angeles, the issue of achieving a new cathedral on the St. Vibiana site is very critical to helping to stabilize the entire historic core. It is time for preservationists to give a little in the interest of the larger whole."[50]

Interestingly the controversy was not restricted to Los Angeles. In New York, for example, a paper complained that "there is some unchurchly bickering between the archdiocese, preservationists, urban planners, municipal planners, state legislators, business leaders and the court over the look and design of the new cathedral." It pointed out that Cardinal Mahony was a "spiritual leader who believes that the work of the Lord includes aggressive involvement in a community's temporal affairs." A reporter asked the cardinal where he would rank Saint Vibiana Cathedral on the list of the world's great churches. He replied "Either last or next to last. There may be one worse, but I can't recall."[51]

A moderately sized book could be and may one day be written about the fate of the venerable Saint Vibiana as it teeter-tottered between the Cultural Affairs Commission, the Community Redevelopment Agency, the Department of Building and Safety, the Historical Landmarks Commission and various levels of the judicial system.

Meanwhile, as the cardinal pointed out in a memo dated June 21st, "everyone in Los Angeles backs our plans to build a brand new cathedral, except the Los Angeles Conservancy."[52] He noted that the mayor, the City Council, the CRA, our Catholic people and our priests want a hasty resolution to the impasse. For that reason Mahony called a press conference for June 25th at which he announced "plans to build a new $45 million facility on the site of the quake damaged St. Vibiana Cathedral in downtown Los Angeles" had been abandoned.[53] Seeing no end in sight to the legal challenges put up by the Conservancy, the cardinal had decided to move on. An editorial in the Los Angeles *Daily News* agreed, noting that "holding a building in higher esteem than the people it serves seriously undermines the very purpose of preservation." The paper went further and wondered if it might be time "to re-evaluate the entire historic-designation process to allow for greater flexibility on the part of land owners."[54]

Ira Yellin wrote a classic editorial for the Los Angeles *Times* in which he outlined how such esteemed persons as Tim Vreeland, a distinguished professor of architecture at UCLA, and Nabih Youssef, a seismic

[50]Los Angeles *Independent,* June 12, 1996.
[51]New York *Times,* June 17, 1996.
[52]AALA, Memorandum, Los Angeles, June 21, 1996.
[53]AALA, Statement for Press Conference, June 25, 1996.
[54]Los Angeles *Daily News,* July, 24, 1996

engineer recognized by the Conservancy for the integrity and quality of his work, had agreed that the existing structure had no architectural merit and relatively minor historical value. Added to that, retrofitting the building would leave it still inadequate as a worship space. The cardinal made one last futile appeal to the Conservancy to "end its destructive and wasteful lawsuits for nothing profound will be achieved by continued litigation except the loss of a historic opportunity for our city and destruction of the Conservancy's credibility and viability, which so many have built up over so many years."[55]

A New Cathedral Site

As early as May of 1996, there were hints that alternative sites were being discussed for the new cathedral. Newspaper reports indicated that Cardinal Mahony "prefers that the cathedral heed tradition in Catholic countries and remain in the downtown historic section," but there were problems beyond those presented by the Los Angeles Conservancy involved. For example, it was reported that some "people who own contingent properties are asking exorbitantly high prices."[56] *The Tidings* reported that negotiations with the owners of the twelve properties to the south of the present site had indeed become bogged down by the owners' insistence that the archdiocese pay at least twice, and in some cases, far higher, than the land is worth. [57]

There were some who argued that the archdiocese was "using the explorations as a bargaining tactic with downtown landowners," while others insisted that the possibility of moving elsewhere was "real and extremely upsetting for hope that a new cathedral would help revive Los Angeles' troubled urban core and Civic Center."[58]

Meanwhile the members of the Cathedral Advisory Board voted unanimously "to support the cardinal's decision to look for a new site unless he can be assured that the archdiocese will not incur costs fighting lawsuits by preservationists." While Mahony was quoted as preferring that the cathedral remain downtown, "he set a deadline of early June for his conditions to be met."[59]

The Los Angeles *Times* weighed in as preferring that the new cathedral remain downtown. Speaking about the obstinacy exhibited by the

---

[55]June 27, 1996.
[56]Los Angeles *Daily News,* May 21, 1996.
[57]*The Tidings,* May 24, 1996.
[58]Los Angeles *Times,* May 23, 1996
[59]Los Angeles *Daily News,* May 23, 1996.

"This is *not* the place!"—Cardinal Roger Mahony.

Source: Los Angeles *Times,* June 11, 1996.

Los Angeles Conservancy, an editorial said that "frustration is stoked by a variety of causes: a clash with conservationists over restoring the old cathedral; the high costs of such a restoration; the likelihood of grueling encounters with city bureaucrats over the permitting and construction of a new facility at the present site and the rising price of adjacent property that the archdiocese has indicated that it would seek to buy to accommodate an expanded cathedral complex." The editorial countered by pointing out "compelling reasons" for keeping the cathedral downtown arguing that the spiritual center of the archdiocese should send a strong affirmation of faith—not just spiritual faith but a belief in a future vibrant and welcoming Civic Center, a place full of more than just buildings."

Downtown is struggling against strong economic tides of business retrenchment, mergers and government downsizing. The invigorating promise of the proposed Walt Disney Concert Hall, among other projects, still hangs in the balance. The flight of St. Vibiana would be a severe body blow to efforts to revive the Civic Center. St. Vibiana is needed right where it is, and city leaders must do all they reasonably can to ensure that the cathedral will be a part of a revitalized downtown when it enters the new century.[60]

By this time public opinion was definitely lining up in favor of the archdiocese. Civic officials began issuing statements advising the Conservancy to back off. Especially targeted was the "pigheadedness" of the property owners who would lose the most if the cathedral moves."[61]

In retrospect, the officials at the Conservancy performed a great service for the Catholics in Southern California by forcing them to select what became an ideal site at another location.

On July 22nd, 1996, Cardinal Mahony announced that the archdiocese would "absolutely not" build on the site of the current Saint Vibiana Cathedral." While unwilling to specify what possible sites might be under consideration, the cardinal said he expected a tentative purchase agreement soon for property "just west of downtown" that would "give the new cathedral a marvelous vista point over the city." A newspaper reported that "knowledgeable sources identified that site as next to the former Union Oil headquarters between Fourth and Sixth streets immediately west of the Harbor Freeway." Other sites were still being discussed, however, but the overall announcement "gave some measure of relief to Los Angeles city leaders who see the cathedral project as a crucial boost for downtown." When asked if there was any chance that the old site would be reconsidered. "Mahony said the project would still move on."[62] It was also on that date that the cardinal, for the first time, revealed that the new edifice would be named "The Cathedral of Our Lady of the Angels."[63]

On September 13, 1996, the cardinal shared with members of the Cathedral Advisory Board the criteria in the selection process that would be followed over several months by the Cathedral Complex Site Acquisition Committee. He considered "the ecclesial and pastoral criteria to be far more important than other criteria that urban planners might recommend."

FUNDAMENTAL PRINCIPLE: The entire final site selection process flows from the clear understanding that the old site at Main and Second streets is to be abandoned, and

---

[60]Los Angeles *Times,* May 26, 1996
[61]*Downtown News,* May 27, 1996.
[62]Los Angeles *Times,* July 23, 1996.
[63]*Downtown News,* July 23, 1996.

that all of those properties are to be sold in order to help fund the purchase of the new site.

I. ECCLESIAL CRITERIA

- Does the site fulfill the cathedral's fundamental role: the Mother Church of the Archdiocese of Los Angeles, a visible sign of unity linking all 292 parishes to the cathedral?
- Does the cathedral serve primarily as the archdiocese's Mother Church, not just the "downtown civic center Church"?
- Does the site offer the cathedral its proper role in the community, linked to, but not dependent on, other community landmarks, structures and institutions?
- Will the cathedral have a sense of "independence" that will prevail for decades and centuries to come, regardless of other changes in the central Los Angeles area?
- Does the site help the cathedral to "bridge" the civic, governmental, cultural and residential dimensions of downtown Los Angeles?
- Does the site offer room for possible expansion of Church programs and services in future years, or is the site too small to accommodate changing future needs? Will the site accommodate any further buildings in the future?
- Given the vast web of Southern California freeways, will the cathedral be truly visible to the millions of people who constantly travel these freeways, thus serving as a beacon of hope for all?

II. PASTORAL CRITERIA

- Is the site so located that large numbers of people can come to the cathedral on foot throughout the course of each day: visitors, pilgrims, downtown employees, and downtown residents?
- Is the site such that both the cathedral and its plaza will be welcoming to all?
- What is the potential for new and increased housing near the site? What strategies are now included in the Downtown General Plan and the Civic Center Plan that would enhance housing near and around the new cathedral?
- Is the site truly "user friendly" to all people?

III. PROPERTY CRITERIA

FUNDAMENTAL PRINCIPLE: All of the Cathedral Complex buildings must be located on the same site, not spread over two separate blocks. The integration of all the cathedral pastoral services demands that the complex be self-contained on a single site.

- The property must be adequate to permit the following project to be developed upon it:
  Cathedral Church: 30,000 to 36,000 square feet
  Rectory/Residence: 20,000 square feet
  Cathedral Center: 24,000 square feet
  Plaza: 20,000 square feet minimum
- Is the property owned by *one* owner? if not, how many owners? How complicated to acquire all the parcels? Prices? What is the realistic time frame for assembling the *entire site* into one property unit?
- Is the property vacant of all buildings? If not, what will it cost to purchase and demolish each building?
- How easily and early can the property be acquired and secured? What is the earliest, firm acquisition date to acquire the entire property free of all buildings—a vacant lot? What will the *total* costs be for such a site?

IV. ACCESSIBILITY CRITERIA

- Does the site have good, easy and simple freeway access thus enabling it to be accessed *primarily* by the Catholics of the Archdiocese of Los Angeles, the members of the 292 parish communities?
- Is the site served by the downtown Metro? How near is the current Metro stop? How extensive is the bus service passing by the site?
- How will downtown weekday "rush hours" impact the site? Will Saturdays and Sundays pose any special problems for the site? Any special advantages?
- Since visibility of the cathedral to people invites them to it, how does the site enhance or diminish accessibility?

V. PARKING CRITERIA

- How would the site accommodate parking needs for the cathedral?
- Are there shared parking possibilities close to the site?
- Will the site require unusual and expensive parking construction?

VI. POSITIVE IMPACT CRITERIA

- Will the site enable the cathedral to be a positive catalyst for other development nearby, especially housing and retail stores?

- Will the site help stimulate and generate new levels of development in its zone of influence, and within a reasonable time frame?
- Will the areas surrounding the site be open to positive development and improvement—whether by private sources or government leadership?
- What are the realistic timetables for such overall development?[64]

Of the original eight sites, four were owned by government entities and four were under private ownership. By September 15th the number had been reduced to three, including a parcel adjacent to the Glendale Freeway, another at the corner of Sepulveda Boulevard and Rinaldi Street in Mission Hills and a third at Temple Street and Grand Avenue adjacent to the Hollywood Freeway.

Acting on the recommendation of the Cathedral Advisory Board, the cardinal called a Press Conference on September 17th to announce the final selection of the site for the new cathedral. It was to be a county-owned plot of land between the city's Hall of Administration on Temple Street and the Hollywood Freeway. The 5.53-acre parcel of land encompassed 241,000 square feet and would cost $10,850,000 which was about $45 per square foot. The area was then being used as a parking lot for the county employees. The cardinal said that the advantages of the lot include the following:

- its relation to the downtown cultural and civic centers, as well as to the 292 parishes of the archdiocese;
- space adequate to build the church, the cathedral plaza, the new cathedral center, the archbishop's residence/rectory and needed parking;
- freeway visibility and accessibility, as well as proximity (one-half block) to the Civic Center Metro Rail station and major bus routes;
- ability to serve three major constituencies—the 4.5 million Catholics of the archdiocese, downtown residents and downtown commuter employees;
- easy accessibility on foot, according to the Civic Center Plan;
- the Cathedral Complex project will help further development of the Temple Street corridor and could act as a catalyst for further residential and retail development in the area;
- the lot is vacant and has but one owner, the County of Los Angeles, which has no other development plans for the site.[65]

---

[64]AALA, Memorandum of Criteria, Los Angeles, September 13, 1996.
[65]AALA, Public Announcement, Los Angeles, September 17, 1996.

Downtown Hillside Site Selected for Cathedral

■ **Church:** Catholic archdiocese hopes to buy 5½ acres, now used as parking lot, from county within 6 months.

By LARRY GORDON
TIMES STAFF WRITER

Now, it is an ugly, 1,100-space parking lot next to the Hollywood Freeway and a steam-belching heating plant. But in four years, the hillside property could be the home of a towering new flagship church for the Los Angeles Roman Catholic Archdiocese, visible from East Los Angeles to Hollywood and including "a wonderfully landscaped plaza" for worshipers, downtown office workers and tourists.

The proposed transformation of the county-owned Lot 20 into the Cathedral of Our Lady of the Angels was announced Tuesday by Cardinal Roger M. Mahony as he formally began the task of acquiring the sloping 5.53-acre parcel across Temple Street from the county Hall of Administration. Church and county officials expressed confidence that the sale can be completed within six months and said architectural design work will begin immediately.

However, money remains at issue. The county is asking $10.85

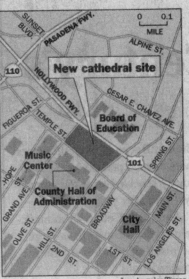

Los Angeles Times

million for the property, based on a recent appraisal. Archdiocese advisors contend that the land is worth $6 million to $7 million.

"There will be obstacles and hurdles along the way that we will have to jump over and around," Mahony said at a press conference Tuesday at the chosen site. "But we do hope to make it work."

Source: Los Angeles *Times,* September 18, 1996.

A non-imaginative writer for the Los Angeles *Times* described the area as "an ugly 1,100 square space parking lot next to the Hollywood Freeway and a steam-belching heating plant." He pointed out that since the county was the sole owner of the entire block, negotiations should be simplified. No demolition would be required except for some wooden shacks. Though the cardinal anticipated no problems with the site, he remained prepared to move to one or the other of the sites, observing that "we will not consider any further downtown locations."[66]

For someone who chooses words carefully, it bears notice that Jose Rafael Moneo, the architect for the new cathedral, picked such adjectives as "wonderful" and "incredible" to describe the new site. He felt that it "embraces both the civic and the cultural center of the city and yet it is not absorbed by their presence." He was also impressed, as was the cardinal, by the heavy flow of pedestrian traffic and its proximity to public transportation. Moneo likened the adjacent freeway to a river in the way it was used to move people and goods from one place to another. He also compared the slope of the hill on which the new cathedral would sit to the view of Notre Dame Cathedral in Paris as seen from the River Seine.[67]

Judging from letters to the editors of local newspapers the selection was well received by the general public. Ethel Rubio, for example, felt that "a lot of false idealism and vision have been associated with this project." She felt that "the new cathedral should be thought of and recognized not only as an icon for the followers of the Catholic faith in Los Angeles, but as a sanctuary for all." She said "Let's just sit back, relax and let the Archdiocese of Los Angeles and Moneo design and build us a new cathedral."[68]

The topography of the site slopes to the east more than twenty feet vertical over a distance of more than 600 feet horizontal. It is mostly filled ground from the days when the adjacent area was excavated for the construction of the Hollywood Freeway. Cardinal Mahony believed that the "site offers a wonderful panorama of downtown Los Angeles, and gently embraces both the culture and the downtown civic communities, while retaining a certain spirit of independence from any other major buildings or institutions."[69]

It was a happy Mahony who announced to Rafael Moneo that "at 12:21 p.m. on Friday December 20, 1996 the new cathedral site legally became ours!"[70] Mayor Richard Riordan was handed a check on that day

---

[66]Los Angeles *Times,* September 18, 1996.

[67]*The Tidings,* September 20, 1996.

[68]Los Angeles *Times,* September 30, 1996.

[69]Quoted in *Cathedral Update,* September 1996.

[70]AALA, Roger Cardinal Mahony to Jose Rafael Moneo, Los Angeles, December 21, 1996.

Future site of Our Lady of the Angels Cathedral.

for $10,850 million, thereby closing a three-month land transaction that involved the County of Los Angeles selling the site to the City's Community Redevelopment Agency which in turn sold it to the archdiocese.

Topographical historians are unanimous in declaring that "location is everything" in the planning and development of a building. Over the next decades, the Cathedral of Our Lady of the Angels will influence, modernize and eventually come to characterize and define the skyline of Los Angeles.

Site of the new Cathedral of Our Lady of the Angels, taken on May 23, 1949. *Source: Air Photo Archives, UCLA Dept. of Geography*

Chapter III

Oversight

With few exceptions, hardly any artistically significant Catholic churches have been built in Los Angeles since the days of John J. Cantwell. That such spectacular houses of worship as Blessed Sacrament (Hollywood), Holy Family (South Pasadena), Saint Andrews (Pasadena), Saint Brendan (Los Angeles) and Saint Monica (Santa Monica) were designed and built in parishes with only local revenues speaks highly of Cantwell's leadership. The only architecturally impressive Catholic church built in recent years was Saint Basil, erected on Wilshire Boulevard in the 1960s, by Msgr. Benjamin G. Hawkes.

An apocryphal story is told that the Blessed Mother, appearing in Los Angeles several decades ago, told the visionaries: "Build here a beautiful church." Whether the Cathedral of Our Lady of the Angels can be regarded as a response to Mary's directive probably hinges on one's definition of beauty. But even with beauty aside, the Cathedral of Our Lady of the Angels is surely a world-class edifice in every respect. While any cathedral is bigger than one person, it would not be an overstatement to say that the catalyst, the one who made it all come together, was the Archbishop of Los Angeles. And there is probably no case in all recorded history where a cathedral has been planned, financed, erected and dedicated within a single archiepiscopate, in barely eight years, something that could only have occurred in California and under the leadership of a dynamic and single-minded churchman.[1]

In God's providence, Roger Cardinal Mahony was the right man at the right time. He had come to the archiepiscopate in 1985 because he had the requisites that Roman authorities felt were necessary for ecclesial leadership of the Church in Southern California.[2] But Mahony had

---

[1] Three of the nation's best-known cathedrals, all of them Anglican, took more than half a century to build: Grace Cathedral (San Francisco) fifty-four years, National Cathedral (D.C.) eighty-three years and Saint John the Divine (New York City), sixty years.

[2] In addition to being native born, he exhibited personal piety, loyalty to the Church's *Magisterium,* theological astuteness, administrative experience, pastoral proclivity, liturgical acumen, lingual facility, diplomatic smoothness, social awareness, political credentials, leadership ability, episcopal seniority and a

other qualities too that served him well for the most ambitious and extensive project ever attempted by the Catholic Church in California, maybe even the nation. He was decisive, energetic, pragmatic, practical and courageous. He was also a quick-learner, a consensus maker and, finally, a workaholic who never allowed himself to be dissuaded by the suggestion of difficult or impossible.

Once the overall project for the new cathedral had been launched, Cardinal Mahony took upon himself the *de-facto* role of Chief Executive Officer and from that moment onwards, any and all major decisions (and a lot of minor ones) were made exclusively by him or with his approval.

The cardinal reckoned that he spent at least twenty hours a week in activities relating to the cathedral. He personally approached any and all potential donors and wrote hundreds of letters to prospective supporters. Only once, in all the mountains of his correspondence, does he exhibit any weariness and that was in July of 2001, when he wrote that "frankly, the incredible amount of time and energy required to complete the new cathedral and its fund raising have brought me to the very brink of total exhaustion." Raising the final $30 million took "every ounce of energy and strength."[3]

Working closely with the cardinal was Jose Debasa and Bill Close who served as Chief Financial Officer, a position in which he directed all fund raising, supervised the complicated dealings with Allied Irish Bank and kept track of all expenditures on a daily basis. A third member of the leadership team was Brother Hilarion O'Connor, O.S.F., who in his capacity as Chief Administrative Officer looked after and implemented all contracts and served as liaison with the Morley and Daly companies. He interacted with sub-contractors, arranged and approved scheduling, oversaw change orders and other deviations from the original plans, as well as coordinated adornments and their placement. The last person on the team, Father Richard Vosko, proved to be a pivotal member who had the difficult task of relating the envisioned cathedral to the liturgical and spiritual level.

The leadership team did not work in a vacuum. Of all the numerous committees and sub-committees that functioned at one time or another, the primacy of honor goes to the Cathedral Complex Advisory Board which gathered for its first meeting in the dining room of Saint Vibiana Cathedral on May 25, 1995.[4] The cardinal outlined the role and function

---

proven track record. See Francis J. Weber, *Magnificat. The Life and Times of Timothy Cardinal Manning* (Mission Hills, 1999), 662.

[3] AALA, Roger Cardinal Mahony to Peter Barker, Los Angeles, July 1, 2001.

[4] Members of the Cathedral Complex Advisory Board, at one time or another were:

Sister Patricia Arnold, C.S.J., Rev. Monsignor John F. Barry, Mr. Louis Castruccio, Sister Faith Clarke, S.N.J.M., Mr. Bill Close, Sir Daniel Donohue, Rev.

of that board by saying that it would work with him and the Vicar General "hand in glove" to shape the overall project. At that gathering, Mahony guestimated the cost of the new cathedral and that construction would take about thirty months. He also expressed his desire to see the completed edifice dedicated in the first days of the new millennium. It would be "built in the traditional, classical California style architecture." He also hinted that the patronage of the cathedral would likely be that of Our Lady.

At the initial meeting, the cardinal handed out a printed copy of *Vision for a New Catholic Cathedral* which outlined his goals for Los Angeles. Here reproduced is the section on the "Symbol of the Shepherd":

> Foreshadowing the mystery of God's true temple, the cathedral "is the image on earth of the heavenly city." In this church only do we see the sign of the archbishop's teaching office and pastoral power, the sign also of the unity of the believers in the faith that he proclaims: the chair or *cathedra*.
>
> For all people of good will, especially the people who follow one of the world's other religions, the cathedral is a holy place, one in which they are prayed for by the local shepherd and his flock. For all the cathedral fosters justice and hallows aspirations. It informs and reconciles. It beckons and heartens. Although "the whole world is God's temple, shaped to resound with the divine name," we build our cathedral so that "here prayer, the Church's banquet, may resound through heaven and earth as a plea for the world's salvation. Here may the poor find justice, the victims of oppression, true freedom. From here may the whole world clothed in the dignity of the children of God enter with gladness your city of peace."
>
> For God's first-called people the cathedral echoes with the same assembling Word that called our spiritual ancestors to make pilgrimage to a place where God always fashions a people and delivers on the promise of his Name, "I shall be there

Source: The Tidings.

The cathedral's proto-pastor, Monsignor Kevin Kostelnik, greets a group of children at the cathedral. *Source: Lee Salem Photography*

for you as Who I Am shall I be there for you." The cathedral weeps, repents and warns, "never again."

For our fellow Christians the cathedral is the font of our common baptism in whose waters the shame of sin is overwhelmed and all die to sin and live again through grace as God's children.

For inquirers, catechumens, the elect, and neophytes, the cathedral is the open gate to the sheepfold, the prime catechumenon of the archdiocese, and the place where the Book of the Elect is annually opened to enroll the names of those to be received for full initiation as Catholic Christians. In the name of the Chief Catechist their local catechists lead them to the Word on whom they will live and in whom "the sheep hear the shepherd's voice. He calls his own sheep by name and leads them out. When he has brought out all his own, he goes ahead of them, and the sheep follow him because they know his voice.

For all faithful Catholics, both lay and clergy, the cathedral is their "house of prayer, their temple of worship, their home in which they are nourished by word and sacrament."

Bill Close, Cathedral Project Chairperson, and his wife, Helen, with Roger Cardinal Mahony. *Source: Lee Salem Photography*

They are eager to make pilgrimage to the place where they can "celebrate the liturgy of the hours with their high priest" gather around the altar of sacrifice to celebrate the memorial of the Paschal Lamb" who is also the good shepherd who lays down his life for his sheep. Parishioners and pastors light their dedication candles annually in celebration of the dedication of their cathedral. From this church they receive with joy the oils blessed and chrism consecrated at the great annual concelebration; with these oils the archbishop's ministry of healing of body and soul.[5]

During the years between 1995 and 2002, there were no fewer than fifty-six meetings of the Cathedral Advisory Board. Sister Lois Anne Linenberger, C.S.J., served as secretary of the committee and her copious notes of the proceedings are on file in the Cathedral Archives.

---

[5] AALA, Catholic Complex Advisory Board , Minutes, Los Angeles, May 25, 1995.

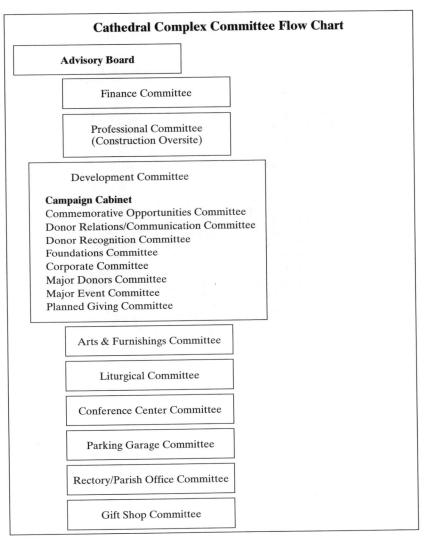

Cathedral Complex Committee Flow Chart

Advisory Board

Finance Committee

Professional Committee
(Construction Oversite)

Development Committee

Campaign Cabinet
Commemorative Opportunities Committee
Donor Relations/Communication Committee
Donor Recognition Committee
Foundations Committee
Corporate Committee
Major Donors Committee
Major Event Committee
Planned Giving Committee

Arts & Furnishings Committee

Liturgical Committee

Conference Center Committee

Parking Garage Committee

Rectory/Parish Office Committee

Gift Shop Committee

At various times during the ensuing years, there were other committees and sub-committees, including ones for Finance, Community and Public Relations, Design/Liturgy, Rectory/Parish Offices/Center and Development. Rarely did the cardinal miss a meeting of the Cathedral Complex Advisory Board and often, he attended meetings of the sub-committees as well. He proved to be a good listener and, while there was never any doubt who was in ultimate charge, he patiently and graciously welcomed and often acted upon suggestions from committee members.

Brother Hilarion O'Connor, O.S.F. served
as Director of Construction for the cathedral. *Source: Lee Salem Photography.*

In the "Letters" section of a national Catholic newspaper, a sub-
scriber from San Gabriel, California, made the preposterous charge that
the decisions about the erection of the Cathedral of Our Lady of the
Angels came about "without apparent discussion, prayer and discern-
ment!" [6] Nothing could be further from the truth! Probably no cathedral
in history was more prayed over and surely none was more widely written and spoken about in newspaper articles, and op-ed pieces in the local
and national press. Likely no ecclesial structure ever erected was the subject of more news conferences, public disclosures, open hearings, clerical
consultations, parochial bulletins and opinion surveys or more spoken
about by radio and television commentators. Newspaper and periodical
editors know what their public wants to read. Perhaps that is why the
Cathedral Archives contain over twenty folders of clippings relating to
the erection of the cathedral between 1995 and 2003.

---

[6] *National Catholic Reporter.*

SOME KEY PARTICIPANTS

Construction of Our Lady of the Angels Cathedral

ARCHBISHOP	Roger Cardinal Mahony
OWNER	The Roman Catholic Archdiocese of Los Angeles
PROJECT CHAIRPERSON	Bill Close
DIRECTOR OF CONSTRUCTION	Brother Hilarion O'Connor, O.S.F.
GENERAL CONTRACTOR	Morley Construction Company
DESIGN ARCHITECT	Jose Rafael Moneo, Madrid
EXECUTIVE ARCHITECT/ ENGINEER	Leo A. Daly
LANDSCAPE ARCHITECT	Campbell and Campbell
STRUCTURAL ENGINEER:	Nabih Youssef & Associates
MECH./ELECT./PLUMBING/FIRE PROTECTION ENGINEER	Ove Arup and Partners, California
CIVIL ENGINEER	RBA Partners, Inc.
GEOTECHNICAL ENGINEER	Law/Crandall
LITURGICAL ART CONSULTANT	Reverend Richard S. Vosko
ACOUSTICAL CONSULTANT	Shen, Milsom & Wilke/Paoletti
ORGAN CONSULTANT	Manual Rosales
ORGAN BUILERS	Dobson Pipe Organ Builders
CURTAINWALL CONSULTANT	Johanson Associates
PARKING CONSULTANT	International Parking Design
ARCHEOLOGICAL CONSULTANT	Brian D. Dillon
CONSULTANT TO ARCHDIOCESE	Stegeman and Kastner
CONSULTANT TO MORLEY CONSTRUCTION	Bovis Lend Lease
SCULPTOR FOR THE GREAT DOORS	Mr. Robert Graham
ARTIST FOR THE GATEWAY POOL	Ms. Lita Albuquerque
ARTIST FOR THE TAPESTRIES	Mr. John Nava

SCULPTOR FOR THE SANCTUARY CRUCIFIX	Mr. Simon Toparovsky
FURNITURE MAKER FOR RITUAL FURNISHINGS	Mr. Jefferson Tortorelli
ARTIST FOR THE SHRINE OF OUR LADY OF GUADALUPE	Mr. Lalo Garcia
SCULPTOR FOR THE NATIVE AMERICAN MEMORIAL	Mr. Johnny Bear Contreras
SCULPTOR FOR THE TABERNACLE & DEDICATION CANDLES	Mr. Max DeMoss
SCULPTOR FOR THE ALTAR TABLE ANGELS	Ms. M. L. Snowden
ARTIST FOR THE HISTORICAL MURAL	Mr. Frank Martinez
CONSULTANT FOR THE STAINED GLASS	The Judson Studios

Father Richard Vosko

Early in 1997, the cardinal launched a search for an art consultant for the new cathedral. Among those suggested was Father Richard Vosko, a priest of the Diocese of Albany, New York, who "had many of the skills" that would be needed. Vosko did indeed have impressive credentials. The recipient of numerous awards and citations, he had been working in the United States and Canada as a liturgical consultant since 1970. He was associated with the Institute for Liturgical Consultants, a Chicago-based training program for the certification of ecclesial advisers in art and liturgy.[7]

In March of 1997, the cardinal wrote to Vosko about the possibility of his becoming " a special consultant who can work with us to plan out the artistic work that needs to be done." There were several items that needed to be considered, including the design of the Baptistry, altar, *cathedra,* ambo and presider's chair; interior space for the Blessed Sacra-

---

[7] AALA, Roger Cardinal Mahony to Gabe Huck, Chicago, February 22, 1997.

Bill Close and the three co-chairpersons of the Cathedral Campaign-Gretchen Willison, Phyllis Hennigan and William Wardlaw. *Source: Lee Salem Photography*

ment and Reconciliation chapels; the crypt chapel, the design of the multiple uses for glass and other elements of artistic adornment.[8]

After speaking with Vosko, the cardinal recommended to the Cathedral Design/Liturgy Committee that he favored Vosko who would come to Los Angeles for a formal interview. In the meanwhile, Vosko sent a copy of his *Designing Future Worship Spaces* to the committee members, all of whom were impressed with his competence and credentials. On July 23, Vosko was named Liturgical Art Consultant for the new cathedral.[9]

In his press release, the cardinal publicly announced that the "design, fabrication and installation of all liturgical art, furnishings and appointments" had been entrusted to Father Vosko. In his response, the priest pointed out "cathedrals are models for other churches. In this

---

[8] AALA, Roger Cardinal Mahony to Richard Vosko, Los Angeles, March 22, 1997.

[9] AALA, Press Release, Los Angeles, July 23, 1997.

The Vicar General, Monsignor Terrence Fleming, was a frequent speaker at the benefactor dinners. *Source: Lee Salem Photography*

sense, it is the wish of Cardinal Mahony that the Cathedral of Our Lady of the Angels be a most beautiful and inspirational place of worship." He said his work would be a collaborative one wherein he would work closely with Professor Moneo and with the Daly and Morley companies. In an interview with *The Tidings,* Vosko emphasized that his would be "very much a team approach. My role here is to create a whole artistic program— that is, a listing of all liturgical art, furnishings and appointments for the adornment of the cathedral." He added that "the priority spaces and objects are first, the Blessed Sacrament chapel—or, more correctly, the Chapel for the Reserved Eucharist—and then, the baptismal font, the altar table, the ambo and the *cathedra* or bishop's chair.[10]

---

[10] *The Tidings,* September 26, 1997.

Father Richard Vosko was liturgical art consultant for the Cathedral of Our Lady of the Angels.

Early in January 1998, the cardinal issued a protocol in which he said that "because nothing will more fully identify and define the Cathedral of Our Lady of the Angels as a Catholic cathedral than the planning, design and implementation of all the liturgical art, adornment and furnishings, it was "paramount that all final decisions with regard to the art, adornment and furnishing must rest with the Roman Catholic Archbishop of Los Angeles:"

To assist in the overall process of designing and planning these artistic elements, the following order and process be in effect.

1) Father Richard Vosko, our Liturgical Art Consultant, will have the primary role in identifying all of the liturgical art, adornment, and furnishings needed to complete the new cathedral. Father Vosko has already developed quite fully a comprehensive Liturgical Program book, together with priorities highlighted and a time-line proposed. The program will serve as the central frame of reference and give direction to the entire project.
2) A new Liturgical Art, Adornment and Furnishings Sub-Committee will be established to assist Father Vosko in organizing the flow

of the work, as well as in helping to make initial recommendations for all elements of the program and plan.

This sub-committee will be comprised of approximately five
persons with expertise in Catholic art, adornment and liturgy.
Father Vosko will work with this Sub-Committee on the occasion
of his visits to Los Angeles, as well as by mail.

3) Father Vosko will then share his initial recommendations for the
   various liturgical art elements to the following persons:
   a) Professor Jose Rafael Moneo for his views, input and recom-
      mendations;
   b) the Liturgy/Design Committee of the Cathedral Advisory
      Board for their views, input and recommendations to Father
      Vosko and to the Cathedral Advisory Board;
   c) the full Cathedral Advisory Board for their views, input and
      recommendations for final decision;
   d) the Roman Catholic Archbishop of Los Angeles for final
      review, input and decision.

4) Once those initial artistic decisions are made, then Father Vosko
   and the sub-committee will seek out several artists and craftsmen renowned for their work in the area of expertise needed.
   These artists–local, national and international–will then submit
   initial drawings to illustrate their proposed treatment of the element in question.

From those initial drawings and submittals, Father Vosko
and the sub-committee will then follow the same steps as in
(3) above to obtain final approvals and to commission the liturgical art, adornment, or furnishings.

This process will ensure that the fullness of Catholic identity, tradition and current liturgical expertise is brought to bear
upon our Cathedral of Our Lady of the Angels. It is essential
that the new cathedral church be very familiar to all our Catholic
people, and that they feel very much at home in the cathedral
itself.[11]

Shortly after his appointment, Father Vosko released a detailed outline of the important scriptural, liturgical and related themes he hoped
to incorporate into the design of the exterior and interior spaces of the
new cathedral.

- The main entrance into the plaza is being designed as a safe and
  attractive sheep gate—a reference to Jesus Christ who welcomes

---

[11] AALA, Memorandum of Understanding, Los Angeles, January 2, 1998.

all. A carillon with thirty-six bells will be incorporated into this sheep gate.

- The main terrace inside the sheep gate is a reference to the scriptural story of Jesus meeting the Samaritan woman at the well. There, a gentle pool of water and a cascading waterfall designed by Lita Albuquerque will greet all visitors. The scriptural reference will be inscribed in the forty-two languages currently used in the Archdiocese of Los Angeles as a gesture of hospitality to all.
- The large public plaza is designed as a welcoming gathering place. A labyrinth will be designed into the pavement as a focal point of the vast area which will be used for many celebrations. Pilgrims will be encouraged to walk the labyrinth as part of their spiritual journey. (Note: Labyrinths have been incorporated in major Marian cathedrals throughout the world.)
- A children's garden will be the site of a playful sculptural depiction of Noah's Ark featuring animals indigenous to Southern California.
- A shrine in honor of Our Lady of Guadalupe will be created in a special setting in the outdoor plaza. Our Lady of Guadalupe is the patroness of the Americas and is very important in the devotional life of the Church.
- A more intimate and cloistered garden has been designed in the shadows of a very tall campanile that will house three major bells. The garden will be used for quiet reflection and prayer.
- The Great Door to the Cathedral is another reference to Jesus Christ as the gateway to salvation. The sculptor, Robert Graham, has designed this main entrance into the cathedral building to foster an experience of transformation for all worshipers. Note: Although there is a second entry, the Great Door is the one that will be used by all who come into the cathedral.
- The first of many chapels in the cathedral is dedicated to the reservation of the Holy Eucharist. Designed to foster private prayer and adoration of the sacrament, this noble, beautiful and conspicuous chapel will be able to accommodate up to 100 people.
- A lengthy ambulatory is designed as a pathway from the main entrance to the baptismal font. It is a reminder of the pilgrimage that faithful people continuously walk. Eventually, the artwork in the wall and floor of this south ambulatory will depict the story of the growth of Catholic faith in Southern California. Memory is important in any religious tradition.
- The chapel next to the Eucharistic Reservation Chapel will be a place of honor for the statue of Our Lady of the Angels commissioned by Cardinal McIntyre in the 1950s and sculpted by Prof. E. Pattarino. Other chapels along this ambulatory will be completed later.

Key members of the Cathedral Complex Advisory Board review plans for the cathedral with architect Jose Rafael Moneo.

- A twenty-foot high seventeenth century Spanish Baroque *retablo* that was purchased by the Archdiocese prior to the Second Vatican Council to be housed in a new cathedral will be situated at the end of this ambulatory. This retablo was originally installed in the chapel of the Congregation of Saint Philip Neri, Ezcaray, Spain in 1687.
- The baptismal font is located at a prominent junction of the journey—where one leaves the south ambulatory and turns the corner into the nave. Flooded by ample natural light the font will be designed to accommodate the current rituals of Christian initiation including baptism by immersion. The living water in the font will serve as a reminder of baptism for all who enter the cathedral. A setting for Christian wakes and an ambry for the holy oils will be in this location.
- The Chapel of Reconciliation is located in the north ambulatory. It will contain a reflective area and three small chapel settings for individual confessions. Other chapels, for example, a Chapel of the Cross, are planned for this ambulatory.
- A unique chapel designed to house major traveling exhibitions of Christian works of art has been planned for the north ambulatory.

- On Good Friday in 1991 Pope John Paul II made the way of the cross using scriptural references. Similar scriptural Stations of the Cross will be incorporated into the cathedral.
- Translucent windows of alabaster stone will emit abundant natural light into the cathedral. At night the cathedral will glow for all to see. The Church is a beacon to the world.
- Over one hundred tapestries are being created by the painter John Nava for the walls of the nave. These tapestries will depict the Communion of Saints including the holy women and men of the Americas. When the commission is completed the cathedral will house the largest collection of religious tapestries in the world.
- A beautiful fixed stone altar table will be designed for the cathedral so that the assembly of laity, clergy, liturgical ministers, and choirs is gathered around it. The Church is a sacrament of unity. Other important ritual furnishings, the *cathedra* and ambo, will be custom designed for the cathedral.
- An appropriate setting for the music ministry has been incorporated into the seating plan. The Lynn Dobson Organ Company is utilizing sections from the instrument once housed in St. Vibiana Cathedral to build a new true pipe organ.
- The undercroft of the cathedral will house the Chapel of St. Vibiana and her relics. A crypt mausoleum has been designed as a place of rest for deceased loved ones.[12]

The team worked exceptionally well. One of the top managers in the construction crew was heard to say that working at the cathedral was the easiest project of his long career because "problems" were resolved quickly and definitively in less than a week, with relatively little of the red tape usually associated with such activities.

The Cardinal and the Architect

Probably very few architects of great buildings had a closer relationship with their "owner" than Jose Rafael Moneo had with Roger Cardinal Mahony. Apart from undocumented phone calls and personal visits, the extensive paper trail indicates an exceedingly close collaboration on practically every aspect of the building. For the most part, the rapport between these two strong-willed men was cordial and productive, even in

---

[12] Robert S. Vosko, "A Preliminary Description of Liturgical Art and Furnishings," Clifton Park, New York, 1997.

Architect Jose Rafael Moneo discusses plans with Roger Cardinal
Mahony. *Source: Tom Wilmshurst Photography*

areas where differences arose. In one of his early memoranda, the cardinal told Moneo that the Cathedral Advisory Board was "very pleased with
the first design concept for the new cathedral." In fact, he said that "most
are very ecstatic about the creative and bold approach, while at the same
time, preserving the tradition of the Church." The building, he observed,
would be "at once new and ancient." He urged Moneo to proceed as soon
as possible with the selection of an executive architect in Los Angeles.
After making some suggestions about the overall site and design, the cardinal thanked Moneo for his "excellent work so far on our new cathedral."
He looked forward to moving quickly ahead with updated and expanded
design.[13]

Though thousands of designs and comments were exchanged in subsequent months, the cardinal sensed that the overall project was slipping

---

[13] AALA, Roger Cardinal Mahony to Jose Rafael Moneo, Los Angeles,
November 17, 1996.

behind schedule. He pointed out that there were enormous cost implications involved in such delays, saying "we must agree to a definite schedule and stay with it. We cannot continue design changes once all have understood that we were dealing with final plans." And he gracefully but firmly said it had to be "absolutely clear that the Archbishop of Los Angeles is the sole and final arbiter" for all liturgical and artistic furnishings and appointments for the new cathedral. It was then that he informed Moneo that Father Richard Vosko would serve as his principal and sole advisor on all these matters and "will be the coordinator of all aspects of our liturgical interior for the new cathedral."[14]

Clearly the cardinal was more concerned about budgetary restraints than was the architect. In mid 1998, the cardinal told Moneo that "the absolute total budget for this project is now firmly set at $163 million. Under no circumstances whatsoever will that budget be raised by even one dollar." To do otherwise, he feared, would cause "such an outcry in this archdiocese . . . that I would have to abandon totally the project."[15]

Moneo was perplexed. He did not feel that the cost of the project should be put "on our shoulders." He complained that he was "only following your mandates." He said he was indeed aware of "how costly construction is in the United States," pointing out that $100 million had been spent on the parking structure alone for the Disney Concert Hall.[16]

When Moneo complained about the role of the Liturgical Art and Furnishings Sub-Committee, the cardinal reminded him of his earlier memorandum and then said that "while your consultation is welcome along the way of the process, all of the final decisions belong to me and to the Advisory Board." It was clear from then onwards, the direction initiated earlier would be the "process which I will follow diligently throughout the coming months."[17] The cardinal thought it might be wise to remind Moneo that "the principal purpose of the Cathedral of Our Lady of the Angels is the solemn celebration of the Liturgy of the Church."[18]

Moneo was especially disturbed about his design of the Baptismal Font which the cardinal said was just "not acceptable." Moneo regretted

---

[14] AALA, Roger Cardinal Mahony to Jose Rafael Moneo, Los Angeles, December 16, 1997.

[15] AALA, Roger Cardinal Mahony to Jose Rafael Moneo, Los Angeles, June 2, 1998.

[16] AALA, Jose Rafael Moneo to Roger Cardinal Mahony, Madrid, June 4, 1998.

[17] AALA, Roger Cardinal Mahony to Jose Rafael Moneo, Los Angeles, May 23, 1999.

[18] AALA, Roger Cardinal Mahony to Jose Rafael Moneo, Los Angeles, March 5, 1999.

The cardinal and the architect. *Source: Tom Wilmshurst Photography*

that the font, along with the altar, *cathedra,* presider's chair and ambo
were going to be designed by others and, while appreciating "your wish to
involve a diversity of artists in order to provide the rich imagery that is
sought for the cathedral" there is "a crucial moment when a certain con-
sistency of form is needed." He was worried that having each liturgical
item designed by a different person "would sacrifice that unity " and end
up with "a more distracting collection of pieces that will seem more anec-
dotal."[19]

In his response, the cardinal went to some effort to "allay some of
your concerns" saying that "if any of my remarks offered you any offense,
I am truly sorry and ask for your forgiveness." As for the Baptismal Font,
he said that "the problem arose because of misunderstanding between
Father Vosko and me. I had always envisioned that the Baptismal Font
would be commissioned by an artist or artisan with the full theological

---

[19] AALA, Jose Rafael Moneo to Roger Cardinal Mahony, Madrid, May 21,
1999.

and liturgical understanding of Baptism in the life of the Catholic Church." Father Vosko had presumed that Moneo would be included among the designers but that was "not the direction that I wished to take." The cardinal thanked the architect for understanding his desires and he wanted "very much for you and your staff to proceed with all of the many details of the cathedral and the allied facilities that so desperately need attention."

> While I surely understand your desire for " . . . the immobile condition of the architectural features," please keep in mind that I see the Baptistry, the Altar, the *cathedra,* the ambo, etc., as more of the liturgical features of the cathedral, not the architectural features. I believe that this is the point where our separate goals do not converge.[20]

Moneo was not totally convinced. He did admit that "the inclusion of works of art coming from different esthetic points of view always has happened in the cathedrals we admire. But it is also true that it happened over a very long period of time so softening the differences and making natural the diversity." But, he argued, that "in a cathedral being built at once, such diversity presents some difficulties and that explains my concern and my request to all of you not to make of the cathedral a *'fritto misto'.*"[21]

When responding to this latest missive from Madrid, the cardinal hastened to say that "in our working relationship with you as our design architect and ourselves as the client, 95% of our relationship has been extremely positive and with great agreement. It is only a very small number of instances where we have had differing viewpoints, but none of these has done anything to lessen my high esteem for you nor the excitement we have with the wonderful design of our Cathedral of Our Lady of the Angels." He went on to say that "we are truly blessed to have you as our design architect and any small differences along the way are very minor in the context of the great cathedral which you have shaped for us."

> With respect to the artwork, we certainly want you involved very much in the process for the art, but I believe that

---

[20] AALA, Roger Cardinal Mahony to Jose Rafael Moneo, Los Angeles, June 6, 1999.

[21] AALA, Jose Rafael Moneo to Roger Cardinal Mahony, Madrid, June 9, 1999.

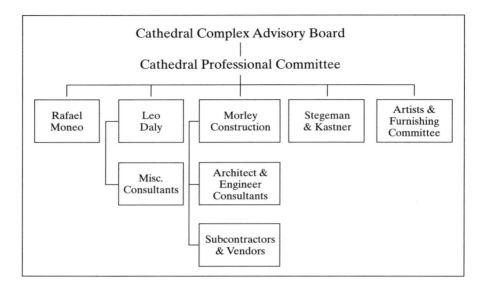

the overall beauty and liturgical function of the cathedral will be enhanced with the utilization of a variety of artists and artisans. As you know, our process does include your input and recommendations along the way, and you have been generous and helpful in offering those thus far. I would expect you to continue to offer Father Vosko, the art committee, and myself your views and ideas.[22]

In October of 2000, after meeting Moneo in Los Angeles, the cardinal said that "we are all so excited to see the new Cathedral of Our Lady of the Angels soar heavenward day after day."

The design is truly awesome, and we are just beginning to comprehend the wonderful sacred space which you have designed with such creativity. It is going to be one of the finest Catholic cathedrals in the world, I can assure you. We have been blessed with a superb working relationship since we began our project together in June of 1996, and this close friendship and working collaboration has deepened ever since. I consider it a joy and a privilege to call you a dear friend.

The cardinal was still obsessed with funding. He told Moneo that "it was quite a bargain, building a remarkable cathedral as well as all the

---

[22] AALA, Roger Cardinal Mahony to Jose Rafael Moneo, Los Angeles, June 14, 1999.

other elements for a total of $152 million. With the Getty Center costing $1 billion, the Staples Arena $400 million and the Disney Concert Hall $280 million, we realize what a stunning cathedral we will be getting for our investment."

But he went on to explain that 'we must rely fully upon free-will offerings in order to raise the money. Keep in mind that the construction budget does not take into account the interest we must pay for the bridge loans to carry us through the construction—a sum of a further $14 million." Given all his other expenses, the cardinal reiterated that " it is simply not possible for me to add even a new dollar to the total approved budget for the cathedral project." He quoted his "great collaborator," Bill Close, as saying that "we are building a plain vanilla cathedral." By this he meant that "we are going to open a splendid new cathedral in the Fall of 2002, but it will not have all the refinements we would like. These will have to come with time and the availability of additional funds for these purposes."23

Moneo was also pleased with the emerging cathedral. For his part, he admitted that his sometimes "stubborn efforts to achieve the best possible cathedral in every detail" may have "occasioned conflicts" but he hoped "that you will sympathize with our attempts to achieve excellence in even the smallest details." He noted that in this profession the actual building always provides some surprise, reflection and reaction."24

With all the occasional differences between the cardinal and his architect, an objective onlooker would have to conclude that Moneo got about 90% of his wishes, which is pretty high for an architect in a venture of this immensity. For his part, the cardinal expected and received maximum mileage in return for his investment of time, money and energy.

Finale

There were, of course, those who did not comprehend the basic notion of a cathedral, why it was important and why it should cost so much. Feeling that it was important to address those negatives when they arose, Cardinal Mahony was always anxious to engage in dialogue and

---

23 AALA, Roger Cardinal Mahony to Jose Rafael Moneo, Los Angeles, October 14, 2000.
24 AALA, Jose Rafael Moneo to Roger Cardinal Mahony, Madrid, October 20, 2000.

often invited the complainant to lunch or dinner for a person-to-person discussion.

Among the massive correspondence in the Cathedral Archives are several letters which raised specific objections to one or another aspect of the overall project. One writer, for example, thoughtfully questioned whether (1) the project had grown beyond what many deemed appropriate, (2) the funds allocated for the cathedral would impact the poor, homeless and aged of the archdiocese and (3) if the funds might better be used for needed medical, housing and educational assistance, especially among the large local immigrant population.

The cardinal's response to that letter is important because it revealed his own thinking and convictions in the matter.

> I would really be very pleased to meet with you in person and to discuss the overall project with you in a little more detail, if you would give me that privilege. I would be delighted to have you visit me at our new Archdiocesan Catholic Center on Wilshire Boulevard, and to have the opportunity for some dialogue and conversation about the cathedral project.
>
> As you must be aware, all of us involved with this project have been concerned about the cost of building a new cathedral. In fact, this same question has arisen over the centuries for every single cathedral built in the world, including St. Peter's Basilica in Rome. There were many who objected to the construction of St. Peter's Basilica for the very reasons that you have given in your letter. And yet, millions of people visit St. Peter year after year and gain a wonderful sense of God's presence in their lives, have their faith renewed and restored, receive the sacraments after long absences, and become inspired with great works of religious art.
>
> It is interesting to note that St. Patrick's Cathedral in New York cost two million dollars to construct in 1858. The equivalent of those dollars today is the sum of $192 million dollars. And yet, what an enormous resource of spiritual renewal and development St. Patrick's has been! That great cathedral is a central point of prayer and worship day after day, and millions of people have been deeply touched by this wonderful house of worship in the midst of a very busy city.
>
> We expect our new Cathedral of Our Lady of the Angels to have an important role in the downtown Los Angeles. In fact, since there are no other churches in downtown Los Angeles anymore, we expect the new cathedral to be a very active place of inspiration, prayer, and worship. I am confident that many millions of people will visit the cathedral and experience God's

presence and love deeply in their lives for many decades and even centuries to come.

I am always somewhat mystified when the only major building project in Los Angeles to be questioned is the new cathedral, while many other enormous projects are designed and built without similar questions being raised. For example, the new Getty Museum cost one billion dollars to construct, and I have never heard a single person question that amount nor its alternative uses for the poor and those most in need. Also, the new downtown Sports Arena will cost some $300 million dollars to build, and a new football stadium is anticipated to be another $300 million dollars. And yet, no one raises a single word or question about these amounts.

A cathedral will be a wonderful point of inspiration, prayer, and worship for all of Southern California, and its cost—when spread over some centuries—is extremely minimal.

What makes the Cathedral Project even more appealing is the fact that the majority of the funds are coming from two Los Angeles Foundations whose record on giving to projects to benefit the poor and needy children are without equal. Fortunately, their assets are such that they can not only help build the cathedral, but they also can continue unabated all of their other charitable projects and programs.

And finally, the Archdiocese itself is totally committed to our service of the poor through our parishes, Catholic schools, and outreach programs. Not one of those efforts will be diminished nor impeded because of the Cathedral Project.[25]

Another person, from Orange County, not even a part of the archdiocese, wrote to say that "homelessness matters; poverty matters; hunger matters." Why do we need a project of this magnitude which "won't revitalize downtown; it won't feed the hungry or shelter the homeless." While not disagreeing about the need of a cathedral, the writer felt that "spending $100 million is definitely an outrage to all Catholics." She argued that "downsizing is the word of the 90s" and maybe it was time to downsize the plans for a cathedral. Finally, she denied being "a disgruntled Catholic with a 'bone to pick'." One again, the cardinal graciously responded that the donors "are the very same people who donate hundreds upon hundreds of millions of dollars to a wide array of charitable causes that help to feed, clothe, house, educate and provide healthcare for the poor. Entities within the Archdiocese of Los Angeles, such as Catholic Charities,

---

[25] AALA, Roger Cardinal Mahony to n.n., Los Angeles, February 25, 1998.

CATHEDRAL ARCHIVES

At the suggestion and encouragement of Bill Close and others associated with the erection of the Cathedral of Our Lady of the Angels, an archival program was organized to house, organize and eventually make available to researchers all the documents related to the design, construction, decoration and operation of the cathedral.

The Cathedral Archives were formally established by Roger Cardinal Mahony in November 2001 and, the following February 1, he appointed Sister Mary Joanne Wittenburg, SND to be the archivist. A portion of the basement at Bishop Alemany High School in Mission Hills, adjoining the annex to the archdiocesan Archival Center, was set aside to house the collection. The archivist would work directly under the supervision of the archdiocesan archivist, but would be a member of the cathedral staff.

The task of identifying and filing the monumental hoard of documents, letters, photographs, blueprints, interviews, committee reports, newspaper articles and periodical essays was envisioned as taking a minimum of three years.

The following mission statement for the Cathedral Archives was formulated:

The Cathedral Archives, located at the San Fernando Mission, serves as a repository for documents, books and all other media resources related to the history of the Cathedral of Our Lady of the Angels. Its purpose is to collect, preserve, interpret and provide access to these materials. The Cathedral Archives also conducts a variety of "outreach" programs involving the editing and publication of materials for the benefit of the historical and ministerial community.

"Together In Mission", and the Catholic Education Foundation, are among the many agencies that help funnel these funds to the needy. Our donors' commitment to charitable works is not diminished by their desire also to gift Los Angeles with a beautiful cathedral church that will be a House of God for all people regardless of the socio-economic conditions."

He went on to assure her that "because so many foundations, corporations and individuals are funding the cathedral through their special gifts, our parishes will not need to seek pledges or raise funds to help in the cathedral effort. One of the donor's intentions is that the Catholics of the archdiocese would not be deflected from supporting their own parishes, schools and religious education programs, as well as participating in "Together In Mission" and other charitable giving. Our cathedral donors make it possible for the archdiocese to continue to expand our services to the less fortunate *and* build a cathedral that will please God and serve all the peoples of Southern California for centuries to come.[26]

---

[26] AALA, Roger Cardinal Mahony to n.n., Los Angeles, April 22, 1998.

Chapter IV

Financial Overview and Funding

The story is told, but never documented, that when Archbishop Joseph Sadoc Alemany was building Saint Mary Cathedral in San Francisco, a bedraggled and elderly lady approached him one day with a verbal pledge of $1,000. The kindly Dominican archbishop smiled and said: "Show me the green of your money." The lady was taken aback and responded that all she had was a thousand dollar gold piece. "Well, in that case, he said, I will grant you a dispensation!"

Perhaps it is characteristic of a mundane society that so many priorities are measured in dollars and cents. From the very moment a new cathedral was announced for Los Angeles, reporters rushed to attach a monetary value to the envisioned structure, perhaps influenced by contemporary reports that the Lakers paid Shaquille O'Neal $125 million to play basketball, the Kings paid Wayne Gretsky $75 million to play hockey and the Dodgers paid Mike Piazza $50 million to play baseball. Rarely, if ever, does anyone speak about the appropriateness or even obscenity of such amounts of money for sports.

The initial guestimate about the cost of the new cathedral for Los Angeles was $50 million, a figure predicated on the hope of building on the original site at Second and Main streets. When preservationists successfully blocked the demolition of Saint Vibiana, the project took on a totally different dimension. While no specific figures were released to the press, one newspaper reported that by March of 1998, the cost had escalated to $102 million, with the Associated Press quoting Cardinal Mahony to the effect that $106 million had already been donated.[1]

Another newspaper told its readers that the $102 million figure for the four-structure complex "does not involve fees for the architect or for attorneys." The cardinal explained that the new site at Temple Street and Grand Avenue doubled the size of the earlier property. No cost figure could be given at the time because so much of the design work had not been completed. Until the design architect, Jose Rafael Moneo, deter-

---

[1]Los Angeles *Daily News,* March 2, 1998.

100

mined such things as the height of the walls and the shape of the roof, there was no way to attach a price tag to it. Two-thirds of the overall cost of the project, at $835 per square foot, would go for the cathedral itself. But the project would also include a three level parking structure, a three-acre plaza, cathedral offices and conference center as well as a residence for priests.[2]

Within a few weeks, the price was pegged at $163 million. At a news conference, the cardinal released the names of nearly a hundred donors who had offered cash or pledges tallying $110.5 million. Among the original donors were Peter O'Malley, Dolores and Bob Hope, Mayor Richard Riordan, Roy and Patty Disney, Phyllis Hennigan, a co-chairperson of the cathedral development effort, said there were eleven committees working on the project which was now fixed at $163.2 million. The Vicar General, Monsignor Terrance Fleming, said that "much of the cost increase is the result of a redesign of the cathedral plaza, nearly doubling the size of the conference center, adding more parking and using a more expensive but sturdier architectural concrete."[3]

In mid-2000, a "policy paper" was issued by Bill Close, Chief Financial Officer, which stated that a little more than 90% of the then goal of $163 million had been raised or pledged with almost two years remaining until dedication. Based on those results, it became feasible "to enhance the construction project by adding certain electives which were not part of the original project."

- The electives (such as Campanile, the crypt chapel, the tapestries, the Bronze Doors, building out the second floor of the conference center, the main entry fountain and waterfall, the carillon entry structure, the Shrine of Our Lady of Guadalupe, and the children's garden) will tremendously enhance the cathedral and the Conference Center and save the extraordinary extra costs of adding these very important elements after construction is completed.
- Even if we can raise the dollars for these electives, the cathedral will still not be a finished product. There are nine chapels that are not being built out as well as other future art elements; for example, instead of stone for the Plaza, we are paving our Plaza with stamped/scored concrete.
- We have learned a great deal about the process of building a cathedral and what it means to the city, as well as its financial impact.
- Our ultimate fundraising goal, set by volunteer leadership with agreement of Cardinal Mahony, is to raise $32 million more than

---

[2]Los Angeles *Times,* March 5, 1998.
[3]*Ibid.,* March 20, 1998.

$163 million for a total of $195 million. We hope even to exceed this goal and set aside money for endowment.

- We need/expect to reach the $195 million goal in cash and pledges prior to dedication in 2002.[4]

The cardinal also repeated his earlier pledge that there would be no parish-based appeal to finance the cathedral. The cathedral itself would represent two-thirds of the construction costs, with a main floor of 63,000 square feet and a lower level of almost the same footage. The cardinal was quoted as saying that he was urging major donors to the cathedral project "not to cut back on their current or future charitable giving," hoping that they "can continue outreach efforts to the poor and build a new cathedral at the same time."[5]

In order to keep the record accurate, it was decided to release a resume of the total construction costs to the press.

The Big Three

Without any question, the linchpin of the Cathedral of our Lady of the Angels was Daniel J. Donohue, president of the Dan Murphy Foundation. He and his late wife, Bernardine, had been long-time supporters of Saint Vibiana Cathedral. They helped to finance the refurbishment of the sacristy and sanctuary during the 1960s, they donated a magnificent new organ in 1989, (which was enlarged and placed in the new cathedral) and they provided funds for a new roof, reinforcement of the tower and walls, choir loft and general maintenance. When Archbishop John J. Cantwell unveiled plans for a new cathedral on Wilshire Boulevard in the 1940s, Bernardine gave $250,000 and, when that edifice was discontinued, she generously consented to apply those funds for the enlarging of the archdiocesan Catholic school system. Given the historical pattern of support to Saint Vibiana Cathedral, it was understandable that Cardinal Mahony would look to the foundation for support after the disastrous Northridge earthquake.

But Daniel Donohue had bigger plans. He recalled that he and his wife "often talked about a new cathedral for Los Angeles."

Several times, I confided to Cardinal McIntyre about the matter, especially at the conclusion of the funeral services for

---

[4]AALA, Memorandum, Los Angeles, c. 2000.
[5]*The Tidings,* March 20, 1998.

The "linchpin" of the Cathedral of Our Lady of the Angels was Sir Daniel Donohue, without whom it would never have been erected. *Source: Lee Salem Photography*

Bernardine. The cardinal was sympathetic but he felt that other needs, like education, were more pressing and I could understand that. For a long time, McIntyre thought the existing property on Wilshire Boulevard, which his predecessor had purchased, would be the site of the cathedral whenever it would be erected.

Donohue went on to say: "Once I spoke about a new cathedral to Cardinal Manning. Obviously he didn't feel up to that challenge and his personal ties to Saint Vibiana, where he had been ordained, consecrated a bishop and installed as a cardinal, didn't incline him to such a monumental challenge."

Donohue felt that "following the Northridge earthquake, there were convincing reasons why the notion of a new cathedral had finally reached the surface. For me, it was the opportunity I had wanted for over fifty years." It was after an ordination ceremony, on the Feast of Saint Joseph, 1994, that Donohue "broached the idea" of a wholly new cathedral with Cardinal Mahony." He noted that "from the beginning, he expressed interest." The cardinal "knew that the cosmetic changes at Saint Vibiana Cathedral would only delay the inevitable." He asked me to come to his office and there we explored the possibility." From the outset, Donohue did not feel his foundation could support any further financial outlays to the old edifice.

Donohue told the cardinal that "the Dan Murphy Foundation would support him financially with a major pledge for a new cathedral." No figures were made because he needed to speak with the board members about the matter. In his reflections, Daniel Donohue said that "the cardinal was most cordial and supportive when I explained that a new cathedral had long been uppermost on my mind. I felt it would be the culmination of my life service to the Church." The cardinal asked for some time to consider the proposal. A few days later, he called Donohue with an affirmative response. After consulting with the Board at the Dan Murphy Foundation, Donohue conveyed the word that a $25 million pledge would be made.[6]

The generosity of the Thomas and Dorothy Leavey Foundation to proposals for restoration at Saint Vibiana Cathedral was related in a prior chapter. As soon as plans were approved for the erection of a wholly new cathedral, Daniel Donohue approached Kathleen McCarthy, the President of the Leavey Foundation, with a suggestion that their earlier gift be re-designated. With the approval of the board members of both foundations, the Leavey and Murphy Foundations became the "lead" donors for the Cathedral of Our Lady of the Angels. In both cases, their original grants were augmented over ensuing months.

It was the intention of Donohue and other board members of the Dan Murphy Foundation that their gift to the Cathedral of Our Lady of the Angels "would inspire others to join with them in generosity" and it was for that reason that they chose not to fund the project completely. For his part, Donohue volunteered "to speak with other potential donors."[7]

It needs to be mentioned in this context that the cardinal wanted the total funding for the new cathedral to come entirely from non-parochial sources. Several times, he pledged to the priests of the archdiocese "that there would not be any parish level campaign of any kind for the cathedral" and he kept that pledge to the very end.[8] That decision was not only popular among the clergy but it guaranteed that no interruption or diminution of parochial services or functions would be felt at the local level.

---

[6]AALA. "Interview with Sir Daniel Donohue," Los Angeles, November 20, 2002.

[7]AALA, Roger Cardinal Mahony to Director of National Philanthropy Day, Los Angeles, July 29, 1999.

[8]AALA, Roger Cardinal Mahony to Rev. Pedro Lopez, Los Angeles, December 2, 1998.

The last of the "big three" donors was the Rupert Murdoch Family Foundations who announced on September 2, 1999 that they were giving $10 million to help build the Conference Center. Cardinal Mahony said that "the Murdochs have long recognized the importance of Los Angeles as a key city for the new century and millennium." The Murdochs were "demonstrating in a significant fashion their commitment to providing this world-class city with a world-class cathedral church and conference center." The Murdochs had long been a major provider for scholarships to enable poor Los Angeles youths to attend Catholic schools.[9] A story in the *Downtown News* reported that "the Murdoch family wishes to designate their major gift to the Cathedral Conference Center where so many various religious, civic and community groups will gather in the thirteen various conference rooms for meetings of all kinds to improve the quality of life for all here in Southern California."[10]

Major Donors

Most fundraisers are convinced that there is more than an adequate amount of money in Southern California. An example would be a fund drive by UCLA, already a state-subsidized institution, which set out to raise $1.2 billion dollars, a goal that was reached two years early. The motivation may have been, especially among Catholics, that never before had they been adequately challenged. Cardinal Mahony decided to tackle that problem personally in a big way, devoting fully twenty-hours a week to the project.[11] He personally contacted any and all potential donors. Because his letters, and their many variations so succinctly described the goals and ideals of a new cathedral, one is reproduced here in its entirety:

> Historically, cathedrals have defined their eras, creating a legacy of enduring and innovative architectural designs. They have served as a focal point for artistic and religious expression through their acquisition from local artisans of the adornments that distinguish and enhance the structure, and through the central role they have played in preserving and expanding the spiritual and liturgical teachings that define the Catholic faith.

[9]Los Angeles *Times,* September 3, 1999.
[10]September 6, 1999.
[11]AALA, Roger Cardinal Mahony to Terrance Fleming, Rome, April 16, 2000.

Rupert Murdoch speaks with the cardinal as his son and Monsignor. Terrence Fleming look on.

Los Angeles has lacked such a visionary and centralizing structure. Today, the erection of a cathedral is finally being realized. The Cathedral of Our Lady of the Angels is under construction in Los Angeles and has begun to generate excitement for its neo-classical design, its fine arts acquisition and restoration program, and its plans to work with our diverse communities to ensure the cathedral is enjoyed to its full potential.

This project will serve a vital role in our society—contributing to the architectural, religious and cultural persona of downtown Los Angeles. World-renowned architect Jose Raphael Moneo, creator of the National Museum of Roman Art in Mérida, Spain, and the Pilar and John Miró Foundation in Palma de Mallorca, was selected to design a cathedral worthy of American's second-largest city. *The Wall Street Journal* cited this undertaking as "One of the five most significant building

Monsignor Kevin Kostelnik leads a group of visitors on a tour of the construction site.

projects in the country," based on a criteria that includes cultural significance and an architectural style that "paves the way for the new millennium."

The cathedral will offer seating with unobstructed views to 3,000 people—more than any other American cathedral, and the adjoining Plaza will accommodate up to 6,000 people for celebrations, concerts, processions and community events. In addition, a Conference Center with capacity for 1,200 people will be available for use by the cultural and business communities.

The Cathedral Complex: Meeting the Need of Our Faithful

The downtown area of Los Angeles has undergone great change over the past five years as it has matured into its role as the city's preeminent transit, civic and business center. The Cathedral of Our Lady of the Angels and its accompanying components will be an integral part of this renaissance and will help lead the city proudly into the 21st century. Frank O. Gehry, a Cathedral supporter and the designer of the nearby Disney Concert Hall and the Guggenheim Museum in Spain has said, "It is an achievement for the city to finally have a big Cathedral . . . it is significant to have a symbolic center."

Los Angeles residents are embracing the Cathedral as an important component of the diverse institutions that play a central role in this changing city. The tremendous impact of Cathedrals in other cities throughout the country is widely recognized. St. Patrick's Cathedral in New York coordinates the feeding of numerous elderly throughout the city; because of Holy Name Cathedral in Chicago, thousands of homeless receive shelter and food; and St. James Cathedral in Seattle is known for its ministry to AIDS victims and immigrants.

The recently completed St. Mary's Cathedral in San Francisco has quickly become a community treasure because of its stunning design and adornments. Visitors have remarked that its breathtaking design and grandeur is so uplifting that it contributes to the spiritual experience. All of these churches draw millions of visitors each year.

This Cathedral Complex will do no less than its peers in other cities. Moreover, it will raise the community's expectation by creating a usable space that, by its very design, will help unify many segments of our city. Designers have sought to create a structure so compelling in design, yet so connected to its surroundings, that guests will likely assume the Cathedral preceded the buildings around it. Current residents and future generations will regard it as a center of culture and education, and an architectural highlight.

In addition to the Cathedral, the full 5.53-acre complex will provide many non-religious benefits. A 2.5-acre public Plaza will offer the largest open public space of its kind in Los Angeles, accommodating up to 6,000 visitors at one time.

The Cathedral Center will serve the city as a Conference Center, an Education Center and an Outreach Center. The state-of-the-art facility will be available for secular as well as religious gatherings. The center will house nine conference rooms of varying sizes, a small museum and a café. A particularly important element will be ample underground parking for all events and conferences. The 600-car parking structure will be available for use by downtown area visitors and employees.

Los Angeles currently lacks a central, non-commercial location in which to hold large events, so this facility will serve as a welcome addition to the hotel and convention space currently in use, or the less desirable municipal space upon which the numerous organizations with limited budgets must rely.

The opportunities for outreach from this strategically located site will be numerous. The Cathedral Center will provide needed facilities to expand programs for the inner city, including education, counseling, and outreach. The Plaza will be open to all individuals to enjoy its beauty and peace on a daily basis.

The facility will also be used as an Outreach Center that will coordinate the Archdiocese's ministry to the poor of our community. Suggested outreach programs include food distribution, family counseling and support services for the homeless. Specific services to children may include designating the children's garden as a safe haven for latchkey children in the downtown area. This center will also be used as a designated earthquake disaster area.

Personal Significance

Never having had a Cathedral in Los Angeles that was large enough to serve the full range of archdiocesan programs, it is difficult for area residents to appreciate the impact the Cathedral of Our Lady of the Angels will have on their spiritual lives. In this regard, the cathedral and its Conference Center will become a focal point for many, if not all, of the multi-parish group activities and missions of the Church.

Viewed in this way, the cathedral will be a prism through which the faithful can see the services, missions and good work of the Church, and

Michael, Wilma and Robert Campion were among the early supporters of the Cathedral of Our Lady of the Angels. *Source: Lee Salem Photography*

through which they will participate in them. From a practical point-of-view, the Cathedral Complex will be used by the missions, their staff, their volunteers and the many whom they serve to extend and expand their good works throughout the archdiocese.

At the very root of its appeal, the cathedral will provide a unifying force for area Catholics. The complex was sited to be central to the entire Archdiocese and will be close enough to most communities to be easily accessible. It will encourage our faithful to expand their perception about the role they play in their church and encourage parish members to see that they are connected to a larger reality—the archdiocese as a whole.

The advent of the cathedral will demonstrate the value of a central, visible sign of faith. Parishes will be invited to attend and make use of the cathedral and to participate in its liturgical life. The addition of an impressive and accessible cathedral will help people to pursue a greater understanding of what their spirituality means to them.

Architectural features of the cathedral take advantage of three unique attributes of its downtown location: its overlook onto the heavily traveled Hollywood Freeway, its elevation above the surrounding civic and cultural properties and its available open space within an urban metropolis.

Overlooking the Hollywood Freeway—one of the two major north-south California highways, the cathedral will be visible day and night from both approaches. The cathedral will offer a stunning image for drivers heading into and through downtown Los Angeles, replacing an asphalt parking lot that offered no visual relief for commuters.

The 150-foot campanile will be visible from Hollywood to East Los Angeles. Centered in a garden and holding the bells from the historic San Fernando Mission and the original bells preserved from St. Vibiana's Cathedral, this tower will add resounding audible and visual elements to the surrounding areas.

Situated at one of the highest points in downtown, and sufficiently away from the highrise office district to ensure unobstructed views, the cathedral has been designed with a "skyward" elan to create the perception that the cathedral is a natural extension of the site's uplifting elevation. The angles of the structure are intended to allow natural light to fill the interior during the day, bringing the desert lightscape inside the cathedral. The use of natural construction materials—more alabaster, in fact, than any other American building—will imbue a sense of permanence in the structure that will anchor the northern section of downtown.

In addition, nearly half the total site will be devoted to landscaped terraces and public gardens to offer needed assembly space in a safe and serene environment. This will provide ready open space for large gatherings but preserves the feel of distinct environments within the Plaza for different experiences.

The traditional layout of California's early missions was used as a guide to design the Plaza and a wide variety of indigenous plants and citrus trees will line shaded walks, fountains and sculptures throughout. Special garden spaces reserved for children have been added, along with meditation gardens that will offer a peaceful retreat for reflection, or simply a place to enjoy a quiet lunch.

A conference center with capacity for 1,200 people sits across the Plaza and will be available to all interested users. The archdiocese will encourage its use among members of Los Angeles' cultural organizations, and anticipates extensive usage by commercial associations as well. The modern and flexible meeting space will adapt to serve all manner of meeting requirements, and is unique in its joint orientation between the practical needs of

Mary Jane Von der Ahe and Bob Smith were enthusiastic donors for the cathedral. *Source: Lee Salem Photography*

downtown business neighbors and the spiritual and community pursuits on the adjoining property.

Every element of the complex has been designed to interact with the adjoining uses of the site, as well as to take advantage of its unique and inspiring location. The cathedral design, with its generous use of space and light to create an expansive and uplifting space, marks a new era in architecture. The Plaza brings needed green space to the community while serving as an exhilarating prelude to the experiences that awaits within the cathedral.[12]

Allied Irish Bank

Allied Irish Bank, a registered company in the Republic of Ireland, whose shares are quoted on the Dublin and London Stock Exchange, is also traded in the United States on the New York Stock Exchange. Operating principally in Ireland, Britain and Poland and in the United States under the name Allied Irish America, the bank has offices in New York, Chicago, Philadelphia, Atlanta, San Francisco and Los Angeles.

With a work force of 25,000, the AIB was formed in 1966 bringing together three distinctive Irish banking traditions, The Provincial Bank (1825), the Royal Bank (1836) and the Munster and Leinster Bank (1885). It was thought that such an alliance was a preferable way of overcoming the often-fragmented nature of the Irish banking industry. The firm has operated in the United States since the 1980s. As of December 31, 2002, the AIB had assets of $86 billion.

Working with the Allied Irish Bank proved to be a pleasant and necessary aspect of building the Cathedral of Our Lady of the Angels.

There was a regional version too, all of which showed that the cardinal did his homework rather well:

---

[12]AALA, Roger Cardinal Mahony, Proposal, Los Angeles, November 1, 1999

Following are the main message points I propose to use in developing our objective case for a linkage between the San Gabriel Valley and the cathedral, as well as some of the narrative proof points that support our argument.

CATHOLIC COMMUNITY
The Sun Gabriel Valley has one of the highest, if not the highest, per capita Catholic population in Los Angeles County.

- On average, Los Angeles County is 31 percent Catholic
- San Gabriel Valley is home to 1.2 million Catholics—63 percent of its 1.9 million population.

San Gabriel's population represents just 16 percent of the archdiocese's 11.7 million population, yet it is home to:

- 23 percent (66) of the archdiocese's parishes
- 25 percent (13) of the archdiocese's high schools

PROXIMITY
The geographical center of the San Gabriel Valley is just 30 minutes from downtown Los Angeles by car. According to the Census Bureau:

- 92.55 percent of households report owning at least one vehicle.
- One-third of those surveyed reported a daily commute of at least 30 minutes—indicating a predisposition to traveling outside SGV.

FINANCIAL COMMITMENT
This year, San Gabriel's large Catholic population has contributed 21 percent of the Annual Appeal—more than its proportional share. It has demonstrated its commitment to support the archdiocese through personal, as well as financial participation.

As of July 1, 1999, the Cathedral Campaign counts 248 donors who have demonstrated their commitment to this project. Over 28% of these donors (70) reside in the San Gabriel Valley—again representing more than its proportional share. Residents of the San Gabriel region have demonstrated that they feel a direct connection to the cathedral project and a desire to see it realized.

The cardinal gave several hundred personal tours of the cathedral as it was being built. Often he would also invite the potential donor to lunch or dinner. Among others taking the tours were such outstanding local religious leaders as Frederick Borsch, the Episcopal Bishop of Los Angeles, Paul Egertson, Bishop of the Evangelical Lutheran Church in

America and Mary Ann Swenson, Bishop of the United Methodist Church.

Corporate Campaign Committee

In 1999, the Corporate Campaign Committee was formed by eighteen highly motivated individuals within the Los Angeles business community. The co-chairs explained that "we looked at perspective candidates who would not only work well together, but who would have the enthusiasm and passion that is so important in going to the corporate community. We needed to find people who not only could be supportive from their own perspectives, but who also understood how the cathedral benefits this entire community." Members of this committee were asked to reach out to corporations rather than foundations. Vice-Chairman Paul Watson, said that a corporate contribution toward building the cathedral is a commitment to Los Angeles itself. Whether animated by faith or informed by practicality, businesses donating to the cathedral should know their contributions would become part of this city and its quality of life for the next 500 years. Richard Ferry contended that "Corporate Los Angeles under-

Ken Olsen and his wife, "Dickie", were active in all phases of the campaign for funds with which to erect the cathedral. *Source: Lee Salem Photography.*

stands the benefits of having a cathedral in this community. It will be a place for people to gather, to worship, and to enjoy the peace and tranquility of the gardens. It's more than a church; it's an integral part of the redevelopment of downtown Los Angeles and will be a stop-over for every tourist visiting the area."[13]

Special Gifts Committee

Largest of the volunteer groups established was the Special Gifts Committee, under the chairmanship of Thomas Romano, which was composed of men and women who were responsible for a substantial portion of the fund-raising efforts for the cathedral. Members spent much of their time arranging tours for groups interested in the overall project. They utilized other occasions to emphasize that the Cathedral of Our Lady of the Angels was a collaborative and communal project to provide a million Catholics with a central church which would be a cultural as well as a religious shrine.[14] There were other subcommittees that functioned at various times, including ones for Donor Relations, Major Events, Planned Giving, Commemorative Opportunities, and Individual Giving. The Community Outreach Committee aimed at working to involve all of the various ethnic groups comprising the archdiocese.

Publicity

In addition to periodic articles in *The Tidings,* a number of monthly topics were sent by the Community and Public Relations Committee to the various parishes for inclusion in their bulletins. The following would be examples:

Month:	Topic:
November 2000	*Why Do We Need a Cathedral?*
December 2000	*Central Cathedral Themes: Journey and Light*
January 2001	*Physical Elements of the Cathedral and Cost*
February 2001	*Liturgical Role of the Cathedral*

---

[13]*Cathedral Chapters,* III, #3, Fall 1999.
[14]Ibid., V, #1, Spring 2001.

March 2001	*Civic and Social Role of the Cathedral*
April 2001	*The People Building the Cathedral*
May 2001	*Artistic Elements of the Cathedral*

Matt Connolly, a nationally recognized and award winning film producer, prepared several videos on the cathedral construction. The one on the theme of "Light and Journey" was used by the cardinal in a presentation in Orlando, Florida. A series of seventeen *Cathedral Update* newsletters were mailed to pastors, potential donors and local newspapers between Easter 1996 and Easter 1998. Featured in those releases were letters from the cardinal, updates on construction activity, announcements of significant gifts and descriptions on the cathedral interior. The following is an example of a release dated September 24, 1998:

The Need

The Cathedral of Our Lady of the Angels will be a much-needed structure to serve the needs of the dynamic Archdiocese of Los Angeles, the nation's largest archdiocese and the fastest growing. A cathedral has a special role that can be served nowhere else in a community; to serve as a point of inspiration and unity. As such, it will also be an important link between the archdiocese's 288 parishes, and greatly enhance the ecumenical spirit of our city.

An Inclusive Complex

Certainly at its heart, Our Lady of the Angels will be a place of worship for Catholics, and a place of quiet reflection for all visitors, regardless of their beliefs. But the cathedral will be much more. We have designed the complex to serve as a vital cultural and artistic force in the city whose name it shares.

A Reflection of our Diversity

The growth of our spiritual community in Los Angeles is inextricably linked to the tremendous diversity of our city. Plans for the cathedral, and its use, have always taken into account our city's wonderfully diverse population.

Continued Service to the Community

The cathedral project is not without its critics; in particular, those that feel that new construction, particularly a project of this scale, is inappropriate in the face of human suffering. We are very mindful of the role the Church plays, and should play, in helping the poor in Los Angeles. The Cathedral Complex will be the focal point for the archdiocese's many successful programs that provide essential assistance to the needy in our community.

Fund Raising

The cathedral will be funded entirely through private donations, large and small, from individuals, foundations and corporations. Not a nickel has been diverted from projects that serve the basic needs of the people, and individual fund raising for those programs has continued to be successful. In fact, we're delighted that excitement about the cathedral has motivated generous contributions from brand new donors to both the Cathedral Building Fund, and to other social service programs of the archdiocese. While we're very happy with fund raising progress to date, we still urgently need donations of every size in order to make the Cathedral of Our Lady of the Angels a reality.

Then in the Fall of 1997, the Cathedral Advisory Board began sponsoring *Cathedral Chapters,* a publication which stretched over the years to summer of 2002, with sixteen issues. There again, the cardinal generally wrote a special letter on some feature of the new cathedral, a major donor or function of the archdiocesan Mother Church. The local newspapers provided a wide coverage of the overall process, most of it favorable.

Finally, there were handsome packets prepared for potential donors. They were enclosed in purple folders and contained several photographs, copies of *Cathedral Chapters,* reprints of essays on artists, a prayer for "A Renewed Church of Los Angeles, A New Millennium, A New Cathedral," several related brochures, an information page, a list of donors, a "Preliminary Description of Liturgical Art and Furnishings" and a letter from Cardinal Mahony. In his letter, the cardinal sketched the need for a cathedral:

Every major city in the world can boast of a great Cathedral Church. Paris has the Cathedral of Notre Dame, New York the St. Patrick's Cathedral, Mexico City has the historic *La Catedral.* For much of Christian history, cathedrals have stood at the center of these great cities, bringing their citizens together in worship and community. They are great gathering places, where communities are formed and strengthened, and where all God's people are welcomed.

Most of us in Southern California have never known what it is like to experience the presence of a great cathedral in our midst. Not only does Los Angeles not have a cathedral church worthy of its importance; it no longer has any major church of any kind in its central city.

Los Angeles has no visible sign and point of inspiration, no beacon pointing its citizens and visitors to the presence of God in their lives. We are diminished because we are missing this spiritual landmark, this place to remind us that God dwells in the midst of His people.

Soon, this will change. The new Cathedral of Our Lady of the Angels will rise atop a prominent hill alongside the Hollywood Freeway, embracing both the Civic Center and the Cultural Center of Los Angeles. Finally, we will be able to point with pride to the grand cathedral in our city, and our children will grow up knowing and understanding the spiritual anchor of the Mother Church of our archdiocese.

The journey has already begun. Please join with me in praying for the successful completion of this endeavor.

Dinners and Receptions

The Cathedral Development team sponsored a series of events designed to either cultivate or recognize donors to the cathedral project. Donor/Benefactor Cultivation events were generally a series of dinners and occasionally receptions hosted by private individuals at which the cardinal was invited to present his vision of the new cathedral. These began in 1997 and the Cathedral Gala Kick-off in September 2001 was also one of these events.

Another cultivation event was *La Ofrenda* which was a gala under Hispanic leadership aimed at raising money among the Latino community. Benefactor/Donor Recognition dinners were a series of formal dinners designed to acknowledge the generosity of various donors. They were held in 1998, 1999, 2000 and 2001. The "Cross-Lighting" was also one of these events. The Cathedral Development Department hosted two breakfasts at Christie's in Beverly Hills to honor specific volunteers, including Bill Close, Robert Erburu and Courtney Adams.

Construction Milestones were events that marked an important facet of the construction—the Winter Fiesta marked the "topping off" of the garage and the five Residence Dinners gave major donors a chance to see the cathedral rectory. Among other events sponsored by the Cathedral Development Department/Committee were "Dinner after the Ground Blessing", special site tours including breakfast/lunch with the cardinal, the Celebration of Dedication, the Paving Stone Campaign, the "Go Back" Campaign and the "Chasuble Opportunity."

Naming Opportunities

In a memorandum sent to his advisers, Cardinal Mahony outlined a "Cathedral Naming Opportunities" program which was designed primarily for prospective donors with the capability of making a major gift to the Cathedral Project. Noting that a substantial percentage of the one billion dollars then being raised for the University of Southern California "came from the Catholic community," the cardinal said he had "no qualms in asking our friends for substantial gifts." He felt that "we do not insult them by suggesting a gift that may be beyond their present means."[15] The list was revised several times before being published in a brochure format in 2001:[16]

THE CATHEDRAL

Sanctuary
$10 MILLION
The sanctuary, a sacred space within the cathedral, contains the altar, the ambo, and the archbishop's *cathedra.*

Altar
$5 MILLION
Designed by Cardinal Mahony, the altar is composed of a solid piece of Turkish Rosso Laguna marble, deep burgundy in color. Its base is adorned with sculpted bronze angels.

Blessed Sacrament Chapel
$5 MILLION
The chapel of the Blessed Sacrament, dedicated to the reservation of the Holy Eucharist, will house the tabernacle and can accommodate up to 75 people for personal prayer and adoration of the Sacrament.

---

[15]AALA, Memorandum, Los Angeles, December 31, 1996
[16]The price of each item reflected its commemorative, not its real value

Cost Description	Total Excluding Mausoleum
Soft Costs:	
100: Architect, Engineering and Professional Consultant Fees	11,881,299
200: Testing and Inspections	1,571,988
300: Management, Administrative & Fund Raising	9,162,070
400: Mock-ups, Contractor Preconstruction	1,246,109
500: Permits, Fees, Bonds, Utility Connections	1,374,944
Total Soft Costs	25,236,410
600: Construction Costs:	
Group 01: General Conditions	15,265,050
Group 02: Sitework, Street Improvements & Utilities	6,340,972
Group 03: Cast-ln-Place Concrete & Formwork	45,135,026
Shotcrete Work	975,285
Concrete Reinforcing Steel	6,893,614
Group 04: Masonry Work	349,447
Stone Work	2,953,870
Group 05: Structural Steel	3,733,562
Steel Stairs & Misc. Iron Work	978,189
Metal Decking	362,083
Ornamental Metals	442,394
Group 06: Rough Carpentry & Wood Framing	698,822
Finish Carpentry & Millwork	966,451
Group 07: Roofing, Waterproofing & Sealants	1,293,877
Copper Roofing & Sheet Metal Work	1,455,541
Thermal Insulation	74,472
Group 08: Doors, Finish Hardware & Trim	951,218
Curtainwall, Storefront & Windows	6,794,852
Group 09: Drywall, Lath, Plaster, Framing & Fireproofing	2,939,742
Floor, Wall & Ceiling Finishes	3,555,708
Group 10: Misc. Specialties	405,075
Group 11: Window Washing & Building Maintenance Equip.	671,548
Kitchen Equipment	582,729
Audio/Visual Systems	613,578
Group 12: Furnishings	3,676
Group 13: Base Isolation System	3,589,860
Group 14: Elevators & Escalators	866,712

Cost Description	Total Excluding Mausoleum
Group 15: Plumbing	2,321,871
Fire Sprinklers	551,661
Heating, Ventilation, Air Conditioning & Controls	4547,593
Group 16: Electrical & Fire Alarm Work	9,232,074
Subtotal	125,566,552
Contractor's Fee	2,788,589
Total Contractor Costs	128,355,141
600: **Other Construction Costs:**	
Alabaster Material—Quarry, Fabricate & Ship	621,740
Security System Installation	577,579
Public Restrooms in Garage	516,621
Transept Acoustic Wood Baffles	382,898
Misc. Owner Directed Construction	630,986
Misc. Construction Cost Transfers	1,008,268
Subtotal	3,738,092
Total Construction Costs	132,093,233
700 **Furnishings, Fixtures, Equipment, Artwork**	
Liturgical Furnishings & Adornments	830,140
Great Bronze Doors	1,554,887
Pews, Chairs & Misc. Furniture	983,152
Organ	2,112,106
Center, Residence & Parish Office FF&E	218,008
Cafe & Gift Shop Buildout/FF&E	666,172
Lower Plaza Entry Fountain	676,855
Tapestries	1,360,431
Native American Recognition Art	52,500
Our Lady of Guadalupe Shrine Art	153,803
Carillon & Campanile Bells	444,886
Cathedral Accessories, Vestments, Vessels	519,610
Total FF&E, Artwork Costs	9,572,550
800 **Land & Financing**	
Land Purchase & Closing costs	10,916,666
Interest	10,000,000
Subtotal	20,916,666
Total Project Costs	187,818,859

The Crypt Chapel
> $5 MILLION
> The crypt chapel, dedicated to Saint Vibiana, is located on the lower floor of the Cathedral. This chapel will be used for small liturgical celebrations.

Nave
> $5 MILLION
> The space where the assembly gathers for worship, the Cathedral nave is lined on both sides with alabaster windows and the *Communion of Saints* tapestries.

Art Chapel
> $3 MILLION
> Located in the north ambulatory, the art chapel will host rare exhibitions of religious art from various museums.

Baptistry
> $3 MILLION
> The baptistry is placed at the back of the cathedral—allowing visitors to move from the granite font to the altar in a natural progression. It features a full immersion baptismal font that incorporates moving water.

The Cathedral Cross
> $3 MILLION
> The Cathedral's six-story cross, which rises above the altar and overlooks the Grand Plaza, features special lighting that will cause the shape of the cross to glow both day and night.

Great South Bronze Doors
> $3 MILLION
> The 30-foot high South Bronze Doors are the primary point of entry into the cathedral. A representation of Our Lady of the Angels is featured in a 10-foot-high tympanum over the doors, which are ornamented by images of faith from around the world.

Reconciliation Chapel
> $3 MILLION
> Located off the north ambulatory, the reconciliation chapel contains a meditative area and three confessionals for the Sacrament of Reconciliation.

South Ambulatory
> $3 MILLION
> The south ambulatory, designed as a pathway from the Great South Bronze Doors to the baptismal font, underscores the cathedral's theme of

pilgrimage. Its future artwork will depict the growth of the Catholic faith in Southern California.

Cathedral Ceiling
$2.5 MILLION

The wood ceiling is both an architectural masterpiece and a crucial component of the cathedral's refined acoustical properties.

Ambo
$2 MILLION

Grafted of fine wood and reflective of the dignity and nobility of the Scriptures, the ambo is the raised pulpit from which the Liturgy of the Word is proclaimed.

North Ambulatory
$2 MILLION

A continuation of the pilgrimage theme, the pathway of the north ambulatory overlooks the meditation garden and campanile, and ends at the reconciliation chapel and the north doors.

Organ
$2 MILLION

The cathedral organ features over 6,000 pipes, many of which were from the original organ at the Cathedral of Saint Vibiana.

Alabaster Windows
$1 MILLION EACH
—North Transept Clerestory Window
—South Transept Clerestory Window
—North Nave Windows
—South Nave Windows

Alabaster windows suffuse the cathedral with a soft radiance by day, and emit a luminous glow by night.

Altar Tapestries
$1 MILLION

Designed to complement the *Communion of Saints* tapestries lining the nave, these beautiful tapestries hang in a place of honor behind, the altar.

Amplification System
$1 MILLION

The cathedral amplification system augments the building's natural acoustics to emphasize music and the spoken word.

Blessed Sacrament Chapel Lamp
   $1 MILLION
   The Blessed Sacrament Chapel is lit by the gentle glow of a candle lamp, symbolizing the constant presence of Christ

Cathedra
   $1 MILLION
   Translated literally as the "Bishop's chair" the cathedra is the symbol of the archbishop's role as a successor to the apostles in his teaching and preaching ministry.

Cathedral Stone Floor
   $1 MILLION
   Made of concentrically placed stones of Jana limestone, the cathedral floor is designed both metaphorically and visually to draw worshipers towards the cathedral altar.

Choir Chancel
   $1 MILLION
   Located beneath the pipes of the great organ, the choir chancel provides a magnificent space for the choir to sing to the glory of God.

Copper Roof
   $1 MILLION
   The cathedral roof is constructed of copper, reflecting light and recalling the natural palette of Southern California's landscape.

Crypt Chapel Altar
   $1 MILLION
   The original marble altar from the Cathedral af Saint Vibiana has been refurbished and will be housed in the crypt chapel.

Mural of the Faith
   $1 MILLION PER CENTURY
   —18th Century
   —19th Century
   —20th Century
   A portion of the wall of the south ambulatory will be adorned with a mural depicting the growth of the Catholic faith in Los Angeles, beginning with the arrival of the Franciscans in the 18th century. Future generations will tell their stories by adding to the mural every 100 years.

Main Sacristy
     $1 MILLION
     Vestments for the archbishop, concelebrants and ministers are kept in the sacristy, along with sacred vessels and liturgical books and materials.

Meditation Garden Vestibule
     $1 MILLION
     The garden vestibule leads visitors from the north ambulatory through a set of glass doors to the meditation garden and campanile.

North Transept
     $1 MILLION
     The cathedral's north transept is framed with alabaster windows and provides seating close to the altar. It houses the music balcony and features access to the sacristy.

Retablo
     $1 MILLION
     Originally installed in the chapel of the Congregation of Saint Philip of Neri in Spain in 1687, the meticulously restored 20-foot high 17th century Spanish Baroque retablo will be placed at the end of the South Ambulatory.

Shrine to Saint Vibiana
     $1 MILLION
     This shrine, located within the crypt chapel, contains the relics of Saint Vibiana, the patroness of the Archdiocese of Los Angeles.

South Transept
     $1 MILLION
     The cathedral's south ambulatory is framed with alabaster windows and provides seating close to the altar. It houses the organ and the choir chancel.

Tabernacle
     $1 MILLION
     The beautifully decorated tabernacle is the place of reservation of the Most Holy Eucharist. It is located in the Blessed Sacrament Chapel so that the faithful can visit and pray regardless of the ceremonies taking place in the main cathedral space.

Tabernacle Canopy/Baldachino
     $1 MILLION
     A baldachino of glowing alabaster hangs above the tabernacle, creating an environment of reverence and beauty.

Archbishop's Sacristy
$500,000
The archbishop's sacristy provides a private vesting and prayerful meditation area for the archbishop as well as storage for vestments.

Baptistry Tapestry
$500,000
Designed to complement the *Communion of Saints* tapestries, this beautiful tapestry hangs behind the baptismal font.

Crucifix
$500,000
The cathedral crucifix, featuring a 10-foot high bronze corpus, is a visible reminder of the Passion of the Lord.

Baptistry Window
$250,000
Constructed of alabaster, the baptistry window will cast a glowing light upon those receiving the Sacrament of Baptism.

Cathedral Choir Rehearsal Room
$250,000
Situated on the lower floor of the cathedral, the choir rehearsal room is designed to accommodate up to 90 singers and instrumentalists and serve as a staging ground for musical performances.

Crypt Chapel Ambo
$250,000
The crypt chapel ambo is originally from the Cathedral of Saint Vibiana and will be used to proclaim the Word in smaller ceremonies.

Holy Oil Ambry
$250,000
The sacred oils of chrism, the sick, and the catechumens, which are consecrated each year by the archbishop at the Mass of Chrism, are preserved in the ambry.

Music Gallery/Balcony
$250,000
Perched above the sanctuary, overlooking the altar, the music gallery is a dramatic location for a single trumpeter.

Presider's Chair
$250,000
When the archbishop is not present, the chair of the priest celebrant stands as a symbol of his role as presider over the assembly.

Relief Carvings of the Evangelists
$250,000 EACH
—Matthew
—Mark
—Luke
—John
Historic carvings of the four evangelists, which previously adorned the Cathedral of Saint Vibiana, are beautifully displayed in the corridor leading to the crypt chapel and mausoleum.

Stairwell to the Crypt Chapel
$250,000
The stairwell to the crypt chapel descends into the mausoleum and provides access to the lower level of the cathedral, where the remains of Saint Vibiana are contained in a beautiful sarcophagus.

Stations of the Cross (Crypt Chapel)
$250,000 EACH
These historic Stations of the Cross, designed and fabricated by famed Italian artist E. Pattarino, are housed in the crypt chapel and will allow the faithful to enter more fully into the Passion of the Lord.

Tapestries
$250,000 EACH
The *Communion of Saints* tapestries, a representation of 133 saints, blesseds and members of the faithful among us, will hang in the nave of the cathedral. The 25 tapestries, each measuring 20 feet high, will be the largest such collection in a sacred space in the United States. The figures are portrayed in pilgrimage, processing with the assembly toward the altar.

Bishops' Chairs
$150,000 EACH
These chairs will be used by bishops concelebrating with the archbishop.

Brides' Room
$150,000
Located beneath the cathedral nave and adjacent to the crypt chapel, the brides' room provides a preparation area for bridal parties.

Crypt Chapel Gates
    $150,000
    Bronze gates adorn the entrance to the crypt chapel.

Lay Ministry Sacristy
    $150,000
    Beautiful cabinetry decorates the sacristy, where the liturgical garments of the lay ministry are kept.

Mausoleum Gates
    $150,000
    Finely crafted bronze gates will open the mausoleum to visitors.

Media Platform
    $150,000
    Located to the south of the nave, the media platform has a clear view to the altar, but does not obscure the view of the assembly.

Nativity Set
    $150,000
    A beloved reminder of Christ's humble birth, the Nativity set depicts the scene at the manger and will be displayed during Advent and Christmas.

Paschal Candle Stand
    $150,000
    The paschal candle, which symbolizes the light of Christ and is used in liturgical celebrations throughout the year, will be placed on this stand.

Cantor's Stand
    $100,000
    The cantor leads the choir and assembly in song from this elegant wooden stand.

Chandeliers
    $100,000 EACH
    Distinctive bronze chandeliers will illuminate the nave of the cathedral.

Chapel Lamps
    $100,000 EACH
    Created specifically for the cathedral, these lamps will provide light for each chapel.

Crypt Chapel Seating
$100,000
Seating for 200 will be available for those attending small liturgical celebrations, or engaging in private prayer.

Deacons' Chairs
$100,000 EACH
These chairs will be used by deacons assisting the archbishop in liturgical celebrations.

Gospel Book
$100,000
A beautifully illuminated Gospel Book has been specially commissioned for the cathedral.

Nave Dedication Holders and Candles
$100,000 EACH
The bronze nave dedication holders feature images of angels and are designed to hold specially made dedication candles.

Stained Glass Windows
$100,000–$350,000 EACH
Stained glass windows originally commissioned for Saint Vibiana's Cathedral have been restored and placed in the cathedral's mausoleum. Backlighting of these windows will contribute to a prayerful and serene ambiance.

Pews
$50,000 EACH
Made of fine American cherry wood, the cathedral pews provide seating for the assembly.

CATHEDRAL EXTERIOR/PLAZA

Grand Plaza
$10 MILLION
The beautifully landscaped Grand Plaza is designed to accommodate up to 5,000 people for outdoor liturgical celebrations, cultural or ethnic festivals and other community gatherings. Its design is inspired "by the California Missions, and it will be filled with gardens featuring plants native to California or those brought by the missionaries.

Sir Daniel Donohue took an active role in what he described as the "capstone" of his many years in the field of philanthropy. *Source: The Tidings*

Campanile
   $5 MILLION
   Soaring more than 150 feet high, the campanile, or bell tower, is an autonomous structure designed by architect Jose Rafael Moneo that will ultimately house 18 tolling bells.

Plaza Promenade
   $5 MILLION
   The Plaza Promenade is a covered colonnade that circles the Cathedral Complex along its northern side and ends at the north doors of the cathedral. It connects all of the gardens and includes the donor colonnade. The promenade will be used as the walkway for all ceremonial processions.

Outdoor Performing Center
$3 MILLION
Set on a raised platform beneath the exterior of the cathedral's 60-foot cross, the Outdoor Performing Center provides the stage for outdoor services and performances with an audience capacity of up to 5,000.

Children's Garden
$2 MILLION
This delightful garden manifests the beauty of God's creation, as seen though a child's eyes. A "Noah's Ark" theme with animal imagery will add to the children's enjoyment.

Shrine to Our Lady of Guadalupe
$2 MILLION
The Shrine to Our Lady of Guadalupe features a double-sided image of Our Lady, the patroness of the Americas, which is visible both from the plaza and from the freeway below.

South Plaza Trellis
$2 MILLION
Covering the walkway from the Lower Plaza to the Great Bronze Doors, the plaza trellis stretches along Temple Street.

Carillon Bells
$1 MILLION
The entrance gateway will host an historic carillon set of 35 bells from the San Fernando Mission.

Docent Room
$1 MILLION
Overlooking the meditation garden, the docent room provides a gathering place for the cathedral's hospitality programs and educational docents.

Entrance Gateway
$1 MILLION
The entrance gateway welcomes within the plaza visitors to the Lower Plaza, as they begin their pilgrimage towards the cathedral.

Gateway Pool and Waterfall
$1 MILLION
Jesus' words to the Samaritan woman at the well—"I will give you living water"—appear in this gateway pool and waterfall in the 34 languages in which Mass is celebrated throughout the archdiocese.

Historic Bells
$1 MILLION
Two of the original bells from Saint Vibiana's, cast in the 1800s and weighing 1,600 and 2,800 pounds, are housed in the campanile.

Lower Plaza
$1 MILLION
The lower plaza is located at the entrance of the Cathedral Complex and houses the gateway pool and waterfall.

Meditation Garden
$1 MILLION
An intimate and cloistered garden in the shadows of the campanile, the meditation garden provides a place for reflection and prayer.

Ministry Room
$1 MILLION
The ministry room provides a central headquarters for one of the archdiocese's vital community outreach.

Oak Tree Garden
$1 MILLION
This garden within the plaza features three oak trees, symbols of growth and wisdom.

Shrine Garden
$1 MILLION
Located beside the Shrine to Our Lady of Guadalupe, the shrine garden provides a peaceful space for contemplation and meditation.

Stations of the Cross (Meditation Garden)
$1 MILLION
Beautifully displayed in the Meditation Garden, the Stations of the Cross allow visitors to reflect on the Passion of the Lord in an atmosphere of quiet prayer.

External Illumination
$250,000
Carefully placed lighting enables the cathedral to be a striking landmark and a beacon in the night for all of Los Angeles.

Easter Fire Hearth
$250,000
Lit once a year during the Easter celebration, the Easter fire hearth provides the flame to light the Paschal candle.

Outdoor Altar
$250,000
The movable outdoor altar allows for open-air celebrations and services.

Olive Tree Grove within the Children's Garden
$250,000
A grove of fruitless olive trees will bring shade and natural beauty to this garden specially designed for children.

Plaza Stairs
$250,000 EACH
These staircases lead visitors to the Grand Plaza of the Cathedral Complex taking them either towards the Great Bronze South Doors or to the Shrine to Our Lady of Guadalupe and the Children's Garden.

Plaza Flags
$200,000 EACH
—United States flag

Monsignor Terrence Fleming explains one of the models of the new cathedral. *Source: The Tidings*

—State of California flag

—Vatican flag

Flags representing the United States, the State of California and the Vatican fly from a cluster of flagpoles on the Grand Plaza.

Glass Angel Panels, Donor Colonnade
$200,000 EACH
Glass panels, intricately etched with a pair of angels in flight, appear in each of the eight openings of the donor colonnade. Measuring 9 feet high and 28 feet long, these images will be clearly visible from the freeway and provide a spectacular backdrop for the cathedral's list of donors.

External Signage
$150,000
Clearly visible signage will assist visitors as they tour the Cathedral Complex.

Lower Plaza Garage Foyer
$150,000
The garage foyer provides elevator and escalator access to the lower plaza.

Native American Memorial
$150,000
Honoring California's Native American heritage, this memorial will be located in the Grand Plaza.

Waterfall Garden
$150,000
A small garden will overlook the magnificent gateway pool and waterfall.

Campanile Gates
$100,000
Crafted of finely wrought ironwork, the campanile gates will be opened during funeral processions.

CONFERENCE CENTER

Conference Center
$10 MILLION
The Conference Center houses the offices necessary to support the cathedral parish ministry, including offices for religious education and for the priests, sisters and lay persons who work within the cathedral. Conference rooms will also be available to the public.

Café
$1 MILLION
Located on the plaza level, the café provides refreshments for visitors and worshipers alike. Café seating accommodates over 200, both inside the building and outside in the gardens.

Conference Room
$1 MILLION
Located on the second floor of the Conference Center, the main conference room has capacity for 1,200 people and dinner seating for 600.

Gift Shop
$500,000
Religious goods and souvenirs are available in the self-supporting gift shop.

Entrance Lobby/Reception
$500,000
A spacious lobby made of the same stone that is used to pave the interior floors of the Cathedral will welcome visitors to the Conference Center.

Grand Staircase
$500,000
Paved with Jana limestone, the Grand Staircase provides a sweeping entrance to the second floor of the Conference Center.

Second Floor Gallery
$500,000
An indoor gathering space featuring a wall of windows, the second floor gallery offers a magnificent view of the cathedral and the Grand Plaza.

Board Room
$250,000
The board room provides a meeting space for the many advisory groups involved with the cathedral's operation and ministries, and is also available to the general public.

Conference Center Kitchen
$250,000
A fully professional kitchen will provide catering service for all events taking place at the Conference Center.

Conference Center Outdoor Terrace
$250,000
Located on the second floor of the Conference Center, the garden terrace overlooks the Grand Plaza and cathedral and will be used for outdoor receptions and gatherings.

Conference Room
> $250,000 EACH
> Located on the first floor of the Conference Center, these conference rooms measure 920 square feet.

Bronze Frieze
> $150,000
> A bronze frieze of the angels adorning the cathedral's altar hangs in the lobby of the Conference Center.

Conference Room
> $150,000 EACH
> Located on the first floor of the Conference Center, these conference rooms measure 450 square feet.

Pastoral Reception Area
> $150,000
> Providing a waiting area for the parish offices, the reception area is comfortably furnished.

Second Floor Lobby
> $150,000
> The second floor lobby provides an open space within the Conference Center and entrance to the second floor gallery.

Pastor's Office
> $100,000
> The cathedral pastor oversees day-to-day operations from this office.

Pastoral Offices
> $1000,000 EACH
> These offices are used by pastoral staff who assist the cathedral pastor in his duties.

CATHEDRAL RESIDENCE

Residence
> $5 MILLION
> The residence serves as the permanent home for the archbishop and priests who serve the cathedral.

Cardinal Manning Formal Dining Room
> $500,000
> The Cardinal Manning Dining Room, named in honor of the ninth Archbishop of Los Angeles, provides a formal dining space for the many functions hosted by the archbishop.

Cardinal McIntyre Formal Living Room
$500,000
The Cardinal McIntyre Living Room, named in honor of the eighth Archbishop of Los Angeles, provides an indoor gathering area for formal functions.

Chapel
$500,000
The residence provides a private chapel for use by the archbishop and other priests.

Cathedral Residence Patio
$500,000
The garden patio provides an outdoor gathering area capable of seating 150 for dining.

Residence Courtyard Garden
$500,000
An interior walled courtyard provides cathedral residents with a peaceful area for private use.

Visiting Bishop's Suite
$150,000
The Visiting Bishop's Suite provides accommodation for the many out-of-town bishops who will visit the archdiocese. The suite provides a magnificent view overlooking the cathedral and Grand Plaza.

Kitchen
$150,000
The kitchen will be heavily used for food preparation for an array of cathedral and archdiocesan functions.

Entrance (Interior)
$150,000
The residence foyer is a gathering place for visitors and those attending formal functions.

Priests' Dining Room
$100,000
A private dining area is available for priests living in the residence.

Priests' Common Room
$100,000
A common room provides a private place of rest and relaxation for priests living in the residence.

Visitor's Suites
    $100,000 EACH
    Designed to provide convenient accommodation for residence guests, each visitor's suite offers a bedroom and a sitting room.

Small Downstairs Lounge
    $100,000
    Located off of the formal living room, the lounge provides telephone facilities and privacy for residence guests.

Children's Murals

An ingenious plan for involving children in the cathedral project was announced early in 1999, when the children in the various religious education programs in the archdiocese were invited to participate in a program whereby the exterior of the construction walls surrounding the site at Temple Street and Grand Avenue would be covered with 180 painted canvases mounted on plywood.[17] More than 4,000 youngsters from parishes throughout the three-county archdiocese participated in depicting scenes of parochial life, local churches, patron saints and regional festivities. Sponsored by Edison International and Architectural Woodworking Company in Monterey Park, the firm provided the four by eight foot wooden panels and all the finishing materials, the prime coat for the panels and the graffiti topcoat for protection over the length of the construction. Cardinal Mahony was enthusiastic about the project because it showed the diversity of people and community in the Los Angeles area. One of the local pastors said, "By using children's drawings, the project re-enforces the fact that the Church always builds upon the presence of the future and our children are the future Church."[18]

Other Opportunities

While the cardinal scrupulously abided by his pledge against any direct appeal at the parochial level, he was convinced that the general populace needed and deserved an opportunity to participate in the overall fund drive, if they so wanted. So he approved a program known in the annals as "One Stone, One Cathedral, One People" whereby people were

---

[17]Cathedral Chapters, III, #2, Summer 1998.
[18]*The Tidings*, January 8, 1999.

Children in the religious education programs throughout the Archdiocese of Los Angeles designed murals for the construction site fence.

invited to dedicate distinctive paving stones that would be placed in a circular pattern in the sanctuary emanating from the altar to form the floor of the cathedral. Approximately 60,000 stones were needed, measuring 5 × 20 inches. Each paving stone was made of Jana limestone, each would be hand-laid, one at a time. Donors were encouraged to dedicate a paving stone which would honor others in a number of ways:

- You will receive a printed certificate and map indicating the location of your designated paving stone.

Children's Fence Art Project. *Source: Warren Aerial Photography, Inc.*

- A personalized card will be sent in your name to any individuals whom you wish to commemorate.
- You and those you remember will be included in a special liturgy planned for the year of dedication.
- Your name will be hand inscribed in the *Archival Register of Donors* located permanently within the Cathedral.
- A computer monitor will display your name and paving stone location at the cathedral site. It is *not* possible for the paving stones to bear inscriptions.
- Paving stone gifts totaling $10,000 or more from an individual donor will be recognized on a beautifully designed donor colonnade along the northern side of the Cathedral's Grand Plaza.[19]

A color-coded floor plan for the cathedral was provided to assist donors in selecting the area they wished to reserve.

Opportunities were also made for vestments that would be used for concelebration in the cathedral. The following brochure was passed among the clergy and others interested in supporting that project.

The Donor Wall

From the very outset, all those involved in the fund raising efforts realized that donor recognition was an important feature, even though,

---

[19]AALA Brochure, n.d.

Honor a Priest

The dedication of our new Cathedral on September 2 will be a historic event for the entire community, but it will have particular significance for the priests of the Archdiocese of Los Angeles. In recognition of this, there are several ways that you can honor a special priest during the Cathedral's dedication—and beyond.

DONOR COLONNADE

You can lead or contribute to an effort to commemorate a priest in perpetuity on the Donor Colonnade. Several motivated parishioners have collected gifts totaling $10,000 or more to have their pastor or pastors emeritus remembered in this enduring way. Cathedral development staff would be able to assist you in coordinating such an effort.

CATHEDRAL CHASUBLES

You can commemorate one of the stunning new chasubles that the priests will wear when celebrating stational liturgies at the Cathedral. Designed by the noted Holland firm of Stadelmaier and specially commissioned for the Cathedral of Our Lady of the Angels, the chasubles are available for dedication with a contribution of $495.

in many cases, gifts were given without concern for public acknowledgement. Gretchen Willison, co-chair of the Cathedral Campaign, pointed out that "our donor colonnade will be a lasting tribute to people who participated. They are not the contractors or architects but are—in a real way—the builders of our cathedral."[20]

A brochure issued late in 2001 embodied the commitment that "Every donor who makes a gift to help build the new Cathedral of Our Lady of the Angels will be remembered in perpetuity in the *Archival Register of Donors*. Anchoring the northern side of the cathedral's Grand Plaza, the donor colonnade was designed as a series of glass panels

---

[20]*Cathedral Chapters*, III, #3, Fall 1999.

engraved with donor's names, and ornamented by beautifully etched images of angels, which are lighted both day and night.

Donor categories will be indicated by the size of the lettering, from larger to smaller. Names will be etched in chronological order, within each category, according to the date that the gift was received. Donors who increase their gift will move to a higher category, but will still be listed according to the date of their initial commitment.

Donors of $50,000 and above may also dedicate an important architectural feature at the Cathedral Complex. When donors select a feature, it will be inscribed permanently in smaller print below their names on the donor colonnade.[21]

Potential donors were reminded that there were several vehicles available to suit the needs and goals of individuals. Listed here were some of the ways that donors could participate in building the cathedral:

- Gifts of Cash or Multi-Year Pledges
- Gifts of Appreciated Property or Securities
- Bequests
- Lift Estate Agreements
- Retirement Funds
- Life Insurance Policies
- Charitable Remainder Trusts
- Charitable Gift Annuities
- Charitable Lead Trusts

---

[21]AALA, Brochure, December, 2001.

CATHEDRAL
OF OUR LADY
OF THE
ANGELS

CHARDONNAY
2000
MONTEREY COUNTY
SAN SIMEON

ALC. 13% BY VOL.

Founded by Santo Cambianica in 1917, San Antonio Winery was able to survive the Prohibition era by selling sacramental wines to local churches. The five colorful labels for the cathedral wines have already become favorites of collectors.

In line with the objective of "bringing into the cathedral the spirit and influence of the early California missions," the Gift Shop at the Cathedral of Our Lady of the Angels offers its own labeled wines, two Cabernet Sauvignons, two Chardonnays and a white Zinfandel to visitors.

The cathedral wines, bottled by the San Antonio Winery, come from the last of a hundred wineries that once dotted the skyline of Southern California. The wines, pressed from grapes grown in Northern and Central California, are bottled and aged at the winery, just a couple of miles north of the downtown area.

CATHEDRAL
OF OUR LADY
OF THE
ANGELS

CHARDONNAY
2000
MONTEREY COUNTY
SAN SIMEON

ALC. 13% BY VOL.

Chapter V

Jury and Architecture

On August 30, 1995, Cardinal Mahony named Ira Yellin to administer the archdiocesan program for the new Cathedral Square. As project executive, Yellin was to be the chief overseer of the program. Married and the father of two grown children, Yellin characterized the envisioned cathedral as the most important building project in the city's history—one that had meaning far beyond denominational boundaries. He felt that the construction of the new edifice would "boost the efforts to renew the city's downtown area." To Yellin, "a cathedral expresses the highest aspirations of human civilization" since it had "meaning for everybody." Part of his goal was to convey that symbolic importance to the broader society as well. A religious Jew, whose father was a prominent rabbi, Yellin said that he was raised "with a deep respect for other religions, including Catholicism." He looked upon his selection as signaling "a remarkable evolution in the Catholic Church since Vatican II." He thought that the cardinal's selection of a Jew to undertake the project said something "about the harmony and the brotherhood in our city."[1]

Yellin's first step was that of commissioning an architect who would clearly understand Catholic liturgy and its requirements in a physical edifice. It was he who came up with the notion of forming an architectural jury who would invite and then screen candidates for that position.

Working closely with the cardinal and his staff, Yellin drew up a fifteen page "Request for Qualifications"[2] which was sent to sixty-seven architectural firms, some of them local and others as far away as Japan, Germany, Spain and England. The RFQ contained, in varying details, an explanation of the Cathedral Square project and its parameters, including cost limits, design, construction specifics and, most importantly, the spiritual and liturgical "vision" for the structure. Those receiving the RFQ were asked to declare their interest by the middle of January 1996.

Central to the RFQ package was the Cathedral Square's "Mission Statement" which laid out the archdiocesan goal of creating a complex "adequate to serve the contemporary and future religious and spiritual

---

[1]*The Tidings,* September 8, 1995.
[2]AALA "Request for Qualifications," Los Angeles, December 1995.

needs of the Los Angeles Catholic community."[3] The Mission Statement stipulated that the new cathedral must give "physical expression to the Church's role in the religious, social and cultural life of the Catholic and general community—symbolically, and as a natural place of meeting, dialogue and prayer for the entire community and for diverse faiths." The Mission Statement also stated that the placing of the new cathedral in the heart of a bustling multi-ethnic area would offer the rare opportunity to bind the city together in a bold gesture, a true crossroads for the City of the Angels.

The RFQ's "Preliminary Program" spelled out some specific features that would be incorporated into the new six-acre building. For example, the new cathedral must be able to accommodate between 2,500-3,000 people for large religious and civic-related functions. At the same time, it must also be conducive to smaller gatherings "which require greater intimacy and community."[4]

The envisioned cathedral, at that time still planned for Second and Main streets, would feature a combination of fixed and flexible seating, all of which demanded an unobstructed view of the altar, assembly, ambo and presider's chair. There would also be seating for up to 100 clergy surrounding the archbishop's chair. Additional features in the new cathedral would include:

- a Blessed Sacrament Chapel;
- St. Vibiana Chapel (to commemorate the saint whose remains rest in the cathedral);
- Chapel of Reconciliation (confessionals);
- side chapels reflecting the ethnic and cultural diversity of Los Angeles;
- a Baptismal immersion font.[5]

Also mentioned were the sacristy, a treasury or library, crypt and bell tower as well as a new rectory for the archbishop and up to six additional clergy, a parish office center, 1,000-person-capacity conference center, parking facilities and an outdoor plaza featuring fountains and gardens. Archdiocesan officials also discussed ways to "memorialize or incorporate" parts of the present St. Vibiana Cathedral into the new complex

On January 6, 1995, the cardinal held a press conference against the backdrop of the earthquake battered Saint Vibiana and there said the

---

[3]*The Tidings,* January 3, 1995.
[4]*Downtown News,* April 8, 1996.
[5]*Ibid.*

new cathedral's appearance would "combine traditional Spanish style architectural influences with modern design elements."[6]

On March 17, 1996, the names of those who would comprise the Architectural Jury were announced. It was indeed a blue-ribbon cadre of experts:

> **Cardinal Roger Mahony**—Honorary Chair, Archbishop of Los Angeles
>
> **Ira E. Yellin**—co-chair, The Yellin Company, Cathedral Square Project Director
>
> **Professor Richard Weinstein**—co-chair, professor of Architecture and former dean, UCLA School of Architecture and Urban Planning
>
> **Professor James Ackerman**—professor emeritus of Fine Arts, Harvard University
>
> **Miguel Angel Corzo**—director, The Getty Conservation Institute
>
> **Professor Kurt Forster**—director, ETH-Honggerberg, Zurich, professor of History of Art and Architecture, original head of The J. Paul Getty Trust
>
> **Professor Robert S. Harris, FAIA**—professor of Architecture and former dean USC School of Architecture
>
> **Sylvia Lavin**—assistant professor, UCLA Graduate School of Architecture and Urban Planning
>
> **Steven D. Lavine**—president, California Institute of the Arts
>
> **Stephen Rountree**—director of operations and planning, The Getty Building Program, J. Paul Getty Trust
>
> **Adele Chatfield-Taylor**—president, The American Academy in Rome[7]

The jury, consisting of "distinguished, informed and accomplished individuals of independent mind",[8] was delegated to select an architect from the dozens of world-class firms submitting proposals.

In "one of the most closely watched international architectural competitions of the decade,"[9] members of the jury moved along quickly, examining and judging forty-six packets received from the architectural candidates for the prestigious job. Names of the five finalists, announced on April 4th, included "some of the biggest names in contemporary archi-

---

[6]AALA, Press Conference, Los Angeles, January 6, 1996.
[7]AALA, Statement on Jury, Los Angeles, March 17, 1996.
[8]AALA, Ira Yellin to Gordon Smith, Los Angeles, May 15, 1996.
[9]Los Angeles *Times,* May 24, 1996.

tecture in the United States and Western Europe." Their number included Frank O. Gehry, Thom Mayne (Morphosis), Venturi Scott, Santiago Calatrava and Jose Rafael Moneo. Finalists were then required to engage in an exercise to design a hypothetical religious shrine which would persuade jury members that his firm could design an inspiring cathedral that at least hints of Spanish Colonial style. A writer for the Los Angeles *Times* said that the finalists "share no common style, but all showed a seriousness of purpose and a depth of exploration associated with building a religious structure at the turn of the millennium."[10]

The national chairman of the American Institute of Architects, Richard Bergmann, said that "the five names are 'pretty heavy hitters'" but all face "the difficult challenge that the building must give you an uplifting feeling of spirit when you approach or walk in."[11]

Other local pundits, in referring to the competition, said that the overall project was "one of the most challenging and coveted architectural projects in the country." The same observer went on to say that "in its own way, the archdiocese may be looking for the 1990s version of Michelangelo. And, although the planned structure is far from the Medici chapel or the dome of St. Peter's in Rome, it will indeed be a cathedral with its own place in California history."[12]

Shrine of Junipero Serra

Of all the celebrated shrines, churches and chapels dedicated to Blessed Junipero Serra, none surpasses the ones designed but never executed by the five finalists competing for the position of chief architect for the Cathedral of Our Lady of the Angels. The jury devised a "sketch exercise" whereby the finalists were required to design a small enclosed shrine dedicated to Fray Junipero Serra as a manner of demonstrating their ability to deal with the local Church's spiritual and religious heritage.

The exercise was designed to allow the jury to see the architects in action—how they thought, how they approached a problem, their attitude toward nature and the surrounding structures and how they would deal with creating a space that has a spiritual component to it. It was determined that the exercise site would be a parcel of land located adjacent to the *Pueblo de los Angeles,* in an area southeast of the *Placita,* bordered by Los Angeles and Alameda streets. At the time, the area was a grass park with an existing statue of Fray Junipero Serra.

[10]Los Angeles *Times,* April 4, 1996.
[11]*Ibid.*
[12]*Downtown News,* April 8, 1996.

Experiencing the new Cathedral from the Inside

As one enters our new cathedral that person should be swept up with several spiritual and human emotions.

At once the aura of God's presence, the immediate recognition that this is God's house, and a deep sense of personal sanctuary should envelop the entrant. The soul should be captivated by the beauty, the silence, and the invitation of the space.

The eyes should be drawn gently but powerfully to the sanctuary where the human community gathers to offer worship to our creator. The progression of one's faith-life should become unmistakable: entry into the life of Christ at baptism and the celebration of the Eucharist and the Church's liturgy and sacraments to sustain that spiritual journey.

At the same time, the soul should seem to float upwards and about as the cathedral structure itself entices each person to the grandeur of God and the irresistible longing to be with God. The limits of creation's "now" should be freed to allow the "eternal" of the Kingdom of God to be in some ways experienced.

The interior setting should unlock for everyone the potential of a glimpse of God's glory and His nearness to us, His creatures.

The space must not distract or confuse. The immediate recognition that this is indeed God's House should capture each person, and instantly affirm that this space is special and like none other in our community.

The cathedral's proportions and beauty should quickly clarify, not confuse, ones emotions: surely this is public space like none other in our community, calling thereby for reverence, silence, joy, and meekness.

The soul, spirit, mind, heart and emotions of each person should begin to merge into a joyful new reality-all elevating the person to a new dimension of God's powerful indwelling.

Roger Cardinal Mahony
November 11, 1995

The challenge was to design a shrine for the statue and its adjoining garden, while providing fifty seats in an environment allowing prayerful meditation. The architect had the option of removing all trees and hardscape from the site and re-grading it in an appropriate way. Cost was not to be a constraint since there was no intention of ever building the shrine.

Among the criteria given to the finalists were:

- The making of a space whose spiritual quality arises from an intense connection between the statue and those who come to venerate it;
- Consideration of what constitutes an appropriate architectural interpretation of the Hispanic tradition in new world architecture;
- The use of natural light to enhance this experience;
- Consideration of Southern California climate and light for the design of the shrine and the garden;
- The garden conceived as an integral part of the experience of the shrine and as possessing spiritual and metaphorical content;
- The thoughtful relation of exterior space to the surrounding urban condition, and the shrine and the participation of landform, landscape and building in support of this relation. Consideration may also be given to the historical and cultural context of the site.[13]

The initial presentations were made on May 4 and 5, 1996 to the archbishop, the chancellor, the jury and several members of the Cathedral Complex Advisory Board. Each of the finalists met privately with Cardinal Mahony and the architectural jury for fifty minutes. It was the cardinal's hope that the building would "unlock for everyone the potential of a glimpse of God's glory and His nearness to us."[14]

Santiago Calatrava placed his shrine at the intersection of four descending wall ways, one of which started at the *Placita* and moved toward Union Station. His simple canonical form was based on an interpretation of the first house-of-worship built by Fray Junipero Serra among the California Indians. The geometry of the trellised roof varied the interval through which light illuminated the statue of Serra. The roof

---

[13]AALA, "Sketch Exercise," Los Angeles, April 1996.
[14]Los Angeles *Times,* May 24, 1996.

was designed to be opened at night. A grove of trees surrounded the shrine in a pattern reminiscent of Serra's trek along *El Camino Real.*

Frank O. Gehry placed his shrine at the high point of the sloping site, designed in such a way that the statue of Fray Junipero Serra was visible from the outside. The composition of the shrine thrust upwards, with natural light emphasizing the figure of Serra. The open roof and predominance of wood suggested a rustic trellis which, as it intersected the strong vertical columns of wood, recalled a variety of Christian symbols, as well as the simple, natural materials employed in the missions. Plant materials associated with the Mallorcan friar were used in support of the design.

Thom Mayne of Morphosis chose to reroute the access road to Alameda, thus enlarging the site. He placed the shrine close to the *Placita,* integrating it into the surrounding landscape. Thus, he emphasized the relationship between life at the missions and California's landscape. The first Mass offered by Fray Junipero Serra at Monterey was represented by an oak tree planted at the focus of the shrine. Care was given to processional aspects of approaching and entering the shrine. The thick profile of roof elements recalled the rounded forms of mission architecture.

Jose Rafael Moneo placed the shrine close to Alameda and located the statue of Fray Junipero Serra outside, opposite Union Station, where it would welcome visitors to Los Angeles. The statue was also visible from inside the shrine whose walls featured a bas-relief of California with its missions, together with a tile mosaic recalling the life of the Mallorcan friar. Light was carefully introduced from the side to illuminate the map. The figure of the friar was dramatized in silhouette. From the *Placita,* one journeyed through a grove of olive and cypress trees recalling the landscape of Serra's native Mallorca. The simple geometry and white walls of the shrine reflected the traditional mission style.

Robert Venturi and his firm of Venturi, Scott Brown and Associates, placed the shrine close to Alameda Street so that it would be seen from Union Station. Believing in the educational role of religious structures, Venturi devised a series of floating walls to tell the story of the California missions. The walls, serving as a peaceful separation, led the public from the Plaza area into the shrine. Visitors entered the shrine though a gateway in one of the wall structures which recalled the silhouette of a mission church. The interior of the shrine contained a large mural of an incident in the life of Fray Junipero Serra.

Since they were commissioned and fabricated solely as an "exercise," the drawings and models for the Shrine of Fray Junipero Serra were not made public. Future historians should take note, however, of the important role that the Mallorcan friar played in the overall process of designing and building the Cathedral of Our Lady of the Angels.

List of the World's Largest Churches		
St. Peter's, Rome	227,069 sq. ft.	713 feet
Mary of the Chair Cathedral, Seville	128,570 sq. ft.	601 feet
Nativity of Mary Cathedral, Milan	107,000 sq. ft.	500 feet
Christ Cathedral, Liverpool	101,000 sq. ft.	619 feet
St. Peter's Cathedral, Cologne	91,464 sq. ft.	511 feet
National Shrine, D.C.	77,500 sq. ft.	459 feet
Washington Cathedral, D.C.	75,000 sq. ft.	534 feet
Notre Dame Cathedral, Amiens	71,208 sq. ft.	521 feet
Santa Sophia, Istanbul	70,000 sq. ft.	350 feet
Notre Dame Cathedral, Chartres	68,260 sq. ft.	507 feet
Notre Dame Cathedral, Paris	64,108 sq. ft.	390 feet
York Minster, York, England	63,300 sq. ft.	486 feet
St. Paul's Cathedral, London	59,700 sq. ft.	460 feet
St. Patrick's Cathedral, New York	57,768 sq. ft.	332 feet
Cathedral of Our Lady of the Angels, Los Angeles	**65,000 sq. ft.**	**333 feet**

Early on the morning of May 25th, the jury presented the Advisory Board with its choice of the three finalists, their names "mentioned without regard to preference":

> **Frank Gehry** of Los Angeles is, perhaps, the world's greatest living architect. We recommend him for his affirmative and humane spirit, and the gift he demonstrated in finding expression for a sacred purpose that connects tradition with our present moment in a way which will remain timeless. He, also, improved the urban circumstance in which he placed his building. While at the height of his creative powers, Gehry, nevertheless, demonstrated the ability to listen and respond to criticism from the cardinal and others and improve the quality of his design. His record in project management, cost control and scope of achievement is unequaled.
>
> **Thom Mayne** of Los Angeles was chosen for the depth of passion he exhibited in the development of his project, his sensitivity to the site and the evocative potential of the landscape.

His work revealed an understanding of the drama of Father Serra's life and he was able to find expression for the tradition of Mission architecture in a wholly contemporary way. An architect of deep conviction, he sought an intense connection with the interests of the client to guide his own creative effort. With a firm understanding of the specifics of the pueblo site, and by implication of the larger city, he nevertheless, made a place of peace and contemplation.

Rafael Moneo of Madrid was chosen because of his penetrating understanding of the program, the site and the meaning of Father Serra's life. We commend the intellectual depth with which he held these complex issues in balance, and the yet decisive simplicity with which they were resolved in the design. Within the simple frame of the concept, he found rich associations and opportunities to bring the shrine into dramatic interaction with the city around it, and to create a garden with resonant memories of Serra's early days in his native Mallorca. An interactive interest in the client's views was coupled with an independent reserve—sometimes humorous and resistant—which would likely promote an intense and productive review of programmatic intentions.[15]

After making its recommendations for the three finalists, based on the proposals for the Serra Shrine, the architectural jury had completed its work and was disbanded. Richard Weinstein, UCLA professor of Architecture and Urban Design, said that "all three finalists could create a contemporary cathedral to heal the wounds between the past and the future."[16]

Cardinal Mahony then called the Advisory Board back into session and acted as its chair for the final phase of the selection process. Saying that he was pleased with all the finalists and could work with any one of them, he entrusted the Advisory Board with the challenge of making the final decision. After several hours of intensive discussion, the name of Jose Rafael Moneo surfaced as the favorite. The final tally fell only one vote short of being unanimous.

The press had already reported that "Jose Rafael Moneo, a prize-winning Spanish architect whose work combined contemporary and historical styles, is the front runner in the competition to design the new cathedral." The writer, Larry Gordon, went on to say that "sources close

---

[15]AALA, Jury Statement, Los Angeles, May 25, 1996.
[16]Los Angeles *Times,* May 24, 1996.

to the press" figured that Moneo was the most "likely choice because his work, such as the National Museum of Roman Art in Merida, Spain, blends present-day and historical elements in a manner that Mahony and financial donors for the $45 million cathedral seem to want."[17] Gordon had been gifted with a "leak" as opposed to a "prophecy." In any event, on June 11, 1996, Roger Cardinal Mahony announced that the Archdiocese of Los Angeles had indeed chosen Jose Rafael Moneo "to serve as the Design Architect for the new cathedral for the Archdiocese of Los Angeles." He noted that we "are at a decisive and defining moment in the history of downtown Los Angeles and with the Historic Core of our great City of Los Angeles."[18]

Moneo was commissioned to perform the following architectural tasks on the existing site or on an alternative site should the archdiocese be required to move the location elsewhere:

1) to analyze fully the site available to us, and to situate the new cathedral and allied structures upon that site;
2) to design a fully new, free standing cathedral church to meet the worship and liturgical needs of the Catholic community of the Archdiocese of Los Angeles for centuries to come, and to serve as a place of civic gathering for all peoples of our city;
3) to design a new archbishop's residence/priests' rectory on the same site;
4) to design a Cathedral Center on the same site;
5) if utilizing the existing site, to work closely with me, my principal advisors, and those interested in historic conservation to meaningfully memorialize the old cathedral on the site, and to integrate various religious artifacts from the old structure into the new structures;
6) to create a great plaza surrounding and off-setting the new cathedral, open and welcoming to all residents and visitors to our city; and
7) to integrate this entire Cathedral Complex into the diverse human and physical fabric of the surrounding blocks so that our new cathedral can serve as the catalyst for the renewal of the historic center of our city.

The cardinal then thanked the "many distinguished architects from around the world who participated in our selection process and especially

---

[17]Los Angeles *Times,* June 10, 1996.
[18]*Ibid.,* June 12, 1996.

our two acclaimed semi-finalists, Mr. Frank Gehry and Mr. Thom Mayne of Los Angeles." In addition, His Eminence expressed gratitude to the architectural jury, the Advisory Board and Professor Richard Weinstein of UCLA and Mr. Ira Yellin, the project executive.[19]

From faraway Madrid, Moneo sent his acceptance note, saying that "my joy is mixed with the sense of responsibility in assuming such a delicate commission. As much as I am aware of the difficulties, I know how rewarding it would be to find a way to offer Los Angeles the cathedral it deserves. Be sure that I will do my best as a professional and that I will draw on all the energy and enthusiasm I possess."[20]

Moneo's selection was well received in all sectors. Washington, D.C. architect Lawrence Cook summed up the feelings of the architectural community when he said that "I think it was the best choice . . . Moneo brings a fresh, creative point of view by incorporating traditional architectural concepts into the very complex technology of the twentieth century."[21]

Jose Rafael Moneo

Jose Rafael Moneo was born in Tudela, Navarra (Spain) on May 9, 1937. Following his years in elementary schooling, Jose Rafael studied architecture at Madrid University. He was a Fellow at the Spanish Academy in Rome and, in 1964, received a doctorate in architecture at Madrid University. At the age of twenty-five, Rafael married Belen Feduchi. The Moneos, their three children, Belen, Teresa and Clara Matilda, live "in twin honey-colored houses four-blocks apart, their plain forms hidden behind rows of Chinese elms, part of a 1930s era garden city plan that was never finished."[22]

Cardinal Mahony visited Moneo in August of 1996 where he witnessed both the renowned architect's unpretentious working style and some of his architectural creations. He discovered that Moneo had no separate office of his own. "He simply moves throughout the building con-

---

[19]AALA, Roger Cardinal Mahony Statement, Los Angeles, June 11, 1996. Shortly after the selection of the architect, Ira Yellin returned to his business interests. He died of cancer in September 2002.

[20]AALA, Jose Rafael Moneo to Roger Cardinal Mahony, Madrid, May 30, 1996.

[21]*Downtown News,* June 1, 1996.

[22]Nicolai Ourousseff, Los Angeles *Times,* August 24, 1997.

stantly reviewing the ongoing work of each associate."[23] He referred to the architect as "a warm, personable man with no pretenses." The cardinal quoted *El Croquis,* a Spanish architectural journal, which said that "Moneo's most memorable buildings are characterized by clarity of image, plasticity of form and a dense texture of detail."[24]

Much of Jose Rafael's life had been spent in academic pursuits. He taught at his *alma mater* for several years and then took positions at the Barcelona School of Architecture, the Institute for Architecture and Urban Studies (New York City), Princeton University and in the School of Design at Harvard University where he served as chairman of the Architecture Department, 1985–1990.

Among the awards and honors received by Moneo over the years are Gold Medals from the Architectural International Union, the French Academy of Architecture and for Achievement in the Fine Arts of the Spanish Government. He also holds honorary doctorates from the Royal Institute of British Architects, the University of Architecture (Venice) and Louvain University (Belgium.) He was also named a Foreign Honorary Member, Academy of Arts and Sciences and an Honorary Fellow of the American Institute of Architects. Moneo has received the Arnold W. Brunner Memorial Prize, the Viana Prize of the Government of Navarra and the Schock Prize at the Royal Academy of Fine Arts.

Finally, and most importantly, Jose Rafael Moneo joined a select group when he became the nineteenth recipient in 1996 of the Pritzker Architecture Prize, architecture's most prestigious honor. The Pritzker jury praised Moneo "as an architect with tremendous range, each of whose buildings is unique, but at the same time uniquely recognizable as being from his palette." In announcing Moneo's selection, the first Spaniard to receive the award, the Foundation president said that "Moneo not only practices architecture in the most real sense of designing buildings, taking into account all aspects of their construction, but he also teaches his theories utilizing all his experience and knowledge. . . . "The Pritzker Architectural Prize, known as the Nobel of architecture, honored "the eclectic architect who was revered for his unusually wide range of accomplishments and his ability to connect the present with the past."[25]

Over his lifetime, Moneo's projects have encompassed residences, banks, art museums, a railway station, an airport, a sport stadium, a city hall and numerous office buildings. His focus has never become diffused.

---

[23]*The Tidings,* August 9, 1996.
[24](1994), #64
[25]Los Angeles *Times,* April 29, 1996.

Jose Rafael Moneo and Sir Daniel Donohue. *Source: Tom Wilmshurst Photography*

One commentator said that "If his small number of executed works possess a very Spanish air of sobriety, dignity and restraint, those qualities are in such short supply worldwide today that his structures fit beautifully into cities as diverse as Pamplona and Berlin, Stockholm and Palma de Mallorca."[26]

A thin, almost frail-looking man who speaks English somewhat haltingly with a pronounced Spanish accent, Moneo launched his work with a promise to incorporate old pieces such as stained glass windows, porticoes and altars into the new cathedral campus. And he promised "to try to accommodate private prayer and large public celebrations." He wanted a "church able to share both the sense of an individual being able to be isolated from the outside world and being able to enhance the value

---

[26]Martin Fuller, "Architect Triumphant," *House Beautiful* (September 1996), 82.

of the community." [27] The only Roman Catholic among the finalists, Moneo was described by Roger Cardinal Mahony as having "an exceptional spiritual depth that we believe essential in designing a wonderful sacred space in the midst of a modern city known for its ephemeral entertainment glitter."[28]

To see that the Architectural Jury's choice of Moneo was indeed a wise one, one has only to review some of the laudatory observations that surfaced after the announcement of his selection. Cardinal Mahony, who confirmed the ultimate choice, said that he was confident "that we now have the best architect in the world to help us all to fulfill our collective dreams."

Architect Dagmat Richter said that "clearly only one person was going to win (the commission), and it is Rafael Moneo because he fit the philosophy of the Catholic Church."[29] In an article written for the Los Angeles *Times* Jose Rafael Moneo made the following observations about a new cathedral for Los Angeles:

> Los Angeles is fortunate to have not one but several wonderful potential sites for its new cathedral. Though each of the competing sites has distinctive and compelling attributes, I believe that the site at Grand and Temple streets announced this week is clearly the preferred choice. Indeed, in my years as an architect, I have never had stronger or clearer feelings about a potential site.
>
> The cathedral's role as the archdiocese's liturgical and spiritual center provides the starting point for my analysis. The fundamental challenge is to find a site that places the Church in its proper cultural and civic milieu, but which also is sufficiently separated and independent of these temporal concerns. A church surrounded by civic facilities, particularly ones as prominent as City Hall, cannot achieve the independence that great churches need to provide spiritual respite. On the other hand, a cathedral that stands by itself, removed from civic and cultural centers, puts the church too far from its proper role in everyday life.
>
> The preferred site strikes a perfect balance. It is very much "downtown," connected to the cultural and civic fabric of the city. It fronts on Grand Avenue, the home of many of the

---

[27]Los Angeles *Times,* June 12, 1996.
[28]*The Tidings,* June 14, 1996.
[29]Los Angeles *Times,* July 24, 1997.

USEFUL FACTS ABOUT THE PROJECT

THE PROJECT AS A WHOLE
- Site area: 5-1/2 acres
- Elevation above sea level, at curbside: Approximately 390 ft. at the corner of Temple and Grand; Thirty-five feet lower at the corner of Temple and Hill.
- Previous structures on the site included residential and commercial structures up to three stories in height, plus a streetcar tunnel. All were removed when the Hollywood Freeway was built in 1949-51.

THE CATHEDRAL CHURCH
- Footprint area: 65,000 sq. ft.
- Floor area of the main space (nave, transepts, and presbyterium): 57,000 sq. ft.
- Basement area (mausoleum, crypt, chapel, ancillary spaces): 63,000 sq. ft.
- Volume of the main space: 3,300,000 cubic ft.
- Interior length of the building along the main axis: Nave— 333 ft.; Crypt Level—365 ft.
- Maximum clear height, nave floor to ceiling inside: 104 ft.
- Maximum height, street level to top of building: 128 ft.
- Number of elastomeric base isolators: 149
- Typical size of an elastomeric base isolator: 40" diameter
- Typical weight of an elastomeric base isolator: 3,100 lbs.
- Number of "slider" base isolators: 47
- Maximum differential movement at the isolator during a "design earthquake": 27 in.
- Fixed seating capacity: 2,400
- Additional movable seating: Up to 600
- Area of alabaster windows: 27,000 sq. ft.
- Building weight, above the seismic isolators: 125,000,000 lbs.

REINFORCED CONCRETE
- Concrete quantity in the entire project: Approx. 59,000 cubic yds. (architectural and structural)
- Quantity of exposed architectural concrete: Approx. 25,000 cubic yds.
- Quantity of reinforcing steel in the project: Approx. 6,000 tons

MISCELLANEOUS

- Area of the outdoor plaza: 2-1/2 acres
- Number of parking spaces: 600
- Seating capacity of the Cathedral Center, tables set in the main conference area: 600
- Seating capacity of the Cathedral Center, theater/lecture configuration: 1,200
- Floor area of the Cathedral Center: 56,000 sq. ft.
- Height of campanile above street level: 180 ft. to top of the cross
- Weight of one bronze door leaf from the pair of main entry doors: 25,000 lbs.
- The longitudinal and latitudinal coordinates for the cathedral property are: 118 14′ 39″ West and 34 03′ 28″ North.
- Address selected March 17, 1997: 555 West Temple Street.
- Website—Cathedral: info@olacathedral.org
- The cathedral is much wider than it is tall. The nave of Notre Dame Cathedral in Paris would fit within the Cathedral of Our Lady of the Angels
- Seventeen churches the size of Saint Vibiana could be stacked in the new cathedral.

most exciting and well-recognized buildings in the city. Yet its borders are clear and distinct, providing an unmistakable sense of independence. The freeway to the north and the Hall of Administration (itself oriented to face in the other direction) act as bookends, placing the cathedral in its own place in the heart of the city. Equally importantly, this independence will continue regardless of how the adjacent sites change through the years.

I have also been struck by how Angelenos live in and with their environments, not insulated or protected as required in harsher climates. Again from this perspective the selected site excels. This site is at the top of Bunker Hill, clearly visible to thousands who travel on the freeways or who live and work to the north. I envision a cathedral that is a prominent part of the urban landscape, a permanent reminder of God's presence in our midst. It will be visible from many points to many people.

Other factors again weigh in favor of the chosen site. It is the largest of the available sites, offering more opportunity for independence and prominence in the urban core. Its elongated shape—in contrast to the square shape of the alternative sites—offers more opportunities for pedestrian and vehicular access. It is easily accessible by bus and metro.

The various sites near City Hall are well suited for developments that will encourage pedestrians to flow through the urban core. But a cathedral is not merely a tourist destination—it must be a spiritual home. The City Hall sites are too small and too close to insulate persons seeking spiritual respite from the political and temporal businesses conducted nearby. At the chosen site, the cathedral will most certainly be freestanding, as it should be.

I am thrilled by this choice and inspired more than ever to design a wonderful new cathedral for Our Lady of the Angels.[30]

With the signing of the formal contract on June 11, 1996, Jose Rafael Moneo returned to Madrid where he and his associates began drawing plans for the new Cathedral of Our Lady of the Angels. The following months in Los Angeles were spent in excited expectations of what the world-renowned architect, theoretician and educator would bring back with him to Southern California. He did not disappoint anyone.

If it is true that "beauty resides in the eye of the beholder," then there really is no valid criterion for what constitutes true beauty, a dictum that carries over into architecture. According to Marcus Vitruvious, for many centuries accepted as the final authority on the subject, all architecture must be accurate and functional before it can qualify as beauty. One elderly lady was heard to say, on the day of the cathedral's dedication, that "it looks like the box it came in." For her that might well have been a compliment.

With the arrival of the secondary preliminary model in Los Angeles during the early months of 1997, Catholics got the first glimpse of their new cathedral. It combined an historical regional mission influence with a radically modern reconfiguration of the traditional cathedral plaza. Despite its mission references, the overall complex was a response to its freeway-bound context.

Some of the more carefully and precisely written commentaries on the cathedral architecture are the ones by Nicolai Ouroussoff. In his role as Architecture Critic for the Los Angeles *Times,* he couched his descriptions in words easily understood by casual onlookers as well as by professional observers.

According to Ouroussoff, the bell tower was conceived as a spiritual beacon. Visitors would park in a multi-level underground garage and

---

[30]*Ibid.,* April 22, 1996.

from there they would walk up a grand staircase to a plaza. Rather than immediately leading visitors into the church, Moneo's design is reversed, with the altar end serving as the principal façade. By turning the church around, the architect reinvented the traditional church layout. In what one expert called his "most striking invention," Moneo's cathedral draws its congregation slowly into the building. Visitors approach the cathedral along the south arcade, entering the main ambulatory and passing by the side chapels before doubling back to finally face the altar. The rest of the design is slightly asymmetrical, as if the space was held delicately off-balance.

Moneo's decision to move circulation outside the main space creates a system of parallel walls. Chapels do not face the main worship space, but outward toward the ambulatory, instead of encroaching on the main nave. Hence the altar receives the main focus. Openings between the chapels allow visitors to glimpse the main cathedral space as they enter. Hence each of the chapels becomes a private meditation sanctuary, while the central worship space is left undisturbed.

Then, along the northern flank, a second ambulatory gives access to the chapels on the other side of the nave. There the exterior of the church is glass and the ambulatory facing chapels overlook the meditation garden and bell tower. Ouroussoff noted that "by individually connecting them [the chapels] to the landscape, they become wonderfully contemplative." Above the chapels, the architect uses the double wall system to filter light into the various spaces, whereas it filters into the chapel from below and into the main worship area from a dramatic clerestory above.[31]

In a subsequent essay, Ouroussoff explained that "cathedrals are meant to elevate the soul." Pointing out that Moneo is obsessed with history and "shuns the chaos of contemporary life," his design is a "spiritual filter; a sanctuary in the life of a city where the soul can be silently healed."

Suspecting that the cool abstractions of Moneo's design may offend some, the commentator points out that the strikingly Modernist "cathedral is a massive, unadorned concrete shell, perched at the southwest corner of the lot . . . The plaza is vast and bare, enclosed by a series of arcaded walkways. Its only trees line a reflecting pool that juts out from the gardens alongside the cathedral, into the open courtyard. There is a rawness to the forms. But it is just that rawness that gives the building its spiritual weight."

Moneo's forms are forcefully dynamic, with everything asymmetrical. The body of the cathedral is placed at a skewed angle on the site, its

---

[31]*Ibid.*, April 30, 1997.

faceted roof slopes up dramatically toward the altar. The architect's "formal language perfectly reflects his belief in the importance of movement in architecture. The cathedral's beauty comes from the architect's ability to translate form into a poetic contemporary vision."

The importance of understanding the architect's view is highlighted by all the commentators. But "once you give yourself over to it, Moneo's plan is also wonderfully inspired."

> He is not preaching an easy, accessible spirituality. He wants the visitor to take time to think, to engage more deeply. Rather than animate the space with loud gestures, he delicately opens views between the chapels to the main nave. By doing so, he creates a sense of anticipation–of spiritual secrets about to be revealed.

Ouroussoff completed his commentary by saying that in a culture that values instant gratification, Moneo is "creating an alternate world–one where the cosmic drama can only be understood by the aristocracy of wisdom."[32]

Five years later, Ouroussoff finished his trilogy on the cathedral by observing that "Los Angeles finally has a spiritual heart. That is the assumption at least, behind the monumental new Cathedral of Our Lady of the Angels." He wrote that "Moneo drew on a range of traditional precedents. He then reworked them for a contemporary world. The result is a structure steeped in memory and yet wholly new." Moneo's design "is an effort to reconcile the tension between traditional forms and the more informal layout of post-Vatican II cathedrals."

> Moneo refuses to let go of the thread that binds him to his spiritual past. His interest lies in the long arc of history, in reconciling the conflicts that periodically rock the church as it attempts to adapt to changing realities. It is an evolutionary strategy rather than a radical surge forward. It is in that sense that Moneo's cathedral echoes the great works of earlier church architects. Moneo's design shows no patience for those who forget the past. Yet it is firmly grounded in the present. Its ability to transcend those differences is the cathedral's most remarkable insight.[33]

In a column on the editorial pages of the Los Angeles *Times,* author Clint Anderson pointed out that Europe's great cathedrals often were

---

[32] *Ibid.,* September 23, 1997.
[33]*Ibid.,* September 1, 2002.

political statements. The awesome Gothic cathedrals of France were intended to advance the glory of the Capetian kings along with the glory of God; Germany's great Romanesque cathedrals were expressly designed to equate the imperial crown with the papal tiara; the Norman conquerors of England erected their massive fortress-cathedrals to overawe the native Saxon population. "But the Cathedral of Our Lady of the Angels is designed purely for the people of Los Angeles, their own House of God. It is a structure that intends to connect them with their defining past and present and with the indistinct future."

The former Professor of English Literature at Loyola Marymount University goes on to say that "all of Moneo's celebrated buildings around the world thoughtfully reinterpret history and spirit in a language for the future. Amazingly his design for our cathedral connects it visually with the entire history of the Catholic Church and beyond. The very positioning of the building to face the rising sun recalls the temple of Ezekiel's vision and the very first basilica of Constantine who prayed to a Persian sun god as well as to the God of Jews and Christians."[34]

There were some naysayers, but a remarkably small number. The distinguished Father Richard John Neuhaus, for example, otherwise a shrewd observer on the ecclesial scene, said, "from the outside the cathedral looks like a very big barge that somehow got beached in downtown Los Angeles, and the inside looks for all the world like a well-lighted warehouse."[35]

Architect and author, Steven J. Schloeder, said that "the building has at first glance everything required for a major cathedral: a majestic sense of space, tall ceilings, light pouring in from above, a generous sanctuary with ample clergy seating, and a vast open plaza to create a sense of forecourt and presence in the urban fabric of downtown Los Angeles." He opined that "as a piece of modern architecture, the new Cathedral of Our Lady of the Angels will be a solid, noteworthy and frequently visited place of architectural pilgrimage. It certainly satisfies Edouard Le Corbusier's dictum that "architecture is the masterly play of light on form," and it adheres to all the tenets of Moneo's modernism: an articulated box, structurally lucid, well-crated and functional."[36]

Emmy award winning reporter, Sam Hall Kaplan, wrote that notwithstanding his fondness for European cathedrals, their welcoming plazas and awe-inspiring structures, he saw the new Cathedral of Our Lady of the Angels as a distinct "new world, a modern interpretation of a

---

[34]*Ibid.*, September 17, 1997.

[35]"The Public Square," *First Things*, LXXXI (March, 1998), 67.

[36]"Our Lady of the Angels: An Architectural Review," *The Catholic World* VIII (December 1998), 54.

sacred space, site specific and Southwestern, sympathetic to Southern California's context, climate and culture, another icon on the historic train of the missions:

> It is, in a word, unpretentious, especially from a distance. It does not soar or sparkle, as do the great cathedrals of the world. It boasts no twisting spires, no dazzling stained glass. It is enclosed, like the founding missions, turned into itself, austere.
>
> But once through the gates and onto the plaza, and inside the cathedral, the artistry and architecture come together to create a distinct space and spirit.
>
> This view has prompted some strong reactions from readers, such as, "Take the gloves off, Sam. Your thinly veiled praise won't get you into the Pearly Gates. (You're Jewish, remember?)" That's why I have further detailed my comments here, and suggest a visit might be in order.[37]

Writing on the "Sky Line" for the *New Yorker,* Paul Goldberger said that "it's hard to make a landmark in Los Angeles," but Moneo "plays with the past and is genuinely inventive at the same time. His best touch is both an homage to the traditional Gothic cathedral and a subtle, brilliant inversion of it." He concluded by observing that "in Los Angeles, Moneo has made a valiant effort to render sacred space on a large scale, and he has not done it with tricks or gimmicks."[38]

Finally there was Richard Lacayo writing in *Time* magazine who felt that Moneo "is a master of interior space, an expert at setting traps for sunlight." Asking the question: What should a church look like in the 21st century, he responded: "Maybe it's a space where the eyes, in the end, are turned inward."[39]

Leo A. Daly, Executive Architect

Chosen by the Professional Committee to be lead local architect was the firm of Leo A. Daly which had, since its inception in 1915, established

---

[37]*Downtown News,* September 2, 2002
[38]"Sanctum on the Coast," September 9, 2002, 94.
[39]"To the Lighthouse," CLX, September 2, 2002, 64.

a reputation for architectural engineering, planning and interior design.[40] As such the Daly team was to implement Moneo's design for the project from the preparation of all drawings and specifications through the administration of all construction contracts. In that capacity, the Daly firm set to work developing plans, blueprints and other materials for the use of the General Contractor.[41]

It was a formidable commission because it involved the more fundamental design issues of building a cathedral in a modern city's downtown area that connects worshippers with their centuries old heritage. Nicholas Roberts, the firm's executive architect, told one newspaper that "the cathedral complex would help redefine the architecture of Los Angeles."[42]

---

[40]Established in Omaha, Nebraska, the firm today employs nearly 900 design and engineering professionals. Projects have been completed in more than fifty countries as well as the United States. Clients include national and local governments, public bodies, non-profit institutions and corporations such as IBM, American Express, Citicorp, Kodak and Motorola. Presently there are sixteen key office locations worldwide. Projects bearing the Daly name are the Lied Library (University of Nevada), Repsol Technology Centre (Madrid, Spain), Ronald Reagan National Airport (Washington, D.C.), Cheung Kong Center (China), Reliant Stadium Complex (Houston, Texas), the Pope John Paul II Cultural Center and the National World War II Memorial (Washington, D.C.) and the Tower at First National Center (Omaha, Nebraska). AALA, Press Release, February 3, 1997.

[41]*Cathedral Chapters*, II, #2, Summer 1998.

[42]*The Tidings,* October 23, 1998.

Chapter VI

Ground Blessing

Several hours prior to the ground breaking on September 21, 1997, Cardinal Mahony met with a group of Native Americans after they had performed a blessing rite of their own on the cathedral property. "He promised them that the archdiocese would treat both the land and the ancient artifacts uncovered during the building with great care and respect."[1]

Then in a brief ceremony in the basement of the old cathedral, the cardinal asked participants to reflect on the many baptisms, weddings, ordinations, funerals and other ceremonies that had taken place in those hallowed surroundings over the preceding 119 years. "As we leave this closed cathedral, we give thanks to God for all the blessings we have found here. Let us remember the generations of prayer and devotion that Saint Vibiana has inspired."[2] At the end of that service, people gathered up tiny bits of dirt and broken bricks which they carried to the new location at Temple and Hills streets. Police on bicycles escorted a hundred or so marchers as they made the five block trek to a site where the freeways of Los Angeles converge, a place where Our Lady would reach out to embrace all of God's people, regardless of race, creed or color.

A multicultural music and dance festival, including a mariachi band, a Polish folk dance ensemble and Tongan tauolunga dancers presented a program prior to the ground blessing. When all was in readiness a procession of colorfully attired people representing some of the sixty-five cultures comprising the Archdiocese of Los Angeles began the slow and dignified trek to the gathering area. At precisely four o'clock the cardinal, accompanied by bishops, priests, religious, laity and hundreds of banner-bearing young people marched to a knoll overlooking the parking lot that would soon make way for the new edifice.

In its description of the event, the local Catholic newspaper said that "the ground breaking ceremony was both sacred ritual and festive celebration, both a time of reflection and a time of commitment, both the ending and the beginning of a process with its roots in a century past and with its fruition in a century to come." Witnessed by a crowd upwards of

---

[1]*The Tidings,* September 26, 1997.
[2]*Ibid.*

Procession from the old cathedral to the new site. *Source: The Tidings*

12,000 people, the blessing was hailed by Mayor Richard Riordan "as a fitting acknowledgement of the city's religious and civic stature on the eve of the new millennium."[3]

The text of Cardinal Mahony's homily delivered on that occasion is well worth recalling in its entirety:

> For many centuries the sun has risen day after day from the east behind us, has shone upon this piece of ground, and has sunk in the west beyond us.
>
> The rays of that sun have fallen upon this special ground year after year. Beginning with the Gabrieleno/Tongva nation, many moons past, one use of this land gave way to another, until in recent times, this five and a half acres finally lay fallow and bore the official note of "undesignated."
>
> But I believe deeply that in God's loving providence, this special ground, this undesignated portion of downtown Los Angeles, has been preserved by God precisely for this moment—the blessing of this site for the new Cathedral of Our Lady of the Angels.

[3]*Ibid.*

Mayor Richard Riorden was a valued ally in the drive for a new cathedral. *Source: Lee Salem Photography*

Just as our Hebrew Scripture reading instructed us, God has indeed laid "a precious cornerstone as a sure foundation." No previous bishop or archbishop of the Archdiocese of Los Angeles ever envisioned building a cathedral church upon this site. No planning process of previous generations fixed their gaze upon this special, hallowed ground as a site for a cathedral.

Neither I nor anyone on the cathedral planning team foresaw our settling upon this unique, elevated, grand site to situate our new Cathedral of Our Lady of the Angels. No, we were led to this site by a wondrous yet mysterious set of circumstances—and in my opinion, all part of God's providence

Catholic populace participates at the ground blessing. *Source: Lee Salem Photography*

for us. It was God who spoke those words, "See, I am laying a stone in Zion"—it is God who does the selecting, and it is God who lays the cornerstone for anything great in human history. The Church of Jesus Christ does not require actual material stones for its identity nor its authentic witness in the world. No, each person baptized into the Lord Jesus becomes a "living stone" in the structure, the body of Christ, the people of God (1 Peter 2:5). Our Gospel today proclaims the establishment of Jesus' church upon Peter: "And I say to you, you are Peter, and upon this rock I will build my church."

But while the dynamic life of the Church does not depend upon visible houses of worship, from the earliest days Christians set aside certain sacred spaces as places for the faithful to gather for "the teaching of the apostles, for the communal life, for the breaking of the bread and for the prayers" (Acts 2:42).

Down through the centuries the unswerving confession of Peter and the vibrant life of the church were marked both by rejection and persecution on the one hand, and by the building of enduring churches and cathedrals on the other. Both the interior and exterior witness to Jesus Christ have gloriously marked our history as a church.

Today, one could visit every major metropolitan city in the world and find in the very heart of that city a magnificent cathedral church—giving striking evidence of the people's faith, stunning architecture and exquisite religious art. The early cathedrals featured frescoes, stained glass windows, and statues to serve as living teachers of the faith. The story of our salvation was revealed in these resplendent art forms that guided a people yet unschooled and without books.

The eminent metropolitan City of Los Angeles and the largest archdiocese in the country—with one of the largest Catholic populations in the world—has remained for decades without a distinguished cathedral church.

At long last, both the people of God and the City of Los Angeles will finally have a cathedral church worthy of our times and the importance of both the city and the Archdiocese of Los Angeles. Situated as a unique gateway to both Latin America and to the Pacific Rim, Los Angeles stands as a beacon of hope and of unity in a world that continues to blend beliefs and cultures in a new fusion of God's people.

Our new Cathedral of Our Lady of the Angels will be remarkable in its ability to serve as a constant reminder of God's presence in our midst, of the unity that must link all peoples, and of the enduring faith of Peter that must take ever deeper root in our lives.

Today, all of you gathered here on this precious ground are witnesses to a unique, unfolding history. Our new cathedral church is being designed to endure for at least five centuries, thus passing on to many generations to come our faith in God and our willingness to express that faith both in our lives and in our sacred buildings. Future generations will marvel at the intensity and foresight of your vision and your dedication and will thank you for the grace-filled process you set in motion this afternoon.

As this revered ground is blessed and dedicated to God for the ages to come, the precious cornerstone of Jesus Christ is being set in place as a timeless blessing for this city and for our archdiocese. May we all acknowledge humbly that this is a work of our loving God, and that our meager human efforts will take form and shape in proportion to the fervor of Peter's faith deep within our own hearts and his words upon our own lips: "You are the Messiah, the Son of the Living God!"[4]

---

[4]AALA, "Ground Blessing Ceremony," Los Angeles, September 21, 1997.

Young people carry the banner from San Buenaventura Mission Parish at the blessing of the site. *Source: Lee Salem Photography*

Professor Jose Rafael Moneo, the architect for the cathedral, also spoke at the event, saying "It would be difficult to find a more magnificent site in Los Angeles on which to build a cathedral." He hoped that the new edifice would "maintain the dignity a temple ought to have, but I would also like it to be a building open, receptive and welcoming."[5]

An interesting feature of the day was the presentation of a stone fragment brought from a tiny church in Assisi, Italy from which the City of Los Angeles received its name. The *pietra preciosa* or precious stone, taken from Saint Mary of the Angels of the Portiuncula, was presented by the Franciscan, Giulio Mancini, who represented the Order of Friars Minor. It was at that place Saint Francis rebuilt Saint Mary's by hand in the thirteen century hearing the words of Christ, "Go and restore my

---

[5]AALA, "The Architect's Vision," Los Angeles, September 21, 1997.

Ground blessing at the new site on September 21, 1997.
Source: Lee Salem Photography

house." The stone was also reminiscent of the long and noble tradition of the Franciscan presence in California which dates back to 1769.

Another focal point of the day was the presence of a "model" of the new cathedral. Most of the onlookers found the model "functional and filled with symbolism." One lady, admitting that she was not overly enthusiastic, said that "the austere interior reminds me of how we need to empty ourselves when we pray, empty ourselves in the presence of God,

The southland's bishops join the cardinal at the ground blessing. *Source: Lee Salem Photography*

both spiritually and materially. And at the same time, you are filled in this great space with God's richness that is found in those you pray with."[6]

There was a handful of dissenters with their placards, standing on the sidewalks during the ceremony. Matthew Hetz was not amused, as he pointed out in a letter to the local press:

> Efforts to eradicate poverty and feed the poor must always be a pressing priority of the Church, and the Church, while imperfect in an imperfect world, has not, I believe, abandoned efforts to feed the hungry. But if everyone has a big house, it only benefits the owners and their private guests. But if men and women use their God-given talents of architecture, art, science, construction, finance and so forth to build house of worship dedicated to God and consecrate it to Jesus as the woman did with her oils, then we have striven to give praise to God with our meager abilities.
>
> The cathedral, unlike a private house, is open to all, and rich and poor can enter and present themselves to God

---

[6]Marilyn Villalobos in *The Tidings,* September 26, 1997.

whenever they so choose, and indeed in it seek spiritual nourishment.[7]

In her account of the celebration, Mary Rourke said that the blessing was a "welcome break with local custom that a parking lot is making way for a bit of paradise."[8]

Not surprisingly, criticism such as this is anything but new in the Catholic Church. In the twelfth century, when Abbot Suger was designing the Gothic cathedral of Saint Denis near Paris, his fellow monk, Bernard of Clairvaux, was startled when he learned about the soaring arches and rose-shaped window shedding light on the altar vessels studded with gems from King Louis VII's court. Caustically, he said: "If you were to continue that pomp and circumstance of yours, it might appear a little too insolent." Unmoved by the chastisement, Suger wrote: "I see myself dwelling, as it were, in some strange region of the universe which neither exists entirely in the slime of the earth nor the purity of heaven. By the grace of God I can be transported to God." Happily the abbot went on to design one of the world's greatest cathedrals. The cardinal's response to the Catholic Worker people was similar to Suger's: "A cathedral isn't a luxury. It's a necessity."[9]

Ground Breaking

The actual breaking of ground for the new cathedral was scheduled for October 14, 1998. At a press conference on the downtown site, Cardinal Mahony unveiled updated plans for the complex which had been enthusiastically blessed by Pope John Paul II.

An aggravating but somewhat amusing incident occurred during the ceremony when a small group of protesters scaled the fence surrounding the property and commandeered a front-end loader which the cardinal had intended to use to dig up dirt and blacktop, thus effectively interrupting the symbolic event. Never at a loss for words, the cardinal responded by asking a rhetorical question: "Can you serve the poor as well as build churches, schools, hospitals and other institutions that serve the community?" His response: "Yes, we can and for 2,000 years,

---

[7]Los Angeles *Times,* October 6, 2002.

[8]*Ibid.,* September 22, 1997.

[9]Quoted in Mary Rourke's article in the Los Angeles *Times,* September 18, 1997.

[10]*The Tidings,* October 23, 1998.

The cardinal and the architect turn the ground for the new cathedral.
Source: Lee Salem Photography

history has said so. This cathedral will be for everyone."[10] "The works of the Church have gone hand-in-hand for centuries," he said. He went on to observe that "on this site will rise a church that will serve as a sign and a symbol of God's presence in our downtown area."[11] The cardinal donned a hard hat and overturned the earth—standard fare at such events while the ceremony continued with observers trying to ignore the protesters."[12]

Tom Higgins, a bystander, told a reporter "a great cathedral has been a visual symbol to the whole population it serves. The significance of the cathedral goes beyond the Catholic community." It will "be

[11]Los Angeles *Daily News,* October 15, 1998.
[12]*The Tidings,* October 23, 1998.

Southland's Chief Shepherd at the ground blessing. *Source: Lee Salem Photography*

a symbol of great prominence and will further the social role of Los Angeles as a community."[13]

Using the occasion as a "teaching moment," Cardinal Mahony wrote an editorial for the Los Angeles *Times* in which he pointed out that protesters of the new cathedral were ignoring the spiritual needs of the poor. In part he said:

> The Catholic Worker and others shortchange the poor when they adopt the stance that the Church should be attentive only to the material concerns of the needy. This is out of step with Church history and with the teaching of Jesus, who said that people do not live by bread alone.

---

[13]*Ibid.*, October 23, 1998.

There are various kinds of poverty, of which material poverty is but one. When the hunger for the spiritual and the aesthetic is unsatisfied, we can experience a poverty in our souls. Throughout the Christian era, believers have built churches and cathedrals as expressions of their love of God and as sacred oases where rich and poor can find refuge, beauty and inner peace.

Churches and cathedrals have been effective teaching tools for proclaiming and explaining the mysteries of the faith. In every age, the Church uses art, including architecture, to satisfy spiritual hunger and the human longing for the beautiful. The Church has done this without neglecting its obligation to feed the hungry, welcome the homeless, nurse the sick and educate the ignorant. In short, the Church has kept faith with the poor.

We have believed for twenty centuries that the Church as the body of Christ must do what Jesus did—preach, teach, heal, reconcile and sanctify. To accomplish this mission, we have built schools, hospitals, shelters, nurseries, homes for the aged, social service centers and, yes, cathedrals.

Contrary to what protesters say, ours is not an "either-or" situation. We do not face the false dichotomy of tending to the dispossessed or building a cathedral. Rather, our circumstances are "both-and," in which the Catholic community ministers to the materially poor and addresses the spiritual needs of all.[14]

That the extreme attitude adopted by a small minority was beginning to irritate people became evident in several editorials. One, in the Los Angeles *Daily News,* said that "there's a time and place to demonstrate. Some are more constructive than others. Last week's disruption of the groundbreaking ceremony for the new Catholic church in downtown Los Angeles by a handful of homeless advocates was neither the time nor the place for it. By intruding upon Cardinal Roger Mahony's presentation of new plans for the cathedral and standing like little children on the skip loader that was to have made the first cut in construction of the building, the tiny band of protesters destroyed what little credibility they had."

The editorial went on to say:

> The Los Angeles Catholic Worker members belittled their own cause, which is seeking more funding for homeless programs, for a publicity ploy. Did they really expect the nation's largest archdiocese to sympathize with them and abandon a

---

[14]Los Angeles *Times,* October 19, 1998.

Cathedral Ground Blessing. *Source: Rick Flynn*

Those opposed to the new cathedral represented a decidely minority opinion. *Source: The Tidings*

project which has been on the drawing board for years and is so important to many devout Catholics, simply because they were playing on the heavy equipment?

In the process, their message was muddied. They oppose the construction of the cathedral because, at a cost of $163 million, it is too lavish. The protesters think it is wiser for the Church to spend its money on underprivileged, hungry people.

It is their right to speak out, even to demonstrate and protest to call attention to the needy. But there is nothing noble about scaling a fence and barreling through the clutches of a brown-robed cleric.[15]

Construction

On April 24, 1997, Bill Close, co-chairperson of the Cathedral Complex Advisory Board, announced that fourteen firms were in competition for the position of General Contractor. Listed among the qualifications were

- The candidates' experience and expertise in using architectural concrete which will be the primary building material for the Cathedral Complex;
- The "project team" of each company, including the principal in charge, project manager, estimator, scheduler and superintendent;
- The candidates' previous projects and references.[16]

It was generally known that the three finalists were Morley Builders, Clark, and Matt Construction companies.

In a subsequent press release, Cardinal Mahony announced the Morley Construction Company had been named general contractor for the projected Cathedral of Our Lady of the Angels. "We appreciate the openness, spirit of cooperation and the tremendous show of confidence in us by the Archdiocese of Los Angeles." Mark Benjamin, Morley's chief executive officers told *The Tidings,* the archdiocesan weekly.[17]

---

[15]Los Angeles *Daily News,* October 18, 1998.

[16]AALA, Announcement, Los Angeles, April 24, 1997.

[17]AALA, Press Release, Los Angeles, April 24, 1997. Morley Construction Company, founded by Morley Benjamin, celebrated its Fiftieth Anniversary on April 15, 1997. Some of their notable projects in Southern California include the $55 million preservation and strengthening of Royce Hall on the UCLA campus and pouring all the concrete for downtown's First Interstate World Center, then

In its commentary on Morley's appointment, the *Downtown News* said that the Santa Monica firm "was credited with doing more research on the construction site than other contenders."[18] C. Terry Dooley wrote to the cardinal on May 17, 1999, "the momentous day, the start of construction" that it was an historic milestone "along the road that we at Morley have traveled with you for two years."[19] From the earliest days, it was evident how closely the cardinal would remain with the project. He wanted huge signs made for the cranes with the word 'cathedral' emblazoned to impress passersby.

That the Los Angeles cathedral was getting national attention is evident from its coverage in east coast newspapers. In its long essay on one of the "five best" projects in America, *The Wall Street Journal* described the project thusly:

> **Description:** The 5.6-acre site is located at the intersection of Temple Street and Grand Avenue in downtown Los Angeles.
> **Cost:** More than $163 million.
> **Owner:** Archdiocese of Los Angeles
> **Analysis:** When complete, it will boast 48,000 square feet and enough pews to accommodated 2,600 people. A series of devotional chapels will line both sides of the cathedral. The thirty-six bells located in the bell tower will be programmed to play hymns throughout the day. They will also call people to worship. The Los Angeles Cathedral, to be built on the site of a former parking lot, will be the mother church for the Archdiocese of Los Angeles. Roger Cardinal Mahony will reside in the new rectory. Construction is scheduled to begin in the fall of 1998.
> **Comment:** Frank O. Gehry, architect for Frank O. Gehry and Associates: "It is an achievement for the city to finally have a big cathedral to represent the Catholic community. Many people from Latin America who come here are Catholic, and it is significant to have a symbolic center.[20]

---

the tallest skyscraper west of the Mississippi River. Other works include seismic strengthening of Los Angeles City Hall and work on the Hollywood Bowl, CBS Studio Center, the Bunker Hill Museum Tower, the Sherman Fairchild Library, Caltech and the City of Hope Diabetes Research Center.

[18]AALA, Press Release, Los Angeles, March 28, 1997.

[19]AALA, C. Terry Dooley to Roger Cardinal Mahony, Los Angeles, August 26, 1999.

[20]*The Wall Street Journal,* April 15, 1998.

**A Renewed Church of Los Angeles
A New Millennium, A New Cathedral**

Lord God,
  you continue to build up the Church of your Son, Jesus Christ,
  through the faithful proclamation of the Gospel
  and the joyous celebration of the Eucharist.

In your plan of salvation
  you establish Local Churches
  to carry on the mission of your Son.

We pray for all the members of our Archdiocese of Los Angeles
  that together
  we may become ever more fruitful channels of your grace
  and faithful witnesses of the Gospel
  to all of Southern California.

As we prepare to celebrate the Third Millennium
  of Christ's redeeming mission,
  we ask your gracious assistance
  as we plan and build our new Cathedral Church.

May our new Cathedral,
  the Mother Church of the Archdiocese,
  serve as a clearer sign of unity
  linking all our Parish Communities
  in a deeper spirit of faith, hope and love.

We pray that our new Cathedral
  be a visible reminder
  of your wondrous presence in our midst,
  and assist us to live out our lives more fully
  in harmony with our Baptismal promises.

We make our prayer
through the intercession of Mary,
Our Lady of the Angels.
Amen!

+ Roger Cardinal Mahony

Cardinal Mahony was anxious that sub-contractors owned by minorities and women have an opportunity for contracting work. All the bidding processes were to make allowances to reflect the ethnic diversity in the archdiocese. The archdiocese requested Morley to set a goal of employing 25% minority-owned businesses and 5% women-owned for the cathedral project. Monsignor Terrance Fleming, Vicar General for the archdiocese, said that:

Historically, the great cathedrals of the world were reflections of the local community. The local craftsmen and artisans took the local materials and fashioned them into a great edifice which brings the community together in their worshipping of God. Thus, the first new cathedral of the twenty-first century

should also be fashioned by local artisans and craftsmen who reflect the local community and will be the worshippers in the new cathedral.[21]

A frequent, almost daily visitor to the construction site, the cardinal noted on one occasion, as he stood in the center of the lot, looking to the southeast, "one can see the top of the 1928 City Hall, while Dodger Stadium stands visible to the north and a little east. The coming Walt Disney Concert Hall will rise nearby, meaning the cathedral will be just part of a downtown architectural super scheme involving government and cultural edifices"[22]

Mahony rejoiced at seeing "all aspects of the construction moving ahead so well." He said that "one of our biggest challenges with the archdiocesan Catholic community is to acquaint them with the reality of the cathedral's presence and construction."[23] All the while he was anxious to provide "the best security" at the site. He wanted at least one security

[21]*The Tidings,* June 26, 1998.

[22]*Ibid.,* December 7, 1998.

[23]AALA, Roger Cardinal Mahony to Lee Castleberry, Los Angeles, September 16, 1999.

guard on site twenty-four hours a day, seven days a week."[24] One measure for guaranteeing safety was the erection of a construction fence around the perimeter of the site. The wall served the additional purpose of allowing youngsters in the religious education programs throughout the archdiocese to design and paint art boards depicting life in their parish to adorn the otherwise boring wooden fence.

On May 17, 1999, after a prayer of blessing, an Our Father and the grunt of heavy machinery, the excavation process began. The cardinal climbed aboard a giant yellow front-loader and moved the first few piles of dirt where the 63,000 square foot, 3000 seat cathedral would be built[25]. The first foundation pour of concrete was scheduled for June 24th at 8 o'clock in the morning. The footing was for the south Ambulatory Moat wall.[26] On August 12th, the cardinal went up in the basket of one of the tower cranes. He told a friend that "it is really spectacular seeing all aspects of the construction moving ahead so well, and as far as I know, we have been devoid of any major obstacles or problems along the way.[27]

On October 27, 2000, those who designed and built the cathedral were named "Building Team of the Year." Here is the message sent to them by the cardinal:

> What a privilege it was to be with all of you on Friday evening, October 27th, as the Los Angeles Chapter of the AIA presented its prestigious awards!
>
> I was so proud that not only did the Cathedral of Our Lady of the Angels receive the Outstanding Achievement Award, but more importantly, all of you received the prestigious "Building Team of the Year" Presidential Award!
>
> Your Award was very well deserved, and the reason that we are progressing so well with our project is that we have the best overall Team in the world working on the Cathedral of Our Lady of the Angels!
>
> It was a grand night for the Cathedral Project, and Monsignor Kevin Kostelnik and I were so pleased to see all of you being duly and properly recognized.

---

[24]AALA, Roger Cardinal Mahony to C. Terry Dooley, Los Angeles, September 23, 1999.

[25]*The Tidings,* May 21, 1999.

[26]AALA, Memorandum to Brother Hilarion O'Connor, O.S.F., Los Angeles, June 22, 1999.

[27]AALA, Roger Cardinal Mahony to Mark Benjamin, Los Angeles, July 17, 1999.

The cardinal and Close were daily visitors to the construction site.
Source: The Tidings

You all looked terrific dressed up with such class! Maybe
you ought to consider wearing those outfits in the construction
trailers![28]

While he was "generally quite pleased with the quality of the workmanship" by the Morley Construction Company, the cardinal felt that
there were far too many private tours being given on the site. He pointed
out that the cathedral was owned by the Archdiocese of Los Angeles and
he directed that "no one is to come into the site except for legitimate construction related business." He pointed out that only prospective donors
were to be accommodated and these would be coordinated by the official
cathedral staff.[29]

---

[28]AALA, Memo, Roger Cardinal Mahony, Los Angeles, October 30, 2000.

[29]AALA, Roger Cardinal Mahony to Mark Benjamin, Los Angeles, November 28, 2000.

Concrete columns are poured into place, April 29, 1999. *Source: Warren Aerial Photography, Inc.*

Construction site, May 21, 1999.

As the months moved on, the cathedral began gradually changing the skyline of Los Angeles. First a vision of faith, then a blueprint, the cathedral was growing from a concept to a reality. Day by day, the monumental new Mother Church for the Archdiocese of Los Angeles was taking on its own distinctive shape and influence.

Local newspapers informed their readers about the building process. An article on March 16, 2001 described how the 47,000 square foot roof of the eleven-story edifice was completed in March of that year. And it was that issue that mentioned, for the first time, that there would be room in the "undercroft" for 1,270 crypts and 4,476 niches for burials. A "two and one half acre plaza would feature waterfalls and a fountain inscribed with Jesus' promise of "living water" to those who thirst for God.[30]

Writing in another newspaper, Brent Hopkins said that

> The new building is intended to represent a blend of elements of California missions and European cathedrals, and is bordered by a 2.5-acre open plaza for community use. Resembling a Gothic cathedral similar to St. Patrick's in New York in size, the structure also pays homage to local architecture with its adobe-like coloring and mission-style layout. Rather than the traditional stained-glass window behind the altar, Our Lady of the Angels has a distinctive, six-story window in the shape of a cross. Made of Spanish alabaster, the cross will bathe the congregation in natural light during the daytime. The whole layout is a bit off-center—on purpose.[31]

Amid the cacophony of hammers, heavy equipment and orders shouted above the dust and din, a sense of the sacred was beginning to surround the massive new cathedral. Hard hatted workers who climb the towering cranes and pour the concrete, who tie rebar and drink from thermos bottles began to feel the hush within the new edifice.

> The design is so geometrically complex that it could not have been built in the past using hand-drawn blueprints. Computer technology has made it possible to meet building tolerances so demanding that none of the handcrafted concrete forms may vary from the design by more than one-sixteenth of an inch. Ordinary projects allow variances at least twice that

---

[30]Los Angeles *Times,* March 16, 2001.
[31]*Daily News,* September 5, 2000.

Aerial view of the site on June 25, 1999. *Source: Warren Aerial Photography Inc.*

Miles and miles of rebar.

large. The complexity and layering of the space enhances the sense of mystery and wonder.[32]

A progress report for the end of 2000, stated that "the nave of the church is now a forest of scaffolding, supporting what our workers call the 'dance floor.' Made of plywood, the floor ranges from fifty feet high near the baptistry to about eighty-five feet behind the altar. It serves as a staging and safety platform for work now beginning inside the roof trusses and around them."[33]

The day-to-day construction activity of the cathedral has been described in many ways. One writer put it this way:

Few people are more cognizant of that evolution than the design team behind Our Lady of the Angels Cathedral, the adobe-colored Modernist temple rising rapidly above the Hollywood Freeway. For the engineers, architects and designers assigned to the project, under the cardinal's leadership, the pri-

---

[32]Los Angeles *Times,* August 17, 2000.
[33]AALA, C. Terry Dooley to Kevin Starr, Los Angeles, December 22, 2000.

Source: The Tidings

mary goal is to faithfully execute the nuts and bolts of Madrid-based chief architect Jose Rafael Moneo's master plan.[34]

Few contractors kept as careful and precise records as did the Morley Construction Company and its senior project manager, Audre Kleven. Between November 13, 1998 and March 31, 2000, the company issued no fewer than nine volumes of *Activity Reports* which traced the overall process in great detail.

Concrete

The "greatest single cost and scheduled element is the architectural concrete of the cathedral."[35] Morley Construction Company had significant experience using architectural concrete as the primary building material for the complex at the County Hall of Administration. Morley had

---

[34]May 22, 2001

[35]AALA, Hilarion O'Connor to Jose Rafael Moneo, Los Angeles, June 17, 1997.

Source: The Tidings

also previously worked on a $55 million preservation and strengthening of UCLA's Royce Hall, as well as the downtown's First Interstate World Center.[36]

As early as 1997, the cardinal was anxious to get a "recipe" for the type of special concrete Moneo had in mind for the cathedral. He was "greatly concerned that the exterior finish not resemble a concrete parking garage or some other utility structure." Rather, he wanted "the exterior finish to be noble and in the tradition of great cathedrals."[37] The early cathedrals had been built of stone, but the contemporary ones could not afford that luxury especially in an area of the world where stone quarries are practically non-existent.

Concrete had been utilized in buildings since Roman times. The Coliseum was built about 70 A.D. with concrete and faced with marble. The Pantheon, built around 120 A.D. and considered the greatest of all Roman buildings, was erected in concrete as was Hadrian's Tomb (Castle Sant

---

[36]*Downtown News,* April 28, 1999.

[37]AALA, Roger Cardinal Mahony to Jose Rafael Moneo, Los Angeles, April 10, 1997.

Work on the cathedral itself begins to move ahead, June 2, 2000. *Source: Warren Aerial Photography Inc.*

Angelo) in 135 A.D. The use of concrete in the Roman Empire had ceased after the fall of Rome when the formula seems to have been lost

In 1824, Joseph Aspdin, a British stonemason, obtained a patent for a process for making cement. He had heated a mixture of finely powered limestone and clay and ground the mixture into a substance that hardened with the addition of water. Aspdin named his product portland cement because it resembled the stone quarried on the Isle of Port off the British coast.

The Morley Company's experience with concrete was probably the chief reason why it was chosen for the cathedral project. One of the first challenges faced was that of insuring that the principal design, using colored, exposed, sandblasted architectural concrete would serve for several hundred years. The walls were to rise to a height of 130 feet, and to be made of approximately 20,000 cubic yards of adobe-hued concrete. Two items which improve concrete durability are impermeability and protection of reinforcing steel. Considerable research, planning and testing greatly influenced the use of concrete for the cathedral. To control and discipline concrete cracking due to shrinkage, vertical crack inducers with integral waterstops were inserted at approximately twelve-foot intervals for the full

View of cathedral construction from the Hollywood Freeway, August 1, 2000. *Source: Warren Aerial Photography Inc.*

height of the walls. Another measure to induce long life was that of preventing corrosion of the reinforcing steel. One internal report concluded:

> Morley's concrete expertise and leadership in technical organizations like the American Concrete Institute provided a solid resource base to help the owner and design team select the best overall system to produce 500-year architectural concrete.[38]

A light colored and sandblasted architectural concrete was chosen for the 435,000 square feet of interior and exterior walls of the cathedral. The same mixture was used for the campanile, carillon, porch, exposed parking structure walls and the structural elements of the plaza. In total the project was composed of an extraordinary 630,000 square feet of concrete.[39]

---

[38]AALA, Memorandum, February 17, 1998.
[39]AALA, "Combining Architectural and Mass Concrete," prepared by Paula Monteiro and David Selna, n.d.

Cathedral interior.

Unfortunately the cost of the concrete work ran considerably over projections. The president and chief executive officer of Morley told the Vicar General that "I'm sure that much of the concern and rancor of recent times stems from the unanticipated overrun in concrete." It was, as he observed, "an embarrassment to our firm and to me."[40] If nothing else, the "concrete chapter" set records. The project "is believed to be the largest use of exposed architectural concrete in California building." Structural walls vary in thickness from twelve to fifty-eight inches. There are few right angles, and 850 non-repeating corner conditions.[41]

---

[40]AALA, Mark Benjamin to Terrance Fleming, Los Angeles, March 20, 2000.
[41]AALA, Memorandum, 2003 Engineering Awards Banquet, August 23, 2001.

Temple Street side of the new cathedral.

Seismic Base Isolators

Los Angeles County, criss-crossed by dozens of earth faults, has a long history of quakes. The underlying rock has proven highly undependable. Despite the fact that the new cathedral was built on the Elysian Park fault line, projections are now that should an earthquake, possibly up to 8.3 magnitude, hit the area, the cathedral would provide a safe sanctuary. The reason is the base isolators.

In a directive issued in mid 1997, the cardinal wanted to utilize and employ "the latest and fullest seismic protection engineering" in the new building. He pointed out that "our fellow Catholics across the archdiocese are presuming that we would not risk an enormous investment in a new cathedral, one destined to remain visible for centuries to come, without taking into account the possible effect that a serious earthquake could create." He went on to note that "the most effective seismic engineering known to date is the Base Isolation system." Though he knew it would increase the cost by as much as $3 million dollars, he felt that there might be some offsetting savings in the thickness of walls.[42]

---

[42]AALA, Roger Cardinal Mahony, Major Policy Statement, May 23, 1997.

Cathedral at the peak of concrete construction, September 29, 2000.
Source: Warren Aerial Photography Inc.

Cathedral structure nears completion, March 1, 2001. *Source: Warren Aerial Photography Inc.*

Nabih Youssef explained the whole concept in a detailed report which stated that he had designed a seismic isolation system comprised of high damping rubber and flat sliding bearings which exceeded the 1997 Uniform Building Code for the City of Los Angeles.

> The use of base isolation reduces the level of seismic force transferred to the superstructure, resulting in lower inter-story drift and acceleration response, and thus, reducing the potential for structural and non-structural damage[43]

Adrian Greenman said that "if the foundations move, gas, electricity and water pipes must move with them. Pipes go through a complex 3D flexible bend linked by several ball joints. For the electrical power lines, the cable loop paths have to be designed very carefully.".[44]

The Los Angeles cathedral is the only one in the world known to be base isolated. In fact, the technology is quite new, being used in the

---

[43]AALA, Nabih Youssef "A Tale of a Base Isolated Structure: The New Cathedral," n.d.

[44]Adrian Greenman, "From Here to Eternity," *Building Magazine,* 2000, n.p.

Aerial view of cathedral construction, April 4, 2001. *Source: Warren Aerial Photography Inc.*

United States for only about twenty years. Developed in New Zealand and Japan, the technology was used by Morley on two earlier buildings, including their revamping of the Los Angeles City Hall. The 120 million pound vertical weight of the cathedral is supported by 200 base isolators.

The key piece of each isolator is a rubber structure forty inches in diameter and nineteen inches from top to bottom. An isolator was placed under every load-bearing column and wall below the basement level but above the foundation of the cathedral. The building will be able to move up to two feet, three inches before banging into a wall.

There were, of course, some who complained on biblical grounds that Christ's Church was founded "on a rock." Scripture makes no mention of rubber. That argument was countered by those who pointed out that rock, long considered a symbol of permanence and dependability, simply does not convey that meaning in areas prone to earthquakes. Cardinal Mahony was enthusiastic, saying that "earthquakes are not an act of God; they are an act of nature. I think if we are going to make God's house beautiful, we might as well make it safe."[45]

---

[45]Antelope Valley *Press,* October 20, 1999.

The reinforced concrete sheer wall structure of the cathedral was designed to the seismic performance level of a fire or police station, which meant immediate occupancy and functionality of all building systems following a major seismic event. Structural engineer, Nabih Youssef said that "we are not protecting for life safety as per code. We are protecting a building and its contents. It's like a museum with a valued collection."[46]

Only the cathedral and the campanile have isolators. It was felt that the other buildings could be patched and repaired, with minimal discomfort and ease. The cardinal wanted the cathedral itself to function as a shelter and sanctuary should a devastating earthquake occur in the region.[47]

Ceiling

The Cathedral of Our Lady of the Angels "possesses one of the unique ceilings in the world, both because of its design and because of the wood material used." The remarkable wood ceiling project required the creative energies of all those involved in its execution.

Moneo conceived the using of massive wooden beams woven into a complex pattern to cover the 100-foot high ceiling in the massive edifice. "The design consisted of 42,000 stylized timbers, or logs, as they came to be called, each measuring twenty-four inches wide and sixteen inches deep spanning the ceiling to its central rib. Each log was separated by six-inch reveals. Rough sawn plywood fir, specially ordered from the only known manufacturer, was used in the returns and ceiling extents. A cedar satin stain finish kept the ceiling within the warm monochromatic color pallet echoed in other interior surfaces." [48] The architectural critic for the Los Angeles *Times,* Nicolai Ouroussoff, said "above, the patterned wood surface of the ceiling sags down like the belly of a whale, which helps give the room an unexpected warmth."[49]

In August of 2001, Charles Coury, project manager for Pacific Wood Systems, contacted the cardinal and offered to include Bible verses on the hidden portion of one of the logs "in order to honor the Lord and to acknowledge the privilege we have felt working on this project."[50]

---

[46]Quoted in "L.A.'s Third Millennium Noah's Ark," *Engineering News-Record* (September 10, 2001), 2.

[47]Los Angeles *Times,* December 28, 2000.

[48]*CISCA Interior Construction,* January/February 2003.

[49]Los Angeles *Times,* September 1, 2002.

[50]AALA, Charles Coury to Roger Cardinal Mahony, Los Angeles, July 18, 2001.

Workers finishing concrete seams.

Concrete walls begin crawling toward heaven.

The rest of the story is told by the cardinal himself in an issue of *Cathedral Chapters:*

> How extraordinary! In all my years of involvement in building projects, no contractor or vendor has ever asked for a Scripture quote to be placed in the new structure.
>
> Since several Scripture quotes came to mind, I sent them all:
>
> *As the sparrow finds a home and the swallow a nest to settle among her young, my home is by your altars, Lord of Hosts, my king and my God!—Psalm 84:4—5*
>
> *I rejoiced when they said to me, "Let us go to the house of the Lord!"—Psalm 122:1*
>
> *My dwelling shall be with them: I will be their God, and they shall be my people. This the nations shall know that it is I, the Lord, who make Israel holy, when my sanctuary shall be set up among them forever.—Ezekiel 37:27—28*
>
> *In my house, says the Lord, everyone who asks, receives; and the one who seeks, finds; and to the one who knocks, the door will be opened.—Matthew 7:8*
>
> *And now I have chosen and consecrated this house that my name may be there forever; my eyes and my heart also shall be there always.—2 Chronicles 7:16*
>
> When the ceiling panels above the altar arrived, a laminated typed copy of those Scriptures was permanently affixed to preserve these Scriptures for centuries. The workers for Pacific Wood Systems signed the laminated verses, and they were permanently installed.
>
> Someday in future years—maybe future centuries—other workers will come across those panels with their hidden Scripture verses, and they will marvel that God's inspirited Word was placed in the ceiling panels directly above the cathedral altar.
>
> This story is just one of the many instances where cathedral contractors, subcontractors, and construction workers have brought a wonderful spiritual sense to the building of our new Cathedral of Our Lady of the Angels.[51]

Subsequently, two other areas were offered. To that request the cardinal added:

> Ceiling above the Baptistry
> *It happened in those days that Jesus came from Nazareth of Galilee and was baptized in the Jordan by John. On coming*

---

[51]*Cathedral Chapters,* VI, #1, Winter/Spring 2002.

Details of the ceiling. *Source: Fred Balak*

out of the water he saw the heavens being torn open and the
Spirit, like a dove, descending upon him. And a voice came from
the heavens, "You are my beloved Son; with you I am well
pleased.—Mark1: 9-11.
   Ceiling above the Vesting Areas/Sacristy
   The sacred vestments of Aaron shall be passed down to his
descendents, that in them they may be anointed and ordained.
   With violet, purple and scarlet yarn were woven the service
cloths for use in the sanctuary, as well as the sacred vestments
for Aaron, as the Lord had commanded Moses.—Exodus 39:1[52]

Acoustics

From the very outset, Jose Rafael Moneo, the cathedral's architect,
alerted his staff to take every precaution against the ever-present possibility of acoustical "dead spots" in the massive structure. Of course, the

---

[52]AALA, Roger Cardinal Mahony to Charles Coury, Los Angeles, August 12,
2001.

Installation of the base isolators. *Source: The Tidings*

Construction of the campanile

View from the top

sheer size of the 65,000 square foot cathedral presented unique challenges to the acoustical engineers. What worked for regular sound often did not satisfy musical needs. Paul Salamunovich, for example, said that "much of the great music of the world was written to be performed in the church and therefore, the cathedral's sound design must be clean and without echoes to ensure a warm, comfortable ambiance."[53]

Originally the engineers wanted to suspend eight large and unsightly loudspeakers, five feet by eight feet in size. Obviously they would have impacted negatively on the interior visuals of the edifice.

Nicholas W. Roberts addressed the problem. He said that it appeared to him "that the sound at the current level of absorption retains the feel of a great cathedral, but significant echoes affect the intelligibility of the spoken word." Opining that the walls were "causing the problem,"[54] he felt that cleverly designed software might solve it. He proposed putting absorbent and/or diffusing material on the nave walls for the first 30 feet west of the crossing and at the east wall of the presbyterium.[55]

---

[53]*Cathedral Chapters,* III, #3, Fall 1999.
[54]AALA, Nicholas W. Roberts to Roger Cardinal Mahony, Los Angeles, October 30, 1998.
[55]AALA, Nicholas W. Roberts to Richard Vosko, Los Angeles, November 71, 1998.

The Grand Plaza

Cardinal Mahony, who wanted to be involved directly and fully with the sound and video systems,[56] suggested designing a light fixture that would incorporate loudspeakers. Thus one fixture should provide both sound and light,[57] a recommendation eventually followed.

The first musical event given at the cathedral was, appropriately a free Neighborhood Concert by the Los Angeles Philharmonic on Friday, September 27, 2002. A reviewer said that "the high ceilings and the volume of space in the large room provide an acoustic ambiance not unlike that of the Crystal Cathedral in Garden Grove." He went on to say that

---

[56]AALA, Roger Cardinal Mahony to Jose Rafael Moneo, Los Angeles, April 30, 1997.

[57]AALA. Roger Cardinal Mahony to Richard Vandersteen, Los Angeles, September 10, 1998.

Interior view of the cathedral nave

"the listener is awed by the perceived distance of the musical sounds coming from the front of the sanctuary. One senses no distortion, only the sort of low reverberation associated with an outdoor setting."[58]

On the other hand, in a review of the first official (ticket mailing) concert in the cathedral, one critic said that "as a place for music making, the new edifice is something of a disaster." He liked the program, at least as much of it that could be heard through the "susurrus of the ventilating equipment and the harsh, dry acoustics of the space that actually seemed to suck the resonance from both singers and organ."

> My guess is that it never occurred to the designers that there might be a time when a proper concert atmosphere—i.e., a background of silence—might be required in that vast space; under normal church circumstances all that mechanical noise could conceivably stand in for the whispers of God and His angels. It was, however, an audible and highly unwelcome presence at this event.[59]

---

[58]Daniel Carriaga in Los Angeles *Times,* September 30, 2002.
[59]Alan Rich in Los Angeles *Times,* November 22, 2002.

Each stone in the floor was carefully cut and laid.

Chandeliers

From the outset, the cardinal wanted "to make absolutely certain that our new Cathedral of Our Lady of the Angels be beautifully lighted whenever the various liturgies are celebrated."[60] There were several designs for the chandeliers. A first mock-up was shown to the members of the Cathedral Advisory Board at Saint Basil Church on April 10, 1999. Most of the members felt that it was too "salad-bowly" and wanted some

---

[60]AALA, Roger Cardinal Mahony to Jose Rafael Moneo, Los Angeles, April 30, 1997

modifications made. Another complaint was that the "lamps above the reflector, which were intended to light the walls, appeared to be too bright. However, it was pointed out that the brightness observed would be accurate for the fixtures at the front of the nave, where lamps would be added to provide the fill light necessary for television broadcast requirements.[61]

Mahony wanted an adjustment made on the speaker enclosures which, in his opinion, "simply do not work." He said they were too large and would hang some six feet below the chandeliers. He suggested that the size of the speaker baffles be reduced and the overall fixtures raised to appear more part of the chandeliers.[62]

By mid June of 2000, the chandeliers had been redesigned. The cardinal found the housing for the speaker system "quite promising," feeling that the "integration of the piece is far better than the previous design efforts." He did stress that the "actual loudspeaker and its baffle should be independent acoustically from the entire trumpet."[63]

Moneo thought the chandeliers would "be a welcome element in the space of the nave. A discreet and homogeneous source of sound and light is important and I hope that they [the chandeliers] will be understood as pipes like those of the organ."[64]

Alabaster Windows

Among its many distinctions, the Cathedral of Our Lady of the Angels has the largest installation of alabaster windows in the world. The use of that substance makes the cathedral not only unique, but the milky light also makes it very spiritual.

Contrary to many of the articles about alabaster, its use for windows rather than stained glass is hardly novel. Churches used it 300 to 400 years ago, according to John Williams, the Project Architect for the cathedral. In Spain, alabaster is used frequently as a window material.

Alabaster is not a man-made product, but a naturally occurring stone which boasts an unusual translucency because it contains moisture and oil in addition to various mineral deposits. The veining pattern found

---

[61]AALA, "Meeting Notes," Los Angeles April 16, 1999.

[62]AALA, Roger Cardinal Mahony to All, Los Angeles, April 21, 2000.

[63]AALA, Roger Cardinal Mahony to Jose Rafael Moneo, Los Angeles, June 11, 2000.

[64]AALA, Jose Rafael Moneo to Roger Cardinal Mahony, Madrid, June 4, 2000.

Chandelier and their audio tubes. *Source: Tom Bonner*

Arastone Alabaster Quarry, Quintero de Ebro, Spain

within alabaster was formed centuries ago when it was in the form of liquid rock.

The color of the veining will vary depending on what else was mixed into the various pools of rock, which could have included anything from dinosaurs and insects to dirt. The alabaster selected for the new cathedral has veins of red, gray, yellow and possibly green, and will be imported from Spain.

Alabaster is not mined; rather it is dug up from the ground in big boulders with dark, dull surfaces. Similar to a geode, the beauty within an alabaster boulder is seen only after giant machining saws slice it into panels.[65]

The patterning of the cathedral windows is strictly one-of-a kind. Panels are cut to a thickness of one and one half centimeters and vary in size from two and one half to six feet wide. By carefully positioning the 11,800 panels, a giant mosaic pattern emerges.

There are approximately 27,000 square feet of alabaster. Designed by Jose Rafael Moneo, the thousands of pieces represent nearly twenty different sizes, set in horizontal courses and ranging from three to twenty-four inches wide and thirteen to thirty-four inches tall. Mined near

---

[65]*Cathedral Chapters,* III, #2, Fall 1999.

Alabaster fabrication factory in Spain

the Spanish city of Zaragoza in northeastern Spain, the alabaster's color scheme ranges from deep green and warm red to dark gray and brown.

As natural light filters through the alabaster, it enters the cathedral by way of large, thick, slanted light shafts that resemble those that occurred in the California missions in provincial times. The windows are protected by a glass curtain wall system that protects the stone from extreme temperatures and climatic conditions. Specially designed back lighting enhances the windows at certain times of the day.[66]

Chemically, alabaster is hydrated calcium sulfate, typically found in boulders made of sedimentary rock formed as salty water evaporates. Etruscan mourners put the ashes of their dead into alabaster jars. An example of alabaster in the Vatican would be the dove, high up and behind the Altar of the Chair in St. Peter's Basilica. The explanation as to why this substance has been so rarely used is that it is difficult to quarry. Soft and delicate, it easily crumbles under high tension.[67]

Initially there had been some question about the ability of alabaster to withstand the repeated high heat generated by the direct sunlight of Southern California. Working with consulting engineers, officials at Morley Construction developed a double-walled system. As described by Terry Dooley: "Fritted glass takes the direct sunlight on the exterior. Inside is

[66]*The Tidings,* June 22, 2001.
[67]Los Angeles *Times,* July 6, 2002.

Workers install alabaster panes in one of the cathedral windows.

a buffer space of from one to eight feet of circulating air, protecting the alabaster membrane. This membrane is directly visible from the inside of the church, and will be illuminated at night by lights within the air space. The lights cause the building to "glow" at night, seen from the outside. Morley worked with subcontractors to refine details and hone expected costs. Benson Industries was chosen as the subcontractor for the window system."

Illumination will be particularly dramatic in the "lantern" area around the cross. This "lantern" climbs the east wall, then wraps as the skylight for 70 feet, extending westward over the roof. It will be visible from the air and from taller structures in the downtown area.

Air circulating with the window system is part of the ventilation flow for the entire building, not a separate system. The cathedral church benefits from the bulk of its concrete walls, the shielding provided by its deep ceiling plenum, and the benevolent weather in Southern California. Temperatures will change very gradually within the building. Air will be circulated regularly, but the consultants have predicted that supplementary heating or cooling will be needed on only 15% of the days of the year.[68]

Workers' Cathedral

It was not just Cardinal Mahony and his fellow priests who rejoiced as the new Cathedral of Our Lady of the Angels edged skyward to an eventual height of eleven stories. The workers who brought the plans to fulfillment experienced the hush within, the wonderment of making common ground holy.

"You go home every day and you think, my God, this is huge! It's gonna be different than anything I've ever seen in my life," said Mark Pineda, a crane rigger. "Everyman out there puts his heart and soul into it . . . When we're all gone and our kids are gone, this thing is still going to be going strong.

Cardinal Mahony recounted the story of an electrician who spoke briefly to him during one of the cardinal's frequent visits to the site.

> The man said, "I finished another job and went to the union hiring hall. I didn't know what work was available. All of a sudden, I find myself working on the cathedral! Of all the projects I've done in twenty-five years, I've never been able to do something as magnificent as this for God. My family, they all want to know what happened when I get home. Before they could care less. Now their lives are touched by this because I'm building a cathedral."[69]

Many people had a part in the cathedral project. But none had as much of a hands-on role as those men and women engaged in the con-

---

[68]AALA, C. Terry Dooley to Kevin Starr, Los Angeles, September 28, 2001.
[69]*The Tidings,* August 17, 2000.

The construction crews became an extended family at the cathedral. *Source: The Tidings*

struction activity—anywhere from160 to 300 at one time, wielding any and all assortment of machines and tools from giant cranes to hammers and screwdrivers. In the future, when memories dim, one will see the results of those people "whose hands laid the stones, poured the concrete, placed the alabaster in the windows, laid the wires."[70] They came from all backgrounds, all cultures, all religions, and collectively from all manner of construction skills—electrical, plumbing, carpentry, concrete and more.

During the many months of actual construction, the archdiocesan Catholic newspaper ran many articles about those involved in the overall project. Among the interviews was one conducted by Mike Nelson, editor of *The Tidings:*

> "All the angles of the walls, the ceilings—they're all different," points out Eddie Perez, project superintendent, as he walks past the south wall where a series of devotional chapels—no two of them alike—are beginning to take shape. "You don't see the conventional 90-degree and 45-degree angles here. That means the tools we use have to be calibrated differently, we take extra care to get the joints to align properly

[70]Los Angeles *Times,* September 2, 2002.

Solar Power to Generate Electricity

As "a sign of religious commitment to the environment," the Cathedral of Our Lady of the Angels was engineered to generate up to 15% of its own electricity with a giant solar panel.

According to a report in the Los Angeles *Times,* "the array of solar photovoltaic cells, which convert sunlight into electricity"[1] is among the largest yet installed as part of the Los Angeles Department of Water and Power's Green L.A. program. The cathedral system is among the first such units installed through the auspices of the Los Angeles Interfaith Environmental Council's Green Sanctuaries program.

The solar panels, which cover 7,000 square feet on the roof of the Conference Center, were engineered to generate sixty-six kilowatts of electricity, an amount equivalent to the power used by sixty-six family units in a single day.

In a press release for the occasion, Roger Cardinal Mahony said that "in our tradition we believe that human beings are stewards of all God's creation. How we care for God's creation and environment are very important to us."[2]

A spokesman for the DWP said that solar electricity costs between eighteen and twenty- two cents a kilowatt-hour, compared to ten cents for conventional electricity.

---

[1]Los Angeles *Times,* August 16, 2002
[2]Press Release, August 15, 2002.

and securely, and that takes extra time. I'll tell you, we're learning so much on this job that afterwards we will be able to do just about anything."

Of course, many came to the project already blessed with a variety of talents. Juan Hernandez, the forty-nine-year-old carpentry foreman who wears a modified Stetson atop his mandatory hard hat, is a "finish" carpenter by trade who designed and built the hand carved doors at his parish, Saint Peter Church in San Pedro.

"This isn't just about building wall," he says firmly, pointing to the shingles he has made that will be sandblasted and placed on the outside cathedral walls. "They need to be strong enough to withstand the pressure of the concrete that is applied on them, and fit together in a way that will enhance the beauty of this building."

Hernandez—whose grandfather and great-grandfather were also finish carpenters—has been working on the cathedral project since October 1998, and admits this project stands out among all he has worked on.

"This is something that reaches deep into my heart," he says with sincerity. "My wife and my priest have both said to me, 'When you work here, you are not doing it for the money; you are doing it for God.' You are building something that people from many generations after you are going to see and use. I'm very proud to be involved in this."

Mike Allende said he has been a carpenter almost his entire life. "I'm third generation—had a hammer in my hand ever since I could hold one," smiles the thirty-four-year-old Altadena resident, who worked on the parking structure for a year. For the last six months, as "south wall" foreman, Allende has directed construction work taking place along Temple Street, where the cathedral's main entrance will be located, along with the ambulatory walk past devotional chapels.

"There is no comparison between this and anything I've ever done," he adds softly, gazing proudly at the walls rising up. "This is a once in a lifetime project." The challenges, Allende says, are many, but are balanced by the satisfaction of seeing the finished work, increment by increment. "As the walls go up, the floor is poured you see the project become a little closer to reality, and you take a lot of pride in that," he says. "When it is finished, it doesn't look as hard as it did when we were building it."

Indeed, the finished work—of each individual component, as well as the entire structure—projects a simplicity that belies the challenges, and often difficult work that went into it.

Monsignor Kevin Kostelnik leads a prayer at the cathedral site for the victims of the September 11th tragedies.

On this project where high standards are demanded, officials say their mission is further compounded by the new cathedral's new angle on construction—literally.

"I've never been on a project life this," adds Joel Hester, the assistant foreman who assists in all aspects of the cathedral construction. "Every day is a new challenge, but it really is exciting to watch it take shape."

"Right now, these are the people making it happen," says Audre Kleven, project manager from Morley Construction, general contractor for the cathedral. "This is truly the work of human hands—it's people, it's brains, it's the essence of human creativity. And the fact that this is such a historical project makes it even more special."[71]

As the premier immigrant city in the United States, Los Angeles belongs to the people who arrive looking for new beginnings and challenges. For Nick Roberts, project manager for Leo A. Daly, the cathedral

[71]*The Tidings,* April 7, 2000.

was reminiscent of his native England. "I grew up with wonderful sacred spaces in Europe; I was confirmed in King's College, Cambridge, and sang in the choir there." The cathedral project gave him a chance to re-create some of the splendor and majesty of the older churches in his home country. He noted that the sacredness here was "as big as the cathedral in Barcelona and half the size of St. Peter's in Rome."

Ukraine-born Mike Minukin managed many aspects of the construction project for Morley, including the manpower. He had to make sure that everything got done to specification, budget and safety regulations. He said that "this project has given me the chance to grow, to do the best job I can."

Lou Phan, the concrete estimator for Morley Construction, saw the cathedral as adding to the skyline of Los Angeles. "My role is to survey and estimate the use of concrete for the cathedral, noting that "the building will be approximately 90% concrete." And there was Jason Chan, the electrical engineer, who was "the one who brings the entire building to life." From light fixtures to coffee machines to air conditioners, his task was to carefully design electrical wires and power supplies so as not to take away from the beauty of the cathedral space.[72]

Throughout the project, Cardinal Mahony endeavored to forge a special bond with the workers. He sent Christmas cards to each of them and wrote numerous letters such as the one to John Rhoten whose mother had died; to Roberto Lopez who underwent surgery for severe back pain; to Bruno Ramirez who sustained a broken leg while helping to load materials; to Tony Pacheco who lost his wife and daughter in an accident and to Oscar Juarez who accidentally fell through an opening in the top deck of the parking structure. When he was informed that Dwayne Brothers, a tower crane operator, had died, the cardinal gathered coworkers for a prayer service.

In order to avoid any potential problems in case of a potential strike, the cardinal asked Morley Construction to guarantee that workers would be paid whatever the prevailing rates were. On a number of occasions, the cardinal set aside time to have his picture taken with any and all workers. He then had the photographs developed and distributed.

Probably no one caught the tenor of the moment better that Father Robert B. Lawton, S.J., president of Loyola Marymount University, who offered this observation at the Conrad Hilton Center for Business on September 26, 2000:

> Few people in the world's history get to see a cathedral rising before their eyes. And none of our ancestors has seen one

---

[72]*The Tidings,* September 26, 1999.

so majestic going up so quickly. Of course, cathedrals don't just "rise" or "go up." They are imagined, crafted and constructed, works of skill and calloused hands. Many such hands. Three hundred people a day work on the new Cathedral of Our Lady of the Angels. Anyone talking with them feels their pride. This job is not simply a job, like building a corporate headquarters, department store or tract of homes. No, not just a job; more like a mission, a supremely significant task giving meaning to talents and labors of every type."[73]

[73]"L.A. Cathedral," *Design/Build Business,* June 2000.

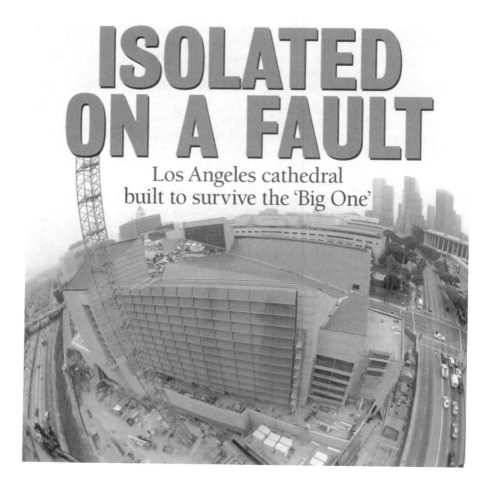

ISOLATED ON A FAULT
Los Angeles cathedral built to survive the 'Big One'

One of the four dedication serigraphs by John August Swanson, this artistic work is based on an acrylic painting, February, 1997

Chapter VII

Ancillary Spaces

The 5.53-acre site of Our Lady of the Angels Cathedral is considerably more extensive than the worship area itself. The outdoor plazas, parking area, conference facilities and the clerical residence are just a few of the many ancillary spaces that are attached and akin to the cathedral.

Crypt Chapel

Walking through the Crypt Chapel at the Cathedral of Our Lady of the Angels is similar to strolling down memory lane. The white Carrara marble altar and former sanctuary lamp, along with the hand-carved wooden lectern and ceremonial chair, are taken from Saint Vibiana Cathedral where they were installed by Bishop John J. Cantwell in 1922. The ceramic Stations of the Cross, removed from Saint Basil Church in the mid-Wilshire District, were fashioned by Professor Eugenio Pattarino in the 1960s for James Francis Cardinal McIntyre.

Shrine of Saint Vibiana

When Bishop Thaddeus Amat brought the wax effigy containing the relics of Saint Vibiana to California in 1854, the huge glass and metallic reliquary was enshrined in Our Lady of Sorrows Church in Santa Barbara. Shortly after that church was destroyed by fire nine years later, the unscorched reliquary was transferred to Los Angeles where it remained at the Plaza Church of *Nuestra Señora de Los Angeles* until 1876 and the completion of Saint Vibiana Cathedral.

Placed in a recessed niche, high above the main altar, the relics were publicly exhibited until 1975 when Timothy Cardinal Manning had them removed from their reliquary and placed in a specially made wooden casket. A marble sarcophagus, fashioned by Louis Carnevale, was then installed along the south wall of the sanctuary and there the relics reposed until 1996 when they were removed and stored in the episcopal vault at Calvary Mausoleum. In 2002 the relics, in the same marble sarcophagus, were placed in the new Cathedral of Our Lady of the Angels

Cathedral towers over the city. *Source: Tom Bonner*

Mausoleum

Remarkably, the mausoleum at the Cathedral of Our Lady of the Angels is one of the few places in the United States where lay people have the opportunity to be buried within a cathedral church. With more than 1,200 crypts and 5,000 cremation niches, the area will likely serve as the final resting place for many of the southland's Catholic laity. Surely it will be among the most visited spaces in the cathedral. A writer in one local newspaper predicted that the mausoleum "promises to be the most prestigious Catholic burial place in the city, if not the country."[1]

As early as September 1996 the cardinal began thinking in terms of a crypt mausoleum beneath the cathedral itself.[2] But as costs began escalating, he subsequently directed that crypt be eliminated, noting that it represents "a very costly part of the cathedral's construction costs."[3] Later he thought it might be wise "to simply rough in" the area allowing the mausoleum to be done in later years."[4]

Meanwhile a request was sent to the Los Angeles Department of Building and Safety about the "permissibility of burial of persons deemed appropriate at the site of the new cathedral to be built by the Archdiocese of Los Angeles." Accompanying the request were several written documents which attested to it being the practice of the Roman Catholic Church allowing this practice:

> Affidavit of Msgr. Francis J. Weber, Ecclesial Historian of the Archdiocese, attesting to the practice of providing burial vaults in major churches and cathedrals.
>
> Article noting the burial of Bishop Thomas Shahan in the Basilica of the National Shrine of the Immaculate Conception in Washington, D.C.
>
> Excerpt from "Saint Vibiana Cathedral" by Msgr. Francis J. Weber noting that the body of Bishop Thaddeus Amat was interred in Saint Vibiana Cathedral until the transference of his remains to Calvary Mausoleum in 1962.
>
> Two articles regarding the Duke University Chapel, noting that it is the reliquary of people important to the University.
>
> Article describing the use of crypts throughout the history of Christendom.
>
> Picture of the crypt of the Cathedral of Our Lady Assumed into Heaven and St. Nicholas in Galway, Ireland showing the caskets of the four bishops interred there.

---

[1]Los Angeles *Times,* February 8, 2002.

[2]AALA, Roger Cardinal Mahony to Jose Rafael Moneo, Los Angeles, September 4, 1996.

[3]AALA, Roger Cardinal Mahony to Jose Rafael Moneo, Los Angeles, June 9, 1997.

[4]AALA, Roger Cardinal Mahony to Jose Rafael Moneo, Los Angeles, June 13, 1997.

Crypt Chapel with the marble altar from Saint Vibiana Cathedral.
Source: Fred Balak

Photos of the crypt in St. Patrick's Cathedral, New York City, noting that the plaques on the doors and adjacent to the doors identify the persons interred therein.[5]

On November 26, 1997, Robert Janovici, the city's Chief Zoning Administrator, replied that based on his research, "it is determined that persons designated by the archdiocese may be buried at Our Lady of the Angels Cathedral by right without need for further zoning entitlements."[6]

A month later, on Christmas day, the cardinal alerted Moneo to those developments:

I wanted to advise you of a very important addition to the cathedral, but an addition that does not affect in any way the design—exterior or interior.

---

[5]AALA, Hilarion O'Connor, O.S.F. to Con Howe, Los Angeles, September 15, 1997.
[6]AALA, Robert Janovici to Hilarion O'Connor, O.S.F., Los Angeles, November 26, 1997.

The Fourteenth Station of the Cross as portrayed by Professor E. Pattarino in the crypt church.

You may recall that from time to time we have talked about the possibility of crypt burials beneath the cathedral. However, until we could get clarification from the City of Los Angeles about this, we have not been able to proceed. We were just notified in writing by the city that there is no problem with our having burial spaces beneath the cathedral, that this is something very much in the cathedral tradition. Moreover, we do not need any conditional use permits.

Given this new information and permission, we are now moving quite actively to plan on a major Cathedral Mausoleum beneath the cathedral–most likely up to 1,000 burial spaces.

Shrine of Saint Vibiana. *Source: Julius Schulman & David Glomb*

Noting that the proposed mausoleum would "not impinge on any other aspect of the cathedral design or function," the cardinal said that "since cemetery and mausoleum construction and management are such specialties, please be advised that we will handle the design, layout and construction of the mausoleum ourselves." He pointed out that "we are constantly building mausoleums in our twelve Catholic cemeteries, and we work exclusively with special architects and construction experts on this specialty."[7]

---

[7]AALA, Roger Cardinal Mahony to Jose Rafael Moneo, Los Angeles, December 25, 1997.

Nativity Window.

The design of the mausoleum was entrusted to J. Stuart Todd, with the directive that "the use of art and iconography is very important. We will want to make sure that all blends well in keeping with our Church tradition of honoring the dead in light of the Resurrection of Christ."[8]

From the outset, the mausoleum was envisioned as a means of providing an endowment fund for maintaining the cathedral. The funds for the construction were borrowed from the archdiocesan cemeteries with the assistance of the Allied Irish Bank.

The mausoleum was envisioned as allowing a quiet atmosphere and a devotional setting combining the long tradition of the Church.

---

[8]AALA, Roger Cardinal Mahony, Memorandum, July 4, 2000.

The mausoleum at the cathedral will accommodate 1,200 crypts and 5,000 cremation niches.

The mausoleum has been crafted of Spanish limestone. Lit by the soft glow of alabaster sconces, it becomes a warm, welcoming place of prayer. Fourteen of the historic stained glass windows, and nine lunettes, from the old Saint Vibiana Cathedral, have been newly restored, and installed within the mausoleum. All are enhanced with dramatic backlighting.[9]

In an issue of *Cathedral Chapters,* the mausoleum was described in these words:

Visitors to the new Cathedral of Our Lady of the Angels will no doubt come to the site prepared to view its stunning modern architecture and extraordinary collections of newly commissioned religious art. What many may not expect to see, however, is a special space that pays homage to one of the oldest practices of the Catholic Church: a cathedral mausoleum.[10]

---

[9]AALA, Promotional Literature "Crypt Mausoleum", 2002.
[10]*Cathedral Chapters,* VI, #2, Summer 2002.

Dome in the central part of the mausoleum. *Source: Fred Balak*

News of the mausoleum in the cathedral made its way to New York, where that city's leading newspaper told its readers that the "prestigious final resting place" would "generate an endowment to pay for the cathedral upkeep and operating expenses." It went on to erroneously say that interment there would be "strictly by invitation and based on one's goodness and contribution to the community."[11]

In addition to the main section of the mausoleum, there are half-dozen semi-private chapels among the stained glass windows and lunettes brought from Saint Vibiana Cathedral, along with the four crypts incorporated into the sarcophagus directly under the cathedral's main altar. Close by are the already entombed remains of James Francis Cardinal McIntyre, Archbishop John J. Cantwell, Bishops Thaddeus Amat, C.M., Francis Mora, Thomas Conaty and Carl Fisher, which were brought there in June 2002.

The article in the Los Angeles *Times* about the mausoleum concluded with this:

A hundred years hence, European tourists may be paying a few extra dollars to see Southern California's saints and

---

[11]New York *Times,* February 10, 2002.

Crypt Plaques

The two plaques on the wall in the Crypt were sent to the Cathedral Of Our Lady of the Angels by the Reverend Robert Dodero, O.S.A. and are copies from Roger Cardinal Mahony's titular church in the Eternal City, the Church of the Four Crowned Martyrs of Rome.

Here is a translation of the plaques provided by Andrew Walther:

First Inscription:

The inscription states that the Chapel was built in honor of St. Stephen, and to the glory and honor of God and Blessed Pope Sylvester, by Reynaldus, bishop of Ostia. The inscription is dated: the Year of Our Lord 1246 fourth week and sixth day before Palm Sunday, in the fourth year of the pontificate of Pope Innocent IV

There then follows a list of the relics enshrined in the Church:

Relic of the wood of the Cross, St. Boniface pope and martyr, St. Januarius, who was subdeacon to Pope Sixtus, Pope and Martyr; St. Tiburtius, Martyr; St. Hippolitus, Martyr; St. Theodorus, Martyr; Saints Mary and Martha, Martyrs; the three boy saints, martyrs, the saints Nrgeius and Archilcus, Martyrs.

Second Inscription:

This inscription lists the relics found in the altar of the Church of the Seven Crowned Martyrs in Rome. The inscription concludes with the indulgence granted to pilgrims who fulfill certain requirements at that Church.

This is the list of relics in the altar: Saints Papius and Maurim, St. Silvester, Pope St. Linus,

St. Lucy Virgin and Martyr, St. Praxedis, Virgin, St. Pudetiane, Virgin, St. Dorothy, Virgin and Martyr, St. Exupantius, VC.

For all of Christian Faithful coming to this chapel on the stated six days, or on seven consecutive days, one year and 40 days from their enjoined penance will be removed.

scholars, its rulers and its elite. The region may not have any kings, but undoubtedly there'll be a celebrity or two. This is L.A. after all.[12]

Stained Glass Windows

The stained glass windows in the crypt impress visitors in a distinct way. Their history and how they came to be there are almost as fascinating as their art is captivating.

In May of 1996, Walter Judson of The Judson Studios was asked to remove the famed Meyer-Munich stained glass windows from the old cathedral. He told how he flattened "a number of those windows, put new bars on, repaired cracks, leaving all the original glass in place." A few of the windows on the south elevation had to be re-leaded; the rest still had the original 1923–1924 lead. When plans were formulated for the mausoleum, "they asked us to reinstall all of the windows."

According to Judson, the windows look far better in their new surroundings than they did at Saint Vibiana. Now they can be seen up close and also studied from a distance. Their painting technique is "wonderful . . . just beautifully made windows."

When asked about some of the challenges in the overall process, the famed artist said:

> Well, as far as the viewing of the windows, at Saint Vibiana the windows weren't really clerestory windows and they weren't really aisle windows. They were sort of halfway in between and they were inset into the wall and when you walked into the church, you really didn't notice the windows. You had to stand and look straight at the window so you didn't really get the feeling that the windows were part of the overall design of the church.
>
> One of the major problems we had was making sure when we took the windows out of the old steel sash, we didn't break anything because they were put in with old fashioned putty and this putty was as hard as concrete. So you had to dig the putty between the steel and the lead of the windows and ease the windows out.
>
> A lot of the windows were actually over-sized, so they fit very, very tightly and when they put the windows into the sash they actually crumpled some of the lead back and just shoved

---

[12]Los Angeles *Times,* February 8, 2002.

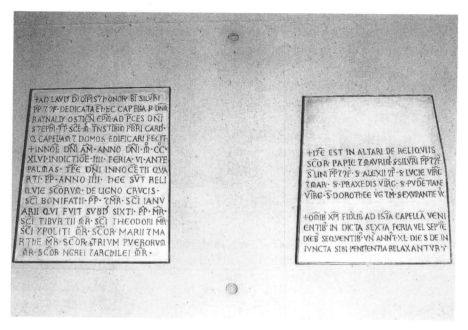

Plaques from the Roman Church of the Four Crowned Martyrs, Cardinal Mahony's titular church. *Source: Fred Balak*

them into place. Now that doesn't show when you put putty over the top of the crumpled lead, but when you start taking it out it does manifest itself. So it was very interesting. That was one of the main things we did when we took them out was to put new lead around the outside of all the sections.

There were a number of broken pieces and in almost every case we were able to use a new reversible adhesive to glue the pieces of glass together and if you can even find any of those cracks that are glued, they just look like a hairline so they are very small. And it's difficult to do that and keep the piece in the proper place and if you do have to take a piece out to glue it, you have to pull the lead back and then put it in, push the lead back again, and to do that and make it look like nothing was ever touched is another challenge.

Asked to give a little bit of background for the Franz Meyer Company, Judson replied:

The Meyer Company is in Munich and has been since the middle of the 19th century. Their style is . . . you've heard of

Workers entomb the remains of the Right Thomas J. Conaty in the cathedral mausoleum. *Source: Fred Balak*

Gothic revival . . . this is sort of Baroque revival because the borders, if you look at them, are very heavily painted—very, very detailed and they look like Baroque illustrations just colored up nicely. The subject matter usually tends to be very heady, almost sentimental in places and when you see windows by other firms where the artwork is not quite so well done, they do look overly sentimental. This was during the Victorian period. But the wonderful thing is . . . that Meyer did these windows in 1922-1923 which is long after Victoria was dead, but Meyer was still doing this work and did it right through the Depression up to the Second World War.

About the style itself . . . the unique thing about stained glass that sets it aside from any other art is that the light is coming through the medium and so you blend colors differently. If you want to do detail, you don't do it the way you would do it with a series of colors in a painting, but you actually use a black line to stop the light. So that a mouth may just be a simple black line in a figure. The drapery is a series of black lines and then to give it a three-dimensional effect, you fire the paint, which is enamel paint, into the glass. Then you put a soft coat of paint, a half tone, over the top of that and rub highlights in it.

Now a lot of the windows also have what we call diaper patterns which makes the robes look like silk damask and what they did there was . . . a lot of the time . . . put a stencil over the top of the glass that has been painted and rub the paint off through the holes of the stencil. So you have this incredible diaper. You'll notice in the Meyer windows, too, that they've used a lot of silver nitrate. Silver nitrate, when it is fired into glass, turns the glass gold. So especially in the borders, you'll notice the gold goes from almost orange to a pale yellow and that just depends how thick they put the silver stain on.

Silver stain fires at a lower temperature so it would be done separately from the other painting and the further you get

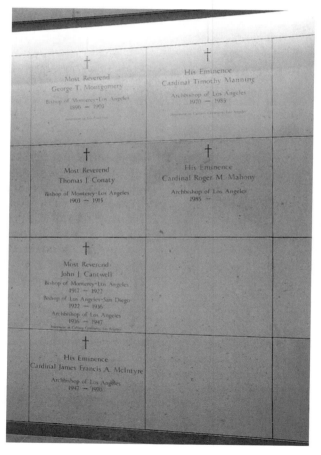

Plaques for the crypts of the southland's bishops.

away from the flesh . . . the heads, the hands, and the feet . . . the more likely you are to have an apprentice doing the work.

So as you look at these windows, the figures themselves would be done . . . Meyer's Studio probably had twenty-five painters, maybe fifty . . . and one of them would paint the Jesus heads and another would do the hands. They all were well in sync with each other so they knew just how to rub the painting and how to make it just right.

A rising apprentice, someone who was almost a master, would do the tracing, putting on the black lines. Then the master would come along and do the half-toning or what we call the matting or painting. Then a specialist would do the garments to give the three-dimensional effect to the drapery. Then you might have another man who might do the background, or the trees, or the sunset. And you know what work the apprentices did was in the borders because it is all fairly straight lines and if you look at the borders carefully in these windows, you can pick out an occasional fingerprint which they would purposely put in there just to make their mark and a few lines that aren't exactly straight.

Judson concluded his interview with the observation that "the Meyer windows are museum quality. I mean it's the kind of thing you see in a museum to point out the most beautiful glass of the 19th century in Germany." He had no hesitation in saying that the large windows and the lunettes, now backlighted and reframed, are as devotional as they are artistic.[13]

The crypt also accommodates a sacerdotal vestry, choir rehearsal room, a Bride's Room, and several restrooms. Along the hallway are the marble plaques of Christ and the four evangelists that formerly adorned the pulpit at Saint Vibiana Cathedral. Opposite the chapel are two marble plaque reproductions sent to the cathedral by the pastor of Roger Cardinal Mahony's titular church in Rome.

Residence Building

Though he insisted that every aspect of the new cathedral be pristine quality, the cardinal was considerably less enthusiastic about the components of his own residence. Several times, he gently urged the

---

[13]AALA, Interview with Walter Judson, April 9, 2002.

architect to tone down the aesthetic features of the residence. He adamantly objected to and then eventually forbade the use of concrete noting that "ninety percent of people in Southern California live in wood houses with stucco walls, and so shall I." While mandating that the cathedral be built well for the ages, he said, "Forget my house. Frame it with stucco."[14]

The cardinal said that adding concrete for the residence and the conference center would cost $700,000. And he reminded Moneo that "the entire parking garage would have to be re-engineered to handle this additional weight." He told Moneo: "Please understand that the final decision has been made, and we will be constructing all of the conference center and the residence using stucco."[15]

When the dust settled, the decision was implemented so that "the residence would have an exterior wall constructed of polymer reinforced cement plaster attached to steel studs, giving the appearance of high quality stucco."

> The construction of the residence will convey a feeling of solidity and permanence. The exterior will require crack repair and repainting every ten or fifteen years. With this maintenance, the life of the building should normally be expected to exceed one hundred years.[16]

The cardinal was sensitive that many priests had voiced deep concerns for such a high price for the residence. And he would hear of no further increases and costs for that purpose. Rather he and the others who would live in the residence were convinced that the steel structure and exterior plaster will stand the test of time."[17]

The building was finished and ready for occupancy during the last week of March 12, 2001. Several days later, he wrote to the project manager:

> It is hard to believe that after all these years of dreaming and planning we have finally completed the cathedral residence and moved in. The layout is working out just as we had envisioned, and once we are all settled and unpacked, I am confident that we will be very pleased for many decades to come.[18]

---

[14]AALA, Undated Memorandum, Los Angeles.

[15]AALA, Roger Cardinal Mahony to Jose Rafael Moneo, Los Angeles, May 31, 1998.

[16]AALA, E. J. Jarboe to Russell Pittelkau, Los Angeles, September 15, 1998.

[17]AALA, Roger Cardinal Mahony to Daniel Donohue, Los Angeles, September 22, 1998.

[18]AALA, Roger Cardinal Mahony to Audre Kleven, Los Angeles, March 20, 2001.

Window detail.

Conference Center

Designed as a multi-use facility, the Conference Center was planned for both service and hospitality and it will serve the entire Archdiocese and City of Los Angeles. "The original purpose of a cathedral centuries ago was to draw the whole community together and, as such, it became a center of life for that community."[19]

Among the components of the Conference Center are offices for the cathedral parish where various ministries are coordinated by the pastor and his clerical and lay associates. Among its uses are youth education programs, parochial outreach, charitable activities, fund raising for the endowment, liturgical and chant ministries, mausoleum services as well as the myriad of other needs of a busy downtown parish.

Also there are a series of conference rooms, the largest of which will accommodate up to 1,200 people. Eight smaller rooms are available, each with such amenities as Pullman kitchenettes, adjustable walls and air conditioning.

---

[19]*Cathedral Chapters,* II, #3, Winter 1999.

The window of St. Mark, the Evangelist, in the
cathedral mausoleum.

A café provides room for up to seventy persons, with ancillary seating
outside in the plaza area. The kitchen provides modestly sized meals and service areas are stocked with cold sandwiches, drinks and pastries. This café is
so arranged as to attract employees from neighboring city and private offices.

The Gift Shop provides a wide range of religious articles, statuary,
books and pamphlets. The goal "is to have Our Lady of the Angels Cathedral Store be distinguished in every respect; in its design, merchandise,
value, service and overall satisfaction".[20]

---

[20]AALA, Peter Kaufman, Draft, July 13, 2001.

View of the residence and conference center taken on December 19, 2001.

Monsignor John Barry, who chaired the committee that helped design the Conference Center, is on record as saying that "the center has a three pronged mission, the first of which is its responsibility to serve the needs of the parish community." He goes on to say that:

> Secondly, the center must also embrace the needs of the civic community. The cathedral and conference center must in some way be there to support the community. And finally, essential to any parish life is an outreach to the poor, and there must be an area within the facility to coordinate the response to the needs of the poor. The archdiocese has been very conscientious about this aspect of the Cathedral Center since its inception. We envision some kind of continuation of service that currently exists within the cathedral community, such as the Adopt-a-Family program, but we cannot place a limit on the type of service offered; as with the cathedral itself, its mission to serve the poor will evolve.[21]

---

[21]*Cathedral Chapters,* II, #3, Winter 1999.

Aerial view of the cathedral Conference Center.

Garage

Since 1951, the site destined for the Cathedral of Our Lady of the Angels had served as a parking lot. Hundreds of people working in downtown or attending performances at the Music Center utilized the area as a safe and convenient place to leave their cars.

Because Los Angeles is a highly mobile community, one of the first considerations in planning for the cathedral was that of providing adequate parking. The three story underground garage was the first part of the complex built, having been started on January 14, 1998 and finished on December 18th of the following year. Initially a large portion of the space was used as construction headquarters for the Morley and Daly firms.

Admittedly not the most attractive part of the overall complex, the garage early became and continues to be a pivotal and surely significant part of the Cathedral Complex. Built to accommodate 620 cars, the garage, operated by the Parking Company of America, provides easy access and egress from either Temple or Hill streets. Competitive rates make the facility attractive and monthly passes and parking validation are available to those attending religious services.

Interior view of the Gift Shop. *Source: Fred Balak*

The interior walls of the garage are color-coded and "painted as brightly as possible so that it doesn't resemble a dungeon," according to Brother Hilarion O'Connor, Director of Construction for the Cathedral Project.[22] A full-scale monitoring system allows security personnel to view each level of the garage on remote cameras. A double-sized escalator and several elevators allow visitors ready access to the upper levels which lead to the plaza or to the Conference Center.

The garage structure contains a number of facilities other than that of parking. For example, it contains space for heating, ventilating, air conditioning and electrical equipment, which supply the other buildings within the complex.

A cast-in-place concrete structure, the garage serves also as the supporting superstructure for much of the plaza, the rectory, the Out-Reach office and the Conference Center. It also provides the infrastructure for the cathedral itself. There are storage areas, a service dock and two service elevators. A utility tunnel leads directly into the crypt area of the cathedral.

_____

[22]*Cathedral Chapters,* II, #2, Summer 1998.

Interior of the Café. *Source: Fred Balak*

Entrance to the Parking Garage from Hill Street.

Gathering Space

Historically, the notion of gathering was connected to the market-place and served as a transitional space for the assembly as it moved toward the place of worship: "The ultimate function of the gathering space is to facilitate the assembly's entrance and participation in the worship space." In today's emphasis on liturgy, the "gathering space" takes on a wholly fresh connotation. After all gathering is a preliminary action of the assembly which needs facilitation.[23] Put another way, "the plaza will serve as the sheepfold, a pasture where people meet and greet each other. We don't want to be just an outdoor public plaza; we want it to be interesting."[24]

Gateway Fountain

On one occasion, the cardinal reminded the architect that "we are looking at the portico from the viewpoint of its theological meaning: that Jesus Christ is the entrance to life, that He is the sheep-gate and that our journey to life eternal begins in and through Him. Consequently, the design of the portico is viewed from quite different perspectives" than simply an entrance way.[25]

Passing through the main entrance of the cathedral plaza, off Temple Street, visitors are immediately confronted by the artistic entrance pool, the constellations on the pavement, translations in numerous languages and the water wall commencing at the upper level and cascading down the cement stone into the lower pool.

In his directive for the Gateway Fountain, the cardinal made three observations: the verbiage needed to be brief; the words should be ones from Jesus' lips and should be "life-giving, active and ones the visitors can take in personally and benefit from." Excerpted from the encounter of Jesus and the Samaritan woman at the well, he recommended that the words should be: "I shall give you living water" taken from John 4:

> John 4:10 Jesus answered and said to her, "If you knew the gift of God and who is saying to you, 'Give me a drank,' you would have asked him and he would have given you *living water*."

---

[23]Sara Michael King, C.S.J., "Gathering Space," *Church Building,* VIII, 16.
[24]*Cathedral Chapters,* II, #3, Winter 1999.
[25]AALA, Memorandum to Jose Rafael Moneo, Los Angeles, August 30, 1998.

Garage for the cathedral complex opened on April 1, 2002.

> John 4:11 (The woman) said to him, "Sir, you do not even have a bucket and the cistern is deep; where then can you get this *living water?*"
> John 4:14 but whoever drinks *the water I shall give* will never thirst; *the water I shall give* will become in him a spring welling up to eternal life.[26]

The words are sandblasted into the marble disk in thirty-six languages spoken in the 290 parishes in the Archdiocese of Los Angeles. The etched reproduction of the constellations delineates the cosmology of the sky on September 2, 2002, the day on which the cathedral was dedicated. Lita Albuquerque was the designer and sculptor.

Jerusalem Fountain

It was in the fall of 2000 that Ira Yellin first suggested that members of the Jewish community, especially those associated with the Skirball Foundation, "might be interested in sponsoring some feature on the Cathe-

---

[26]AALA, Roger Cardinal Mahony to Richard Vosko, Los Angeles, March 7, 1999.

dral Plaza."[27] In his response the cardinal said that "we are all grateful for your vision and energy in realizing this monument in our city."[28]

From the start, the cathedral was planned and designed to serve as a unifying symbol for the entire Catholic populace. It had long been evident that "the world is in need of a place where people of all faiths can gather together as a community to praise God and to celebrate the civil liberties and democratic rights we cherish."

Further consultation with Rabbi Uri D. Herscher resulted in a plan, which was graciously financed by a $2.5 million grant from the Skirball Foundation whose chairpersons were Morris Burgreen and his wife Adelle. The gift was to acknowledge the "longstanding and cordial relationship between the Jewish and Roman Catholic communities in Southern California,"[29] a long standing idea of the late Rabbi Jack H. Skirball.

Located on the north side of the plaza, adjacent to the Children's Garden, the fountain, with its inscription on the rose and gold limestone from an ancient quarry outside the Walled City, recalls the words of Shimon the Righteous, a prominent high priest of the Jerusalem temple: "Three pillars uphold the world: divine teaching, ethical service and loving kindness." That famous motto portrays the ideal person as one who strives to remain close to both God and man. The gift of this foundation is probably the first-ever Jewish contribution to a Christian cathedral.

Mediation Garden

In contrast to the communal gathering places in the plaza, the Meditation Garden is a place for individual or private prayer, contemplation and reconciliation. Nestled against the north side of the cathedral, the Meditation Garden has a fountain splashing onto an outcropping of ancient stones. The water flows over a giant boulder into a pool filled with lilies and assorted tropical fish:

> This garden speaks of the sacred mysteries within the natural world. The oaks, the magnificent elders of the indigenous Southern California landscape, will mature with the cathedral over the centuries.[30]

---

[27]AALA, Ira Yellin to Roger Cardinal Mahony, Los Angeles, September 15, 2000.

[28]AALA, Roger Cardinal Mahony to Ira Yellin, Los Angeles, October 31, 2000.

[29]*Cathedral Chapters,* V, #2, Winter/Spring 2002.

[30]*Cathedral Chapters,* II, #1, Spring 1998.

Meditation Garden. *Source: Fred Balak*

Landscaping

Late in 1997, the Professional Committee chose the firm of Campbell and Campbell was appointed landscape architects for the cathedral. Noted for its design of numerous landmarks, plazas, streets and campus settings throughout the west, the firm was charged with the task of designing "a sense of sacred space while utilizing the naturally abundant beauty that is an integral part of California's culture and heritage."[31]

Probably the greatest influence of the Franciscan friars on the cathedral is not in the architecture, but in the horticulture and landscape. In 1769, when the friars came to Alta California, they began to transform the region with their garden making, methods of agriculture, designing of waterways and planting of trees which were common in their Mediterranean homes. It was they who "designed the first outdoor chapel, sanctuary and prayer gardens; built the first fountains and pergolas; planted the first rose and herb gardens, the first orange,

---

[31]AALA, Press Release, December 11, 1997

Gateway Pool. *Source: Fred Balak*

date and olive orchards, the first vineyards, the first pepper trees and much more."[32]

The Campbells used their research to design the more than two and one-half acres of open space in the cathedral plaza. Noting that "plants and trees connect people to the natural world around them," the designers said that "the cathedral will offer the people of Los Angeles a sanctuary from the world. We envision it as an oasis."[33]

In a description of their plantings, Campbell and Campbell noted that

> As integral formal, aesthetic and symbolic elements of the landscape design, the specific plant materials of the cathedral gardens were selected for myriad, synergetic reasons. Although the design establishes a successionary landscape, one which will change as relatively short-lived species succumb to maturing species, all the plants possess horticultural abilities to thrive in the urban environment of the cathedral over their normal life spans with relatively low resource and maintenance requirements.
>
> Additionally each plant type carries inherent meanings regarding Scripture, Catholic garden traditions especially as represented in the Franciscan missions of California, the liturgical calendar and/or the diverse cultural communities of the archdiocese.

Among the twenty-eight trees mentioned perhaps the most appropriate is the "Mission Fig" tree:

> One of the characteristic trees of the Franciscan missions—Mission Figs—have twisting, smooth gray trunks, which mature into striking silhouettes. Their great leaves are bright green and heavily lobed, their delicious fruit is purple black.
>
> Both fresh and dried figs have been an important food in the Mediterranean region since biblical times (1 Samuel 25: 18; 1 Chronicles 12:40; Hosea 9:10; Amos 8: 1-2). They were not only grown as orchard trees, but were also used ornamentally as vines and shade trees in gardens (Zechariah 3: 10; John 1:48). Figs were used by Jesus in his parables (Matthew 7:16; Luke 13: 6ff; Luke 21: 29-30) and he cursed a fig tree which

---

[32]*Cathedral Chapters,* II, #1, Spring 1998.
[33]Quoted in "Creating an Urban Oasis," *The Tidings,* April 17, 1998.

Jerusalem Fountain

On Monday, December 9, 2002, more than 130 members of the Skirball Cultural Center staff and their families joined Founding President and CEO Uri D. Herscher at the newly completed Cathedral of Our Lady of the Angels in downtown Los Angeles to celebrate the dedication of a fountain that was a gift from the Skirball Foundation, New York.

withered and died in Mark 11:13 and 20, Matthew 21:19. Fig leaves appear in Genesis as clothing (3:7). These trees are often representatives of the sacred Tree of Life in many regions most notably in Egypt, India, Southeast Asia and parts of the Pacific. In Judaism figs are sometimes used as a symbol of prosperity and abundance. In Islam the fig, like the olive, is used to represent the forbidden fruit tree in Paradise.

Mission Figs are used as vines to climb the trunks of palms at the north cathedral entry. There is also an espaliered fig in second phase of the garden of the cardinal's residence.[34]

---

[34]AALA, Kevin Kostelnik to Roger Cardinal Mahony, Los Angeles, August 10, 2001.

One commentator said that "the planting around Our Lady of the Angels is so young, it will take years to attain the kind of scale that will cast a cooling shade. As the construction winds up, the gardening has only just begun."[35]

> Rich in meaning and symbolism, these beautiful landscapes will recall the great landscape traditions of the Catholic Church, especially those of Southern California. Rather than restorations, these gardens will re-envision this venerable legacy to produce a vital, authentic expression of the Church firmly rooted and wholly integrated into California and its future.[36]

Children's Garden

Among the gardens featured in the plaza of the Cathedral of Our Lady of the Angels is one dedicated to children, the *spes gregis* (hope of the future) for God's people. It is a grove of olive trees, the branches of which have traditionally symbolized peace in a troubled world. There is a collection of fabricated animals, including a dog (faith), a monkey (loyalty) and a lion (authority). The donkey is inscribed: "It is better the donkey you must encourage than the one who won't carry his load."

---

[35]Los Angeles *Times,* August 8, 2002.
[36]*Cathedral Chapters,* II, #1, Spring 1998.

Chapter VIII

Native American et al.

During the early days of the excavations for the cathedral, someone informed the press that in August of 1957 fragments of an ancient skull had been found in the ground being removed for the building of the Hollywood Freeway. Fearing that "ancient graves might be paved over once more," a group of Native Americans urged further archaeological testing. The Gabrielino-Tongva Tribal Council warned that the property might contain more graves as well as artifacts of a settlement located upland from the Los Angeles River. The Los Angeles Community Redevelopment Agency suggested that a team be appointed to monitor future excavations and possibly conduct test borings. If human remains or artifacts were found, the tribal council would claim ownership and want to determine their fate. The agency noted that the skull discovered in 1957 was under eleven feet of fill and soil and may well have been moved there from another site.[1]

"With great respect to the Native American culture," Cardinal Mahony met and consulted with the Catholic leadership group of the Kateri Circle of the archdiocese. He invited members and others to a meeting "to seek your counsel and advice."[2]

That there were other issues involved is evident in a letter to Mahony in which a member of the Tribal Council of Pima "questioned the motives of the archdiocese in performing a ground blessing." Vera Rocha complained about "the tragic history of the village of Ya', where refugees escaping persecution from predominantly European Christianity sought solace and the opportunity to live as had their ancestors" for countless generations. While "not objecting to the construction of the cathedral (although, historically, the Catholic Church has left scars on our lives)," she asked:

1. Acknowledgement of the genocidal and abusive history of the Church with the Gabrielino-Tongva.
2. That the design of the cathedral be finalized only after it had been confirmed with absolute certainty that there are no burials which will be removed or violated during construction.

---

[1]Los Angeles *Times,* August 8, 1997.

[2]AALA, Roger Cardinal Mahony to Vera Rocha, Los Angeles, September 2, 1997.

3. That because of the coincidental location of the cathedral, in close proximity to the historic village of the Ya', we ask that the archdiocese assist the Gabrielino-Tongva in documenting the history of Ya', so as to assure that the Los Angeles community has an increased awareness of this tragedy.[3]

There was some question as to who truly represented this local contingency of Native Americans. In any event, just before the actual ground blessing, the cardinal joined with a group of Indians and "prayed their traditional Native American prayers over the site." After further consultation, it was decided that "a certified archaeologist and a monitor acceptable to the developer and Native Americans watch over construction."[4]

Predictably, the local press made much ado about the matter. One reporter demanded to "know the whereabouts" of the bones unearthed in 1957, saying that "the skull may be evidence of an ancient cemetery beneath what is now a parking lot pavement at Hill and Temple streets."[5] More likely, the skull was probably moved to the property in the early 1950s in the landfill that was used to close off an abandoned streetcar tunnel. No mention was made that the Indians of earlier times had no fixed cemeteries, but customarily buried people where they died.

Brian D. Dillon, a consultant hired by the archdiocese, made a search for the missing skull. He located the archaeologist called to the scene in 1957 who recalled that he had determined that there had been no recent homicide. But Dillon was unable to locate the skull. Eventually the skull surfaced at the Los Angeles County Museum of Natural History where it and several other bones had been stored for decades. Museum curators emphasized that the remains had been "curated with a sensitivity that respects our reverence for human life." There had never been an in depth study of the remains.[6]

Meanwhile an archaeological investigation of the site, conducted according to the cathedral's environmental impact report, showed that there were "no sacred burial grounds or ruins of an ancient Native American settlement on the site."[7] Vera Rocha, speaking for the tribe, objected saying that "the spirits of the dead remain in the land and should not de

---

[3]AALA, Cindi Alvitre to Roger Cardinal Mahony, Los Angeles, September 18, 1997.

[4]*Downtown News,* October 20, 1997.

[5]Los Angeles *Times,* October 26, 1997.

[6]AALA, Robert Lavenberg to Roger Cardinal Mahony, Los Angeles, October 28, 1997.

[7]AALA, Press Release, September 28, 1997.

disturbed."[8] Further it was stated that "there is no current evidence of a remaining archaeological site since research reveals that the surface was erased by various forms of land use since 1859 and subsequent residential use, beginning in the 1870s and continuing on into the 1940s."[9]

All the while, archdiocesan officials stated that "if these human remains are indeed those of Native Americans, we would work with the Native American community to be sure that the remains are interred with respect and dignity."[10] In an internal memorandum, it was stated that the "archdiocese will support memorialization in the context of the Public Art requirement and would entertain the tribal nomination of a qualified artist to work with our lead artist, Father Vosko, and other artists who will be commissioned at a later time for the Public Art."[11]

Bowing to the concerns of some who believed that the cathedral site was located on an ancient burial ground, the Los Angeles City Council voted on November 19, 1997 "to add representatives from the Shoshone-Gabrielino Nation to monitor construction work." In so doing, the council members let it be known that "there is no proof that the land . . . was ever a burial site".[12]

About a month later, the Shoshone-Gabrielino Nation filed a $50 million lawsuit against the archdiocese charging that the cathedral site was indeed an ancient burial ground. Early the following year, the cardinal sought assistance from Blessed Kateri Tekakwitha Council because he was worried that the whole incident was "just one more obstacle in our path towards having a new cathedral church."[13] A court hearing was scheduled for March 5, 1998 and, a few days later, the California State Court of Appeals denied the request for a preliminary injunction saying that the plaintiffs were unlikely to win a lawsuit against the city's Community Redevelopment Agency.[14]

Cathedral officials "gave a sigh of relief" when the request for an injunction was denied. At the same time, local papers were reporting that "archaeological testing of the land, which began last week, has revealed nothing beyond railroad ties and rubble."[15] Unusual things did appear in

---

[8]Los Angeles *Times*, September 29, 1997.

[9]Statement on Possible Rediscovery of Bones, October 28, 1997.

[10]*The Tidings*, October 31, 1997.

[11]AALA, Hilarion O'Connor, O.S.F. to Roger Cardinal Mahony, Los Angeles, November 2, 1997.

[12]Los Angeles *Times*, November 20, 1997.

[13]AALA, Roger Cardinal Mahony to Hermitage of Christ the King, Los Angeles, January 28, 1998.

[14]Los Angeles *Daily News*, March 20, 1998.

[15]*Downtown News*, March 23, 1998.

Father Gregory Coiro, O.F.M., Cap. addresses representatives of the press following the announcement that human remains had once been found at the site.

the digs, however. Crew members found a prescription medicine bottle, chicken bones and an Anheuser-Busch bottle, each believed to be more than 100 years old. "The crew also uncovered the foundation of a home believed to have been built around 1888."[16]

On June 5, 1998, the judge dismissed the petition by a small splinter group of Native Americans who were trying to delay the cathedral project. "This is a great victory for us," the cardinal stated, "since there are no more legal challenges to our project."[17] In discussing the decision, the archdiocesan lawyer, John McNicholas said that "the archdiocese has been, and will continue to be, very sensitive to the concerns of the Native American community."[18]

It was an outgrowth of concern for Native Americans that brought about the offer to Johnny Bear Contreras to design a commemorative piece on the cathedral grounds to memorialize his people. In his commission, Father Vosko told the artist that while there was great importance to this memorial, "we do not intend it to be a monumental piece. Rather it should be a simple, yet powerful statement conveying that the land was

---

[16]*Ibid.,* April 5, 1998.

[17]AALA, Roger Cardinal Mahony to Jose Rafael Moneo, Los Angeles, June 6, 1998.

[18]*The Tidings,* June 12, 1998.

Archaeologist sifts the ground for other significant mementoes of another era.

indeed the Native Americans' natural habitat, and through this memorial, it is being honored as such."[19]

A member of the Kumeysay tribe of San Diego, Johnny Bear presented five designs for consideration. The cathedral's adobe color, its brightness and light motivated the artist to design a work "that looks like an extension of the earth." It portrays the notion of "pilgrimage", a

[19]AALA, Richard Vosko to Johnny Bear Contreras, New York, November 17, 2000.

Memorial to the Native Americans.

journey of faith. Measuring about four by eight feet and roughly three and one half feet wide at its broadest point, the bronze weighs 600 pounds.

Shrine of Our Lady of Guadalupe

From the beginning Cardinal Mahony said that the Shrine of Our Lady of Guadalupe was "an incredibly important feature of the Cathedral Complex" and he felt that it would "be the prime destination point for so many members of the archdiocese and across the southland." The cardinal wanted to make sure that "this statue is to be very traditional and very beautiful." He did not feel that there was any place for an unusual representation and he reserved the right to be "very intimately involved

Portrayal of the Virgin of Guadalupe.

with the selection of an artist."[20] Chosen to be the lead artist for this work was Lalo Garcia, a Mexican-born artisan from Mission Hills, California.

Located on the north wall overlooking the Hollywood Freeway, the depiction was to be that of the appearance of Mary to Saint Juan Diego near Mexico City in 1531. The shrine was to be constructed of special talavera tile mixed in clay from *Pueblo de Los Angeles.*

> It will provide a central gathering place for people of all races and cultures and feature the popular digitized image, which will face the cathedral's Grand Plaza. On the opposite side of this shrine, a sculpted image of Our Lady will face the Hollywood Freeway.[21]

---

[20]AALA, Roger Cardinal Mahony to Jose Rafael Moneo, Los Angeles, September 9, 1999.

[21]*Cathedral Chapters,* VI, #1, Winter/Spring 2002.

The twelve-foot mural of Our Lady of Guadalupe is visible from the freeway and the three-sided shrine on the verso opens into the plaza. The center panel of the shrine is a stylized version of the *tilma*. On the bottom is the phrase: *Non fecit taliter omni natione* which recalls the psalm used by Pope Benedict XIV when he spoke about Our Lady's apparition at Tepeyac. The plaza image is digitized which renders a more authentic reproduction.

Donor Wall

A related artistic work, the Donor Wall, which is built along side and above the Hollywood Freeway, is the work of Jacob Jambazian. It consists of a series of eight sets of angelic hosts in five panels for a total of sixteen angels. Each panel measures just less than thirty feet in width and slightly less than nine feet in height. The design of a pair of angels floating toward the center of each panel is so arranged that it can be seen through the panel. Instead of using sand for the etching process, the artist carved the glass with drills and diamond drums. The names of the donors are on a separate piece of glass suspended in front of the etched glass. In an interview the artist noted:

Celebration of the Feast of Our Lady of Guadalupe on December 12, 2001.

CATHEDRAL FIRSTS

First Mass	Msgr. Terrence Fleming
First Entombments	August 19, 2002 Victor and Loretta Mahony
First Baptism	September 13. 2002 George Acuna, III
First Funeral & Inurnment	September 25, 2002 Beverly J. Kostelnik
First Knighthood	October 6, 2002 Brother Timothy Arthur, O.F.M.
First Marriage	October 10, 2002 Estella Ramos and Jaime Garcia
First Wedding Anniversary	October 13, 2002 Joan and Bert Lamberti
First Rite of Election	March 9, 2003
First Call to Conversion	March 16, 2003
First Holy Communions	April 19, 2003 Diana Maria Guevara Julien Martinsons Christian Martinsons
First Confirmations	April 19, 2003 Saydha Thomas Russell Robert Thomas
First Visit by an Asian Head of State	May 17, 2003 Gloria Macapagal Arroyo, President of the Philippines
First Archdiocesan Ordinations	May 31, 2003 Rev. Christopher Bazyouros Rev. James Bevacqua Rev. Abel Ramos Rev. Samuel Ward
First Ordination to the Diaconate	June 7, 2003
First Religious Ordination	June 14, 2003
First Visit by a European President	July 11, 2003 Jose Maria Aznar
First Episcopal Ordination	February 11, 2004 Bishop Oscar Solis

The rough, carved side of the Donor Wall is outside because it will age better, gaining a patina (dirt) that will bring out the highlights and lowlights in the glass. Visitors standing on the opposite side of the plaza will see a series of flowing angels. As they near the Memorial Wall, they will begin to see the lettering of donor names. The letters are more opaque because they are carved with aluminum particle blasting rather than acid etching or carving. They will look through the carved letters on the interior side that are about 5/8th of an inch of clear glass. Through this glass they will continue to see the sixteen angels forming a continuous band. The angels are carved from the same full-sized drawings, but each is different because the drawing was only a guide for the artist.[22]

---

[22]*Downtown News,* August 23, 2002.

Chapter IX

Sanctuary Adornments

Altar

Roger Cardinal Mahony was echoing Catholic teaching since apostolic time when he said that "the most important and central liturgical feature of the entire cathedral" is the altar. He went on to proclaim that "the cathedral's altar makes visible the holiness, unity and charity of the entire Church, but most especially of the local Church of Los Angeles. The altar and its continuing renewed sacrifice of Christ link the local Church with its apostolic origins and catholicity."

> Since our design architect, Jose Rafael Moneo, has chosen a circular pattern stone floor emanating from the altar and reaching to the far corners of the cathedral, it is appropriate that the grace and power of the sacrifice upon the altar be seen to flow down and throughout the cathedral. The single round altar pillar, then, fits in beautifully with the theology of the altar and the design of Professor Moneo.[1]

Another liturgist observes that "the altar should be the focal point of the attention of the congregation. It should be freestanding to allow the celebrant to stand behind it as well as to walk around it for the incensing.[2]

The cardinal had his own "rather strong feelings" about the altar. Wanting it to be the focal point of the entire building, he also directed that it be fabricated of "a beautiful stone" substance. Finally, he preferred a rectangular altar, not a square, one to allow adequate space for principal concelebrants.[3]

Louis Carnevale, a local marble master who had done work for many of the archdiocesan churches, was delegated to serve as agent for designing,

---

[1]*Cathedral Chapters*, IV, #2, Spring/Summer 2000.
[2]Peter Nugent, "The Altar," *Church Building*. VIII (n.d.), 5–6.
[3]AALA, Roger Cardinal Mahony, FAX Memorandum, Los Angeles, July 6, 1997.

Main altar viewed against the freestanding crucifix.

ordering and shipping the altar.[4] Searching for a burgundy strain of marble, he discovered that only one quarry was then producing Rosso Laguna. On a journey to Izmir, Turkey, to examine the quarry, Carnevale made arrangements to have several huge blocks of that marble shipped to Carrara, Italy for final fabrication. The shade was "truly stunning in every way." In Carrara the traditional five crosses were carved into the *mensa* or table part of the altar.[5]

---

[4]AALA, Roger Cardinal Mahony to Louis Carnevale, Los Angeles, October 24, 1999.

[5]AALA, Louis Carnevale to Roger Cardinal Mahony, Los Angeles, December 9, 1999.

Raffaelo Giovetti, the Italian marble master commissioned to oversee the carving of the marble pieces at Carrara, reported that the blocks of marble were "uniquely colored." Besides the altar and its *stipes,* Giovetti also provided additional pieces that could be used for the Baptistry and other areas of the cathedral.[6]

Anxious to see the marble being cut to specification, the cardinal journeyed to Italy in mid-year where he personally inspected the overall process. By the time the marble altar and its *stipes* were ready for shipping, the sizes were enormous; forty inches in diameter for the stipes, weighing 2½ tons. The actual *mensa* was eight feet by ten feet and ten inches thick. Especially attractive was the magnificent white and gray veining. It was shipped by sea in late November.[7]

Officials at Los Angeles were alerted that the shipment would arrive on December 12, 2000. A week later, "the altar base and its *mensa* were lowered into the sanctuary area of the cathedral,"[8] a monumental task because the tower crane was at its outside weight limits. Estimates placed the crated *mensa* as weighing six tons. The following day, the beautiful Rosso Laguna pieces were anchored in place. The cardinal said a prayer and blessing:

> Loving God, today we rejoice in your presence and praise you for your goodness as we celebrate the formal installation of the new altar for the Cathedral of Our Lady of the Angels. As we continue forward on our Advent Journey to the renewal of the graces of salvation in the birth of your Son, Jesus, may our hearts be ever open to the saving transformation you continue to work out in our lives through the power of the Eucharist.
>
> May this altar be the place where the great Eucharistic mysteries of redemption are accomplished, a place where your people offer their gifts, unfold their good intentions, pour out their prayers, and echo every meaning of their faith and devotion.
>
> Pour out your blessing upon all who gather for this historic moment in the life of our cathedral, and continue to journey with us towards the final completion of this magnificent temple of your presence in our midst! Amen.[9]

---

[6]AALA, Louis Carnevale to Roger Cardinal Mahony, Los Angeles, January 19, 2000.

[7]AALA, Undated Memorandum "Cathedral Altar Completed," Los Angeles.

[8]AALA, Roger Cardinal Mahony to Jose Rafael Moneo, Los Angeles, December 23, 2000.

[9]AALA, Press Release, December 20, 2000.

The cathedral's main altar. *Source: Tom Bonner*

Following the installation, a substantial wooden "house" was erected over the entire altar. It was then carefully wrapped with styrofoam. A steel frame was then fitted and heavy planks placed atop the frame, all in the effort to protect the altar from any damage as the roof of the cathedral was put in place.

The local press was out in great numbers for the blessing. A reporter for the *Downtown News* said he envisioned that the altar's color "will interact with light shining through the alabaster windows!" Noting that it was the first "installation" in the new cathedral, the writer observed that it had come 7,000 miles to serve as the focal point in the city's most recent and elaborate church.[10] Another local journalist quoted the cardi-

---

[10]December 25, 2000.

One of the angels which adorn the base of the altar. *Source: Snowden Studios 2003*

nal as saying that "today we're installing the first element of worship and the most important" one in our cathedral. "For us Catholics, the altar signifies stability and continuity of God's presence in our midst."[11]

Altar Angels

Chosen to design and sculpt the angels for the round pillar or *stipes* was M. L. Snowden. She was requested to develop her design from Revelations 8: 3: "There was another angel that came and took his stand at the altar, with a censer of gold, and incense was given him in plenty, so that he could make an offering on the golden altar before the throne, out of the prayers said by all the saints."

The artist planned angels in flight, hued in rose gold to compliment the altar's Rosso Laguna shade. The angels are thirty by thirty by thirty

[11]Los Angeles *Times,* December 21, 2000.

A Dedication Candle holder.
Source: Cathedral Archives

inches in four panels, forming one long length that creates a harmony of
intertwining wings and energy. Each of the angels is related to the others
in a slightly different proportion and design.

The unique Jana stone flooring of the sanctuary captures dramatically the underlying theological significance of the altar.

> By creating a concentric paving of stone that begins at the
> very heart and base of the altar and radiates outward to fill the
> interior of the cathedral, Professor Moneo has presented us
> with an extraordinary visual representation of the theology of
> the altar: the power of the sacrifice of Jesus Christ radiates out
> to touch every member of the assembly gathered for worship,
> while at the same time, the joys and aspirations, and the sor-
> rows and trials of the people of God are channeled back to the
> altar of sacrifice. Consequently, the floor design by Professor
> Moneo provides a vibrant and harmonious representation of
> Catholic worship, while at the same time, highlighting the
> unique role of the altar in that worship.[12]

---

[12]AALA, Roger Cardinal Mahony, "Theological and Artistic Understanding,"
September 4, 1999.

Sanctuary Crucifix

A vast majority of the visitors to the Cathedral of Our Lady of the Angels identify with Simon Toparovsky's crucifix. So many pilgrims and others have kissed or touched the feet of the crucifix that the patina of the bronze figure is turning to a gold shade.

The artist was inspired by Pierre Barbet's book, *A Doctor on Calvary,* wherein the French surgeon studied the crucifixion from every conceivable angle. After carefully reading and studying that book, Simon Toparovsky was able to depict the savior's body without exaggerating the various contusions of the anatomy.

Main cathedral crucifix. *Source: Fred Balak*

The artist constructed the basic shape of the six foot, six inches, 410-pound corpus as a single piece. Using pieces of chicken wire, foam, tape and plastic tubing materials, he coated the outside with burlap and wax from which the bronze casting was molded. His inspiration for the crown of thorns came from a plant in the Holy Land called *euphorbia mili*. Wanting to portray a Semitic Jesus, Simon then mounted the slightly larger than human *corpus* on a fourteen foot tall American sycamore cross.

Cathedra

The latest edition of the *Ceremonial of Bishops* declares that the cathedral church is the site of the bishop's chair or *cathedra* which signifies his presidency over the local church. From the *cathedra* the bishop (archbishop or cardinal) preaches, governs and sanctifies in the name of Jesus Christ. As a symbol of the bishop's teaching office and pastoral authority, the *cathedra* also serves as a sign of the unity symbolizing the shepherd and his sheepfold.

In his design of the *cathedra,* Jefferson Tortorelli fabricated a basic chair and then extended the two ebony arms outward to welcome the congregation: "If you looked to a friend, or if your children were approaching, you would just open your arms in greeting."

Each of the horizontal and vertical lines of the crosses is made from a different wood; olive from Israel, carob from Lebanon, ebony from Africa, holly from the United States, coca bola from Central America, lacewood from Australia and buena burrow from Thailand. The inlay crosses in the front of the *cathedra* have two side pockets, while the verso of the chair is composed of interlinked, inlaid crosses which float in the framework. Also symbolized by the woods are the various ethnic components which comprise the greater Los Angeles community. The pieces of the *cathedra* are joined together in a locked pattern much the same as a puzzle. The seventy-four inch steel substructure, fabricated by welder Dan Tillbury, forms the framework of the 880-pound *cathedra*.

The Presider's Chair

Except for a higher-ranking prelate or the President of the National Conference of Bishops, the *cathedra* is never used by any other prelate without the express authorization of the local bishop. Hence the need arises for a Presider's Chair for the use of the pastor, priests attached to the cathedral staff or visiting presbyters. The Presider's Chair is made of the same woods as the *cathedra*. To the rear of the Presider's Chair, on

Sanctuary crucifix with the organ pipes in the background.

the Presbyterium Wall, is John Nava's tapestry depiction of The Holy City based on a text from the Book of Revelation.

Ambo

Catholics believe that all scripture is inspired. It is God's sacred Word that is proclaimed at the readings during the liturgies. Hence it follows that the readings take place on an elevated or raised place. Good visibility is essential so that all present can see and hear the bishop, priest, deacon or lector when the Word of God is proclaimed.

Traditionally the ambo is a fixed structure used solely by those empowered to read and then preach about the Word of God. Logically the ambo is manufactured or constructed of fine materials. In Our Lord's time, the Jewish rabbis read the scriptures from an elevated platform or pulpit. The notion was introduced into Catholic churches about the fourth century. The one in the Cathedral of Our Lady of the Angels, fabricated around an internal steel mechanism, is fully adjustable to allow for its being raised and lowered for readers of differing heights.

The *cathedra* is the official seat or teaching chair of the Archbishop of Los Angeles. *Source: Tom Bonner*

Presider's Chair. *Source: Jefferson Tortorelli*

Jefferson Tortorelli, the designer, says that he was inspired by reading the part of Matthew's Gospel portraying Jesus climbing to the top of a mountain where he turned and addressed the people. There was no barrier between speaker and listener. The ambo weighs approximately 1,500 pounds and is carved from reddish-toned jarrah wood from Australia. The exterior is accented with bloodwood which is sometimes called cardinal wood or satine.

Adjustable Ambo or Lecturn. *Source: Jefferson Tortorelli*

Chapter X

Ecclesial Furnishings

Baptismal Font

The prominence of the Baptismal Font has always been featured in Catholic ecclesial architecture. Baptism is a priority in the life of the Church's members since it is the sacrament that signifies entry into the community and life of God. At the same time, it is important to emphasize that water is the reminder of Baptism, not the font itself. "The design principle of a font is the emphasis on living, flowing water."[1]

Early in the design phase of the cathedral, the initial concept for the baptismal font was "not in accord with our desires and plans" and, at that time, the planning for that pivotal part of the cathedral was entrusted to Father Vosko.[2]

In his directive for the overall adornments of the cathedral, Cardinal Mahony pointed out that "the altar must be linked theologically and artistically with the Baptismal Font since it is through Baptism that we enter the Body of Christ, gain membership in the Assembly of God's people and become eligible to share in the Eucharist offered upon the altar." While he did not think that the altar and font needed to be made of the same substance, he did suggest that pieces of the altar marble might be used "by way of trim."[3]

In his earliest designs Father Richard Vosko disclosed that "we are exploring the possibility of an octagon perimeter and a cross shaped interior. The three steps in and a second set of three steps out could go into the arms of the cross on the east-west axis." He was thinking of a fifteen foot diameter font.[4]

The cardinal expanded on the design in an issue of *Cathedral Chapters* in which he disclosed that the font would be located at the west end of the cathedral:

> Our font is quite large and in the form of an octagon–a very often used figure in Christian iconography. One will see four

---

[1] Kevin Kostelnik, "The Baptism Font," *Church Building* (VIII, n.d.) #5 and 6.
[2] AALA, Roger Cardinal Mahony to Jose Rafael Moneo, Los Angeles, June 1999.
[3] AALA, Roger Cardinal Mahony, Memorandum, September 4, 1999.
[4] AALA, Richard S. Vosko to Nicholas W. Roberts, July 7, 1999.

Baptismal Pool at the Cathedral of Our Lady of the Angels.

beautiful granite pillars each about three feet high. Each pillar will be filled with moving water, and small spouts from each spill into the larger immersion pool which is just below the level of the floor. Steps lead from the west side down into the immersion pool, and then up the other side towards the people and the altar.

This symbolism is critically important: we descend from our sinfulness down into the waters of Baptism, and there immersed, we are freed from our sins through the power of Jesus Christ. We then emerge on the nave side where the People of God are assembled, and we then belong to that community. Our journey forward then takes us to the altar where we share in the Eucharistic Presence of our risen Lord.

Some pieces of the Rosso Laguna marble that is being used for the altar will highlight the font, thus linking even visually these two important liturgical pieces.

Each of the four granite pillars has a body of water adequate for the immersion of infants for Baptism, as well as for the taking of holy water to bless ourselves as we enter into the cathedral–and are reminded of our Baptismal promises and urged to renew them in heart and spirit.[5]

---

[5]*Cathedral Chapters,* IV, #3, Fall 2000.

The gates to the font are adorned with the Greek word *Ixcthus* which means fish, an acronym for Jesus Christ. The fish was a secret symbol used by the early Christians to identify themselves to fellow believers during the centuries when the members of the Church were persecuted. High above and back of the font, hanging on the western wall, is John Nava's masterful tapestry portraying the baptism of Jesus in the River Jordan by John.

Ambry

Nearby is the Ambry, a specially made enclosure where the Holy Oils are exhibited in an open-faced cabinet. Oils have been associated with the Church's liturgy since apostolic times. On the level of natural symbolism, oil signifies protection and preservation, strength and healing, cleansing and beauty. "Though rooted in this natural symbolism the anointing with oil in Jewish practice was primarily seen as a sign of divine blessing. Priests, prophets and kings were anointed with oil as a sign that they were chosen by God to act in His Name."[6]

Since the holy oils are an integral part of the liturgical life of the Church, their blessing and retention is an important element. Considering their rich symbolism, surprisingly little has been legislated about their placement in churches.

The handsome cabinet for the Holy Oils, referred to as the Ambry, was also designed and fabricated by Jefferson Tortorelli. Carved from jarrah wood, it is inset with hand-cast glass from The Judson Studios. The flasks, designed by Marirose Jelicich, contain the oils blessed each year by the archbishop for use in administering the sacraments of Baptism, Confirmation, Holy Orders and the Anointing of the Sick throughout the archdiocese.

Tapestries

Documents generated by Vatican Council II call for "a new understanding of public worship in the Catholic Church by placing an emphasis on the liturgical section of the assembly and the primary symbols used in worship." Father Richard Vosko acknowledged that many houses of prayer erected in recent times have been "rendered all too barren and

---

[6]Kevin McCracken, C.M., "The Holy Oils," *Church Building* VII (n.d.) p. 12.

Ambry. *Source: Jefferson Tortorelli*

devoid of any iconography thus depriving the worshipper and the pilgrim of a familiar and uniquely 'Catholic' ambience."

Given the strong reference to Jose Rafael Moneo's mission style of architecture, Vosko suggested that a theme stressing the "communion of saints" would be highly appropriate for the cathedral. He noted that liturgically the "walls provided ideal surfaces for iconography, which would strengthen the graceful angularity" of the building's ascetic interior.

The theological rationale for the communion of saints is based on an ancient belief. In the Catholic religion it is understood

Artist completes Saint Joan of Arc for the Communion of Saints.

Loom at Flanders Tapestry Mill, Bruges, Belgium. *Source: Archives of the Cathedral of Our Lady of the Angels*

that when the living organic Church gathers to worship God it is, in some mysterious manner, enjoined by the entire Church including the dead. Thus, the presence of the sainthood surrounding the assembly makes good sense, not for the purpose of private devotion (although this is inevitable) but to complete the assembly of worshippers as it praises and blesses its God. In fact, the *Catholic Catechism* asks, "What is the Church if not the assembly of all the saints? The communion of saints is the Church.[7]

The talented California painter, John Nava, was entrusted with the challenge of portraying a representative group of the saints. Originally Nava's artistic renditions were envisioned as life size figures painted on canvas which would then be mounted on or applied to the walls. Later,

---

[7]Richard S. Vosko "Foreword," *Art for the Cathedral.* (Los Angeles, 2000), n. p.

when it was discovered that the cathedral was acoustically too reverberant, sound experts suggested some sort of textiles would serve the additional purpose of absorbing a portion of the excess sound. It was at this juncture that Nava and his colleague, Don Farnsworth, decided on a technically sophisticated method for creating tapestries.

For centuries tapestries have served as a most effective manner of artistic expression, vividly telling the stories of the Greek, Roman, Medieval and Renaissance periods. Even in modern times, tapestries are recognized as an art form of great size and intricacy.

In the fall of 2000, John Nava was commissioned to provide a total of thirty-six cotton tapestries, including a series of twenty-five that would

Roger Cardinal Mahony inspects the fabrication process for the tapestry depicting Blessed Teresa of Calcutta. *Source: Cathedral Archives*

GALERO

The *galerum rubrum* has been in California's ecclesiastical nomenclature only since January 15, 1953, when Pope Pius XII formally bestowed the "red hat" upon the Archbishop of Los Angeles, as the first and most distinctive feature of the princely role entrusted to James Francis McIntyre.

Next to the Roman Pontiff, there is no office in the Catholic Church higher than that of the cardinalate. Since the early eleventh century, the College of Cardinals has functioned as the pope's principal advisory agency in the administration of ecclesial affairs.

This vital role was emphasized by Pope Eugene IV who stated that just "as the door of a house turns on its hinges, so on the cardinalate does the Apostolic See, the door of the whole Church, rest and find support."

As a recompense for their numerous responsible duties, both tradition and canon law have long accorded cardinals privileges more ample and extensive than those enjoyed by any other ecclesiastics. The actual wearing of the colorful appendage was discontinued after the loss of the Papal States, in the1870s. As a sign of "mourning," cardinals were directed to express their displeasure about the loss of the Church's civil autonomy by refusing to wear the *galerum rubrum*

Traditional norms stated that after its acceptance, the *galerum rubrum* was to be stored in a safe place in the cardinal's residence. At his death, it was to be placed at the foot of his catafalque, after which it was to be suspended from the ceiling of the cathedral or church to which he was attached as evidence of the spiritual authority exercised by princes of the Church. There is was to hang until crumbling to dust!

The design of the unique hat, formerly reproduced in each cardinal's personal coat-of-arms, is as simple as it is singular. Its crown is small and shallow; the brim flat, rigid and very broad. Attached to the crown are two crimson-colored cords, each of which terminates with fifteen tassels arranged triangle-wise. Prior to 1953, the *galerum rubrum* had been conferred on only eleven American bishops. The conferral of the *galerum rubrum* was discontinued following the investiture of 1967 when the ceremonial for installation was simplified. Hence the red hat entrusted to James Francis Cardinal McIntyre was both the first and last formally presented to a Californian. Because Cardinal McIntyre was retired at the time of his demise (and therefore, no longer canonically attached to his former cathedral), the *galerum rubrum* was initially hung at Saint Basil Church where His Eminence resided during his final years.

One of the Flanders' craftsmen adjusts a thread so that the weaving process can continue.

adorn the nave of the cathedral. The series was appropriately named the "Communion of Saints."

Designed and created by California artist John Nava, The Communion of Saints feature 136 ten-foot high figures representing saints from around the world, including the holy men and women of North America canonized by the Church. The faces are life-like, and were modeled after actual people, painted portraits and other well-known images of saints. "It's important to convey that these saints were real, accessible people," says Nava. "These are people we would see walking down the street."[8]

Once he had selected and painted a subject, Nava scanned the artwork into digital files. Then he designed a digital program to weave the

---

[8]*Cathedral Chapters,* IV, #3, Fall 2000.

depictions into enormous tapestries at the Flanders Tapestries mill near Bruges, Belgium. What probably would have taken twenty years to craft by hand was completed in a matter of weeks. Nava directed the weaving of his twenty-five Communion of Saints, some measuring as large as twenty-one feet by seven feet in just forty-five days. The artist designed the tapestries in a blend of colors that compliment the sandy hue of the cathedral walls. The complete set of tapestries constitutes what may be "the largest single installation of its kind ever hung in a Catholic Church."[9]

Concerned about overly complicating the process, Nava worked with Farnsworth and the weavers at the Flanders Tapestries mill:

> Their collaborative efforts led to the development of a method of making weavable digital files for tapestry designs. Nava and Flanders Tapestries developed a custom palette of two hundred and forty colors based on sixteen colors of fiber going in two directions, eight in the warp and eight in the weft, to create the images. All of the tapestries are made of cotton with a small percentage of viscose to ensure that the colors, a subtle interplay of neutral tones evocative of the ancient frescoes of Italy, would remain true. Multiple tests conducted during the months of intense work brought about a precise calibration of the computer monitors and the woven output so that what Nava saw in his studio was what the mill produced. After numerous trials these final weaving files were then e-mailed directly to Flanders Tapestries from Nava's studio in California. The result can be considered as traditionally drawing and painting combined with the best use of contemporary technology![10]

In an interview, Nava said his saints "run the gamut of races and ethnicities, a fitting tribute to the diversity of the Roman Catholic Archdiocese of Los Angeles with its five million parishioners speaking forty-two languages." The artist explained his casting system to a reporter.

> I would say, "Look, we need an Asian twelve-year-old boy or a thirty-year-old woman who is Lebanese," and the casting director would go into Ojai and look. But we had people from all over the world model. I wanted them to look like modern

---

[9]Los Angeles *Times,* November 11, 1999. There may be some dispute about this statement. The Apocalypse Tapestry in Angers measures 16' by 360" or 5,760 square feet. The one at Los Angeles measures only 3,675 square feet.

[10]Ronald E. Steen "About the Tapestries," *Art for the Cathedral,* (Los Angeles, 2002) n.p.

Blesseds John XXIII and Teresa of Calcutta take their places in the Communion of Saints. *Source: Tom Bonner*

Walter Judson of The Judson Studios, with his wife Karen, arranged an exhibit of the cathedral tapestries before they left Belgium. *Source: Cathedral Archives*

people dressed like saints. That is the historical tradition, people in the paintings looked like those using the church. Some people aggressively lobbied to be saints, though they were a minority. A lot of people who modeled were extremely devout. Most of the time they did not know what saint they would be, but most were thrilled to be included. After photos were taken, Nava painted intricate, individual portraits of the faces and hands of his subjects. He worked seven days a week, turning out 136 paintings in twenty months. His models ranged from three months to more than ninety years.[11]

Ezcaray Reredos

In the late 1930s, the Archdiocese of Los Angeles was given the sanctuary furnishings of a chapel in Spain that had been damaged in

---

[11]Los Angeles *Times,* February 7, 2003.

Tabernacle on the Ezcaray Reredos. *Source: Fred Balak*

that nation's civil war.[12] They were later consigned to the never-built cathedral that Archbishop John J. Cantwell envisioned on Wilshire Boulevard.

The reredos and its several hundred accoutrements were placed in storage for many years. In 1954, parts of the pieces were installed in the chapel of Queen of Angels, the minor seminary in Mission Hills.[13] When the seminary was closed, a priest of the archdiocese suggested to Cardinal Mahony that the Ezcaray furnishings at Queen of Angels Seminary

---

[12]Francis J. Weber, "The Ezcaray Chapel Furnishings," *The Tidings,* June 30, 1967.

[13]In 1991, the remaining parts of the reredos were reconfigured and placed in the chapel at San Fernando Mission.

might be appropriate in the new Cathedral of Our Lady of the Angels. On June 2, 1995, the cardinal responded to the suggestion asking for "fuller advice about utilizing the reredos . . . in the new Cathedral."[14] Jose Rafael Moneo, the architect for the new cathedral, journeyed twice with staff members to Mission Hills to measure and otherwise prepare for incorporating the reredos in his designs.

Early in 2001, Robert Erburu, recently retired chair of the Getty Trust and retired Chairman of the *Times Mirror* Company, approached the Getty Trust, pointing out that the reredos, once installed, would be "the most distinguished work of art in the Cathedral of Our Lady of the Angels." And it would help to enforce Mahony's wishes that the cathedral "be a reflection of the history of California and the Spanish influence in California."[15]

Later, officials at the Getty Museum were asked to underwrite the removal, refurbishing and reinstallation of the reredos. In one of his letters, the cardinal thought it was interesting that the late Archbishop John J. Cantwell had intended the 1680 *retablo* "for the new cathedral in Los Angeles. With great foresight he prepared for the future, and we all now benefit from his vision."[16]

---

[14]AALA, Roger Cardinal Mahony to Francis J. Weber, Los Angeles, June 2, 1995

[15]Chelo Alvarez, "The Altar of Ezcaray: Journey of a Lost Masterpiece," p. 15.

[16]AALA, Roger Cardinal Mahony to Deborah Marrow, Los Angeles, August 10, 2001. The history of the Ezcaray altarpieces can be found in Appendix 5.

Chapter XI

Instrumental Tonalogy

Campanile

As is customary in many great cathedrals, the grand campanile or bell tower in Los Angeles stands as a detached structure. Designed by Jose Rafael Moneo, it bears an architectural likeness with the cathedral itself.

Located at the northeast corner of the complex, the 156-foot freestanding campanile, built in the same fabric as the rest of the cathedral, was meant to complement the edifice. With few openings, the tower emanates solidness at its highest levels. It serves a different function at ground level, according to architectural associate, Hayden Salter. "Its positioning as the centerpiece of the cloister garden—placed to create a tranquil space against the rush of the freeway—was important." Architecturally the campanile reflects a vision of tomorrow, while incorporating the inspiration of earlier times. Salter noted that the tower changes form as it rises from the ground; it is a "discreet piece of sculpture that relies on subtle transformation. The slight shifts in the planes of the campanile reflect different lights on each surface."[1]

The tower has three "shelves" for its bells. The bells swing as they are rung, as opposed to remaining static and being struck by hammers. This creates a Doppler effect which intensifies the sound. The entire campanile rests upon four base isolators specially designed to diffuse and separate ground shock during earthquakes from affecting the tower itself.

Historically the campanile served several purposes, a belfry for the cathedral bells, a watchtower to guard against invaders and a civil monument in a town or city. The Florentine painter and architect, Giotto, is credited for inspiring towers for churches. His work can still be seen in the Florence Cathedral which was completed in 1334. The original Giotto Campanile was faced with marble and ornamented with sculptures.

The campanile for the Cathedral of Our Lady of the Angels was designed to be slightly taller than the highest point of the cathedral which it adorns. A thirty-foot cross stands atop the campanile. Lighted at night, the campanile will become a landmark as well as a beacon for all who seek God's house. Cardinal Mahony believes that one will be able to

---

[1] *Cathedral Chapters,* III, #1, Winter 1999.

Cathedral Campanile. *Source: Tom Bonner*

Campanile from across the Hollywood Freeway.

see the great campanile from many distant vantage points, and its great bells will be heard far beyond the Cathedral Complex.

Bells

Eventually, plans called for sixteen bells to hang in the campanile. The two bells from Saint Vibiana, both about four feet high,—one weighing 1,600 pounds and the other 2,800 pounds—were removed from the tower in 1965 when their rungs became infested with dry rot. One, dedicated to the memory of Manuel Dominguez and his wife Maria Engracia Cota by their daughters, was cast at the McShane Foundry in Baltimore in 1888. The other, said to be "one of the giant bells from San Juan Capistrano Mission," was cast in 1828 at a foundry in Massachusetts. It was blessed by Bishop Thaddeus Amat on July 4, 1876 as part of the cathedral's consecration services. These two bells were cleaned and burnished to a stain finish and mounted (as opposed to swinging) in the east niche of the campanile.

The third bell, referred to as the "Jubilee Bell," was made at the Marinelli Foundry in Agnone, a firm active in the field for over a thousand years. The latter bell, designed by the sculptor Armando Marinelli, was first rung for the dedication of the Cathedral of Our Lady of the Angels in 2002.

> *"For bells are the voice of the Church;*
> *They have tones that*
> *Touch and search*
> *The hearts of young and old"*
>   —Longfellow

Carillon

Bordering the Temple Street entrance, the Carillon Wall consists of thirty-six bells programmed to ring the hours as well as liturgical hymns and the "calls to worship." In October of 1996, a priest of the archdiocese offered the thirty-five bell carillon from San Fernando Mission for use in the new cathedral. Mentioning that it had been installed at the Old Mission in 1974, he pointed out that "because we have never been able to afford to have the ringing system modernized, we are only able to use it for the *Angelus* and funerals."[2] Attached to the offer was a written description of the carillon and its fascinating history.[3]

---

[2]AALA, Francis J. Weber to Roger Cardinal Mahony, Los Angeles, April 30, 1996.
[3]Cf. Appendix Four

The cardinal was "really excited to learn about this magnificent set of bells" and was confident that if properly computerized and outfitted with modern ringers and electrical wiring, they would "be a great addition to our new Cathedral of Our Lady of the Angels."[4]

Architect Moneo was alerted about the proposed gift. The cardinal early on decided that the bells "should not be part of the Campanile" but rather housed elsewhere in the plaza where they could be heard primarily by people in and around that area. He suggested that "the carillon bells could be incorporated somehow in the main entrance portico—this would surely reflect the California Spanish tradition. Possibly the bells would be an attractive part of our main entrance from Temple Street."[5]

The Verdin Company was contacted about "physically removing the existing thirty-five bells from the tower at San Fernando Mission." They would be transported to a warehouse and packed for shipment to the company's headquarters in Cincinnati. Included in the contract with Verdin was the following:

Removal of the Bells

The Verdin Company will supply all necessary labor and equipment to remove the existing thirty-five bells from the tower of the San Fernando Mission. The bells will be removed though the interior of the building and will be transported through the courtyard. They will be loaded on a vehicle provided for proper handling and shipping to a site where the bells will then be properly crated, protected and shipped to Cincinnati, Ohio where in the Verdin plant the following work will be completed.

Renovation of the Bells

Each bell will be thoroughly checked to be certain there are no cracks. The bells will then be drilled for proper support bolts. Stainless steel support bolts of proper size and length will be fabricated with necessary interior plates for the future support of electrical striking mechanisms to be constructed. It is understood that the striking mechanism will not be fabricated at this time; however, the bells will be prepared for concealed wiring to be installed when the future strikers are furnished. Verdin will coordinate the length of the bolts with

---

[4]AALA, Roger Cardinal Mahony to Francis J. Weber, Los Angeles, October 3, 1996.

[5]AALA, Roger Cardinal Mahony to Jose Rafael Moneo, Los Angeles, July 23, 1998.

the Project Manager so they are properly constructed for support in a frame provided by others or by the I. T. Verdin Company. The bells will then be properly crated and shipped to the jobsite and Verdin will provide complete supervision of installation in the frame that has been provided.[6]

Added to the carillon when its parts were mounted was a large bell which had been stored at Saint Timothy Church in West Los Angeles since 1956. It was one of a series commissioned by William Randolph Hearst in 1926 for the bell tower at San Simeon. Cast at almost thirty-nine inches and weighing 1,200 pounds, it bears two inscriptions: "Ring out the darkness of the land, Ring in the Christ that is to be" and "Ring in the Valiant men and free the larger heart, the kindlier hand."

Organ

Early in the planning stages of the new cathedral, three of the largest organ building companies in the United States were asked to submit sketches for what was envisioned as an organ "of awesome presence and magnificence." After considerable negotiations, Dobson Pipe Organ Builders, Ltd. of Lake City, Iowa, a builder with "vision, artistic capability and financial resource," was selected to design and install the finished instrument.[7]

From the outset, Manuel Rosales, the organ consultant, felt that the organ would probably be the third largest in the United States, surpassed only by the ones at the Mormon Tabernacle in Salt Lake City and the Washington Cathedral. And it would be one of the few grand organs in the country in a spacious church setting and, as such, would be a well-known concert organ.[8]

The Dobson people invested no fewer than 38,000 man-hours by the time the instrument was finished, installed and voiced. The casing for the organ, designed by Jose Rafael Moneo, is cherry wood, probably the biggest such cherry wood case in the world. The forty-two-ton organ is supported on a steel structure built into the wall. It has 105 ranks of pipes for a total number of 6,019.

---

[6]AALA, Contract, May 19, 1999.

[7]AALA, Manuel Rosales to Frederick C. Stegeman, Los Angeles, November 18, 1999.

[8]AALA, Frederick C. Stegeman to Roger Cardinal Mahony, Los Angeles, November 22, 1999.

Dobson Pipe Organ Console.

Lynn Dobson, owner and president of the Dobson Company, says that "most of the pipes are made of tin and lead alloys:

The biggest pipes at twenty-four inches square are made of wood. Other pipes are made of brass. They are arranged into six divisions, on the console there are four keyboards and a pedal board, or four manual divisions and one pedal division, and a floating division that can be played from any of the other manuals or pedals. Therefore, there are six divisions total. There are three blowers with a total of twenty-seven horsepower and a pressure of twenty inches that make wind for the organ. A twenty-inch wind pressure is very high. The reason for such a high pressure is that the cathedral itself is so large that to generate enough sound to fill the room adequately we had to go with higher wind pressure. There are forty-eight pipes in front of the organ from the thirty-two feet principle and the sixteen feet principle. The largest pipe in the front stands about forty-one feet tall and weighs about 1200 pounds. It is a very big pipe by anyone's standards. The front pipes are 85% polished tin, and are speaking pipes. They all play and are graduated in size because of their pitch. As they get smaller, they rise in pitch. This is probably the largest new façade in the United States made of polished tin.[9]

The design of the organ is more dignified, grand and appropriate for the architecture than wave upon wave of visually insignificant mixture pipes:

A simple arrangement of bases from the Great 32' Prestant and the Solo Principal 16' is given interest by varying foot lengths and the layered placement of the 16' in front of the 32' pipes. Made by Carl Giesecke and Sons of 83% tin, they are the largest such pipes in North America. As massive as they are (low C is over 40 feet long, with a seven-foot-long foot), the scale of both organ and building are so harmonious that these enormous pipes appear perfectly proportioned. The three Fanfare reeds provide horizontal counterpoint. Like the Prestant 32', low C of the full-length 16' Trompeta magna is the largest pipe of its kind on the continent.[10]

Close to half the pipes came from the vintage Wangerin and later Austin organ at Saint Vibiana which was installed in 1926 and expanded in 1989. The older pipes were taken to the Dobson company where they were rebuilt and revoiced. Many of the ranks have new pipes for the lower notes and other have moved up in order to allow for bigger scales.

The Dobson firm built what could be called an "eclectic" organ that can easily play different repertories of music, Baroque, Romantic, French and German classics.

The cathedral's organ is a true pipe organ, not a mechanical action organ. It has an electric key action so the console is moveable. The ramp rising to the choir space allows the console to be on the choir level or on the sanctuary level. Because it is electric action it has a multiplexed control system allowing a

---

[9]AALA, "Lynn Dobson: Cathedral Organ," n. d.
[10]John A. Panning, "Cathedral of Our Lady of the Angels-Dobson Pipe Organ Builders," *The American Organist* XXXVII (April, 2003), 40.

fast electronic action and necessitating only six little wires to connect the console to the huge organ. Electrical outlets have been placed in different areas on the floor, near the audience for concerts, elsewhere for an orchestra or choral concert.[11]

To insure the organ's tonal quality in the vast nave, the voicing and finishing was performed on-site over several months.

---

[11]*Ibid.*

Chapter XII

Other Accoutrements

Blessed Sacrament Chapel

The Cathedral of Our Lady of the Angels follows the age-old pattern in all the world's major cathedrals and most of its larger churches insofar as the Blessed Sacrament chapel is located apart from the central or main altar of the worship area.

Focal point in the Blessed Sacrament chapel is the artistic, angular tabernacle designed and fabricated by sculptor Max DeMoss at his studio in Hemet, California. Wanting to design something that would be juxtaposed to the angular and linear architecture of the cathedral itself, the artist devised a structure based on the Ark of the Covenant, an ancient sign of God's relationship with His people. The Ark is visible whether the doors are open or closed. Its three towers also encompass ark shapes and, when the doors are ajar, there is an ark of space between them and the main body of the tabernacle:

> Viewing the tabernacle from the bottom up reveals a representation of chaffs of wheat, representing the Body of Christ or the bread, rising up, transitioning into grape leaves, becoming clusters of grapes, representing the Blood of Christ or the wine, surrounding an oval that comprises a cross. The cross is a piece of wood formed in the shape of a cross, then cast in bronze. Therefore, the tabernacle in its symbols represents the Eucharist.

When opened, the 400-pound tabernacle becomes a triptych about forty-two inches wide with sentinel angels visible looking towards and protecting the area where the Holy Eucharist is reserved. DeMoss explains that the structure "resembles a flame, symbolizing Christ as the Light." The angels are tipped in polished silver.

> The ten feet tall tabernacle is a vertical composition cast in bronze and designed to play with the changing light that is reflected by the tall, alabaster light shaft, and changing with the mood of the person who enters the chapel. The surfaces are juxtaposed between rough textures and smooth surfaces, and

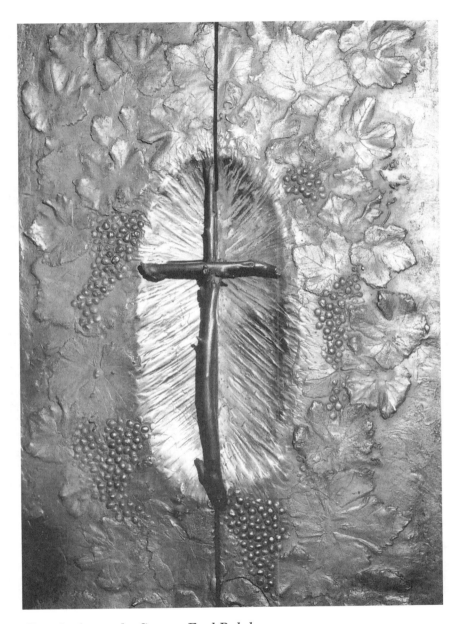

Closed tabernacle. *Source: Fred Balak*

a patina that transitions from darker to lighter as it rises from bottom to top.[1]

DeMoss also designed the Sanctuary Lamp for the Blessed Sacrament Chapel, described as a "disc-like shape with a polished, variegated surface, which allows the candle flame to flicker." That adornment repeats the theme of the Ark of the Covenant. It hangs about eight feet off the floor and is roughly six feel tall and twenty-six inches wide.

The artist also designed the twelve Dedication Candles which are located at crucial parts of the cathedral. Representing the twelve tribes of Israel and the twelve apostles, these candles are lighted each year on the anniversary of the dedication and also on the Feast of the Basilica of St. John Lateran, the cathedral church of Rome and the mother church of the Catholic faith.

Bronze Doors

The use of monumental bronze doors dates to the Golden Ages of Athens and Rome. The portals of the Greek temples were often cast bronze grilles. The Romans characteristically used double doors, much like the twenty-four-foot doors of the Pantheon. The monumental bronze portals in the United States Capitol, installed in 1863, were the first such doors in this country. "Passing through such a threshold on a ceremonial occasion can be an overwhelming experience, even for non-Catholic Christians," says Cecil M. Robeck, Jr., Pentecostal professor of Ecclesial History at Pasadena's Fuller Theological Seminary.[2]

Mexico City born Robert Graham, described by one source as "a perfectionist annoyed by inefficiency and mediocrity,"[3] was chosen to design the Great Doors because of "his understanding of the spiritual and theological traditions of the Catholic Church."[4]

Cardinal Mahony played an active role in the whole concept of the doors, expressing his overall thoughts as follows:

> Robert Graham is the artist whom I have commissioned to design the Bronze Doors for both main entrances to the cathedral. As a result of this commission, I have entrusted into

[1]AALA, Interview with Max DeMoss. March 12, 2002.
[2]Los Angeles *Times,* February 21, 2000.
[3]Lorenza Munoz, Los Angeles *Times,* March 5, 2000.
[4]*The Tidings,* January 1, 1999.

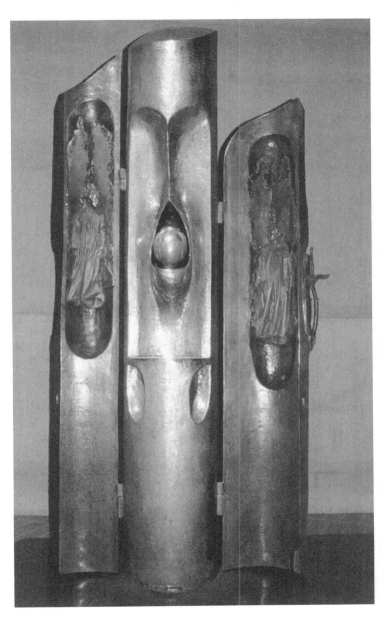

Opened tabernacle.

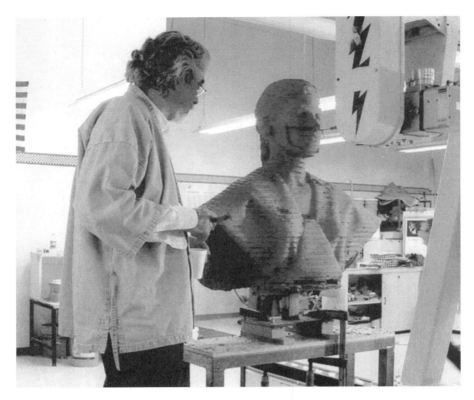

The artist carefully checks the milling process for the face of Our Lady of the Angels.

his hands the overall design and execution of the doors—working in harmony, of course, with all of the design and construction team members.

Our main and principle concern is how the worshippers move through the Bronze Doors into the ambulatory. We want this movement to be inviting and natural. Consequently, the Bronze Doors will be at right angle to the south wall of the cathedral so that the doors will face along the south colonnade sight line, rather than at an angle facing the northeast sector of the plaza. This decision enhances the flow of the worshippers into the vestibule and through the inner glass doors.

We desire the maximum amount of natural light falling upon the Bronze Doors, and no structural hindrances should impede that light. I am very pleased that we will now have maximum light available through the south opening in the

Cardinal Mahony inspects the Great Doors at their formal blessing on May 19, 2002. *Source: William Nettles for Robert Graham Studios*

wall and structure, as well as the light coming from directly overhead.

The porch canopy will extend a maximum of two feet from the top of the Bronze Door structure, giving us a maximum of six feet overhang from the inner door structure to the outer door structure. The decision guarantees that the maximum amount of natural light will now flood over the doors throughout the day in differing degrees, angles, and intensity—creating the interesting light effects upon the doors.

The official press release, coming later that same month, gave some of the salient details of the commission:

> Roger Cardinal Mahony announced today that he has awarded the commission to create the great bronze doors for the new Cathedral of Our Lady of the Angels to renowned Southern California artist Robert Graham.
>
> Mr. Graham said, "The design and realization of The Great Doors of the Cathedral of Our Lady of the Angels in my home city is, in scope, size and importance, a daunting task.
>
> The Great Bronze Doors, the main portal to the cathedral (on its south side facing the Grand Plaza), will be thirty feet tall, including a two-foot tympanum, thirty feet wide, and will weigh an estimated five tons."
>
> Mr. Graham's early plans for the tympanum include an image of Our Lady of the Angels while the large doors beneath will bear ancient iconography in low-relief.
>
> Smaller inset doors will carry, in high relief, images of various manifestations of the Blessed Virgin Mary, as well as the grapevine—emblematic of Christ and his Church—and symbols reflecting the ethnic and cultural diversity of the Catholicism in the Archdiocese of Los Angeles.
>
> Mr. Graham will also create the north bronze doors which will measure thirty feet by twenty feet and will weigh approximately three tons.[5]

For his part Graham said he was "honored and humbled in receiving this commission of such magnitude and relevance."[6]

There was some discussion about the statue of Our Lady of the Angels. The cardinal felt that it would "best be rendered without the presence of the Christ Child." He explained that "the mystery of Our Lady of the Angels is really a post-Resurrection mystery, and Mary gained that title once she was assumed into heaven. This follows the Resurrection of the Lord, the coming of the Holy Spirit upon the apostles and the Church and the Ascension. Consequently, the statue of Our Lady of the Angels is best rendered without the presence of any form of the infant or child Jesus."[7]

As described by another reporter in similar language, the doors rising three stories, including a crowning tympanum, two and a half feet

---

[5]AALA, Press Release, December 21, 1998.

[6]*The Tidings,* January 1, 1999.

[7]AALA, Roger Cardinal Mahony to Robert Graham, Los Angeles, May 3, 1999.

Installation of the Great Doors on May 21, 2002. *Source: Roger Cardinal Mahony*

thick at the hinges and so massive that they must be opened with a motorized hydraulic system" are cast bronze weighing five tons.[8] According to Graham himself, the doors would "serve not only as the physical entry point but also as a symbol of the unique nature of Catholicism in the Americas, a fusion of indigenous influence and iconography with Roman Catholic hierarchy and dogma."[9]

The doors were described, at the time of the their installation, in *Cathedral Chapters:*

> The two doors are cast in bronze, and each door has a smaller door built into it. It is the smaller ten-foot-tall by thirteen-foot-wide doors that act as the entrance for parishioners. The smaller doors will have the most activity, as they will be the ones to open and close on a regular basis. The larger doors will open for special and large occasions requiring a higher capacity of pedestrian traffic in and out the cathedral.

---

[8]Los Angeles *Times,* February 26, 2000.
[9]Quoted by Lorenza Munoz in Los Angeles *Times* Magazine, March 5, 2000.

The smaller doors include ancient Christian symbols and various images of the Virgin Mary in the New World. The doors also feature a depiction of images and symbols of the ethnic and cultural diversity of the Los Angeles Archdiocese. [10]

Graham's statue of Our Lady of the Angels is not only distinctive but also somewhat controversial. One account notes that the statue is

> Unlike any other. Suspended above the bronze doors, she is youthful with a feminine sinuousness and understated athleticism. She stands on an upturned crescent moon in keeping with the Catholic view of Mary as Queen of Heaven. She is wearing a full-length dress with billowing sleeves.
>
> Behind Mary's head is a bronze rectangular backdrop through which a round skylight is cut. As the sun courses through the sky, its light will pass at various angles through the skylight to create a halo effect around her,[11]

Another commentator, Pulitzer Prize winner Jack Miles, told *The Tidings* "the figure of Our Lady has various meanings. She changes to some extent depending on what's happening to moveable parts of the doors. When the doors are closed, she is an image of prayerful humility with her hands outstretched and eyes downcast. She reminds viewers of the scriptural saying, "Behold the handmaid of the Lord." However, the meaning of her downward gesture changes when the doors are open. Then she beckons people through the doors and into the cathedral sanctuary. The figure is presented as a woman standing on the moon and clothed in the sun. She reminds viewers of the Book of Revelation, Chapter 12, when a woman traditionally identified as the Blessed Virgin appears at the end of time."[12]

Another writer said that the eight-foot statue of the Virgin Mary "could be the woman piloting the No. 3 bus along Sunset Boulevard, the one who served you lunch today in Little Tokyo or wiped your brow as you lay in a Boyle Heights hospital bed. She could even be that statuesque supermodel type—those sinewy arms, those lofty cheekbones—breezing by on the Santa Monica Promenade."

> Hovering twenty feet above the cathedral plaza, the statue of Our Lady is set within a gold T-shaped section of the tympanum, a rectangular area above the doors. The tympanum is

---

[10]*Cathedral Chapters,* VI, #2, Summer 2002.
[11]Los Angeles *Times,* February 26, 2000.
[12]Los Angeles *Times,* May 31, 2002.

Great Doors of the cathedral. *Source: Julius Schulman & David Glomb*

scored with three horizontal lines that, according to Miles, represent the Father, the Son and the Holy Spirit. A halo of natural light, created by a large opening in the tympanum, surrounds her head.

Her feet are bare, as are her long graceful arms, and she wears no headdress—one of several striking departures from traditional Medieval and Renaissance images of Mary.

Her palms are turned outward, as if welcoming worshippers into the House of God, and she stands on a crescent moon, an allusion to the biblical description of a woman presumed to be Mary, "clothed in the sun with the moon under her foot." Some observers have told Graham that the statue's powerful bearing puts them in mind of another strong, devout female servant of God: Joan of Arc.[13]

The magnificent book by Robert Graham on *The Great Bronze Doors for the Cathedral of Our Lady of the Angels*[14] identifies and explains the symbology of the doors thusly:

Left Inner Door, left to right

1. Virgin of Pomata—This image from the Andes village comes from the late-colonial School of Cuzco. Mary wears a feathered Inca headdress and a billowing dress suggestive of Pachamama, the Inca mountain goddess.
2. Apocalyptic Virgin/Immaculate Conception—Inspired by Revelations 12, Mary is depicted with powerful wings crushing the satanic serpent. The lily symbolizes her purity.
3. *Ex Voto* to Virgin of Guadalupe—As the text below the image indicates, the child was healed by the mother's prayers to the Virgin of Guadalupe. The mother has left this picture at the Guadalupe shrine as an offering, an *ex voto* to thank Mary for her intercession.
4. Divine Shepherdess—Mary is depicted reclining in the field with four sheep to commemorate her appearance to a holy Spanish monk.
5. Virgin of the Candlestick with Virgin of Belen—The large image shows Mary again in a billowing dress from the School of Cuzco. She holds a blanket over her arms and cradles the Infant Jesus. The small images are of Mary as she appeared in Belen, Peru.

---

[13]Reed Johnson in Los Angeles *Times,* September 1, 2002.
[14]Los Angeles 2002.

6. The Virgin of the Rosary of Chichinquira—Saint Andrew flanks Mary on the right and Saint Anthony on the left. Saint Anthony, known as "the Christographer" is depicted with an image of Jesus on a book. Robert Graham used his mother's rosary to adorn the image.
7. Virgin of Mercy—The souls in purgatory are protected by the Virgin' cloak as they beg for her intercession.

Right Inner Door, left to right

8. Virgin of Guadalupe—In remembrance of her appearance to the Aztec peasant, San Juan Diego, the image depicts the thornless roses she instructed him to pluck in the cold of winter. Mary stands on the moon, with the sun over her head.
9. Virgin of the Cave—In the Spanish Caribbean this image of Mary was miraculously recovered from a cave and could bring about miracles.
10. Virgin of Montserrat—One of the "Black Madonnas" of Europe, Mary holds a black Jesus in this image from Catalonia.
11. Pieta—Depicted often in historic works of art, this is the image of Mary embracing her crucified Son.
12. Chalice with Sheep—The sheep of Christ's flock drink His blood, which spurts from a pierced hand into the chalice, reminiscent of the Holy Eucharist.
13. *Mater Dolorosa,* the Sorrowful Mother—At the top of Mary's image are the instruments of the Crucifixion.
14. *La Mano Todopodereosa,* the All-Powerful Hand—Anna, Mary, Jesus, Joseph and Joachim are depicted on the five fingers. Anna and Joachim were Mary's parents.
15. Virgin of Loreto with the Litany of Loreto—Mary is depicted with angels. Excerpts from the Litany of Loreto fill in the background, including "Queen of Poland" in honor of Pope John Paul II.

Left Inner Door, beginning first row on the left, top to bottom

1. Goose
2. Southwest Indian Flying Serpent
3. Chumash Man
4. Peacock Barge
5. Griffin
6. Chinese Turtle
7. Ibis
8. Griffin
9. Fish
10. Hand of God

Cardinal Mahony, Robert Graham and the statue
of Our Lady of the Angels. *Source: William Nettles
for Robert Graham Studios*

11. Eagle (St. John the Evangelist)
12. Dove
13. Bee
14. Celtic Serpents
15. Stag
16. Croatian Cross
17. Chumash Condor
18. Peacock
19. Falling Man
20. Tree of Jesse

Paschal Candle in front of the tapestry depicting the Baptism of Jesus by John.
Source: Fred Balak

Right Inner Door, beginning first row, top to bottom

21. Energy (soul)
22. Lion
23. Water
24. Lamb
25. Hand (listening symbol)
26. Chinese/Japanese Heaven Symbol
27. Pair of Ostriches
28. Rooster
29. Bull (St. Luke the Evangelist)
30. Trefoil (Celtic Trinity)
31. Dog
32. Sicilian Legs (regeneration symbol)

33. Bull
34. Serpent/Dragon
35. I Ching/Ti Chi
36. Samoan Kava Bowl
37. Foot
38. Celtic Monster
39. Raven Eating Man's Liver
40. Dolphin

Pews and Chairs

The 138 cherry wood pews adorning the Cathedral of Our Lady of the Angels were fashioned by Norberto Gutierrez in his workshop in Tijuana, Mexico. After submitting a prototype of his work, Gutierrez was commissioned to provide pews that would seat approximately 3,000 people.

Gutierrez and his twenty co-workers labored for ten months fabricating the pews; each one is a different length and angled to fit with the

Cardinal Mahony and Monsignor Kevin Kostelnik inspect the pews at the workshop in Tijuana. *Source: The Tidings*

sloping of the cathedral's walls. The aesthetic simplicity of the pews allows for comfort, because Gutierrez recalled Saint Therese of Lisieux's dictum that "the first ingredient for prayer is getting into a comfortable position."

Gutierrez told one reporter that the cardinal required, as part of his contract, that he pay a "living wage" to his co-workers. And, he noted, that the cardinal checked to see if he was abiding by his contract. The longest of the pews is thirty-three feet. "Visitors have commended the simplicity and beauty of their design and their surprisingly high level of comfort."[15]

Pews and chairs. *Source: Fred Balak*

[15]*Downtown News,* August 23, 2002.

Chapter XIII

Dedication

That the new cathedral, reported to be the "third largest in the world"[1] could have been envisioned, designed and erected within the span of four and one half years is unparalled in the construction trade. C. Terry Dooley said that without Cardinal Mahony's day-to-day involvement, it would never have been completed on schedule: "The cardinal is a hard-driving American chief executive officer. Once he decided to do it and got backing from a number of important people, he wanted to get it done."[2] And he did it on schedule.

The previous dedication of a Roman Catholic cathedral in the United States occurred in 1971 with the opening of Saint Mary Cathedral in San Francisco. The Bishop of Dodge City likes to claim that his Cathedral of Our Lady of Guadalupe was the first built in this millennium, dedicated as it was on December 9, 2001. Cardinal Mahony disputes the claim, however. He was there when the church opened and has said that Our Lady of Guadalupe didn't really fit the definition of a cathedral: "I was there and it was very nice," he said, "but it was built primarily to be a parish and they designated it as a cathedral as well." Mahony believes that in the classical sense, a cathedral should be located in the heart of a city where it can engage "in conversation with the public, political, civil and cultural community." Our Lady of Guadalupe is built on an eight-acre parcel of land located in a rural setting on the outskirts of Dodge. [3]

The Labor Day weekend was chosen for the dedication, not only because it recalled the Feast of Our Lady of the Angels, but as a holiday weekend, it guaranteed that the downtown area would be relatively free of traffic. It was an ideal occasion for Catholics and their friends and admirers to gather for the inauguration of the southland's most prestigious religious edifice. One commentator said that "the Labor Day service may have been the grandest church ritual ever performed in Los Angeles."[4]

A year and a half before the scheduled dedication, Cardinal Mahony issued a list of dedicatory events that would surround the Feast of Our Lady of the Angels in the year 2002. He announced that the 600-car park-

---

[1]San Diego *Union Tribune,* September 3, 2002.

[2]*Ibid.,* August 30, 2002

[3]See an essay by Sandra Marquez in the Antelope Valley *Press,* September 4, 2002.

Blessing of the Foundation Stone on March 19, 2002.

ing garage would be open on April 1, 2002 and, the Cathedral Conference Center on April 5. Shortly thereafter the Plaza Gift Shop and Café would be ready for public use. Noting that the new cathedral would maintain "the visible presence of the Catholic Church in the historical center of Los Angeles," the new house-of-worship would "serve as a vital spiritual center for millions of Catholics as well as the general community for centuries to come."[5]

Less than five years after its ground was broken and blessed, thousands of people gathered in the new Cathedral of Our Lady of the Angels for a three and a half hour dedicatory ceremony which began with the ritualistic tapping on the Bronze Doors by the pastor.

Under a sky billowing with clouds, in sweltering 95-degree heat, 565 cardinals, bishops, priests and several thousand invited guests moved into the air-conditioned interior in a procession that lasted forty-five minutes. Guests entered to the accompaniment of Beethoven's "Ode to Joy" booming from the huge organ, punctuated by Scottish and Nigerian drums. "What followed was an elaborate multicultural ritual to

---

[4]Los Angeles *Daily News,* September 3, 2002.
[5]AALA, Dedication Events," June 19, 200.

consecrate a building sunlit through alabaster into a Catholic church whose members profess the light of Jesus Christ."[6]

The cardinal greeted everyone with the words: "Welcome to the city's and to your new cathedral."

> This cathedral must be much more than an optical delight for those who chance upon its beauty in the shifting shadows of the day. Is all this splendor and architectural artistry enough for us? Can we rest content with the beauty arising from this spot? We must answer an emphatic, "No!" Not as a kind of cultural treasure was the cathedral built. As a vibrant symbol of God's habitat in our city, this outer form must find an echo in the inner graces of a people who listen intently to God's Word as it comes to us as challenge and consolation.

The Mass was highlighted by the rites of dedication, anointing of the altar, the incensation and lighting of the church. The fifty-five-voice choir rendered music from the early ages as well as more contemporary composers. In one part of the ceremony, the cardinal singled out three lay people for their contribution:

> Architect Jose Rafael Moneo, for his "artistic genius and vision." He has given the entire church a new path on which to travel for decades to come.
>
> Sir Daniel Donohue, head of the Dan Murphy Foundation, whose lead gift set the financing for the cathedral in motion. "He stepped forward in a heroic manner and because of the leadership of the Murphy Foundation, the Thomas and Dorothy Leavey Foundation [the other lead donor] and so many wonderful people–Catholics and others—the cathedral is now fully funded."
>
> William Close, Cathedral Advisory Board vice-chairman, who "represented the totality of dedication and commitment from so many volunteers. No one has exemplified the role of the cathedral builder more than he."[7]

Cardinal Mahony confided to a friend that he spent "many hours" preparing his remarks for the dedication homily which is printed here in its entirety:

> It is truly fitting that we begin today's celebration at a site alongside the *El Camino Real*. The 18th century Spanish

---

[6]Los Angeles *Daily News,* September 3, 2002.
[7]*The Tidings,* September 6, 2002.

Franciscans trod, up and down that fabled road, as California's first evangelizers. They inaugurated God's active plan of salvation for all who, ultimately, came north and west to make their home in this Golden State. Today we are writing an important chapter—not, assuredly, the last—to that unfolding story of God's saving intentions for the people of California. We celebrate the liturgical dedication of the altar and the cathedral of Our Lady of the Angels in our state's most diverse and decidedly most global city.

Today, we offer our praise to God for this new cathedral church. Yet we do not gather here simply to celebrate its architectural and artistic achievements. These give homage to God and, together, we speak our thanks for the inspiration and artistry engraved in this soaring edifice. But we gather here mainly to reflect more deeply on the significance of this cathedral church.

We have just heard Scriptures which invite us to understand the cathedral, not primarily in the context of the sweeping Los Angeles skyline, but more profoundly, within the rich faith tradition paved, as a layered memory, in the *El Camino Real.* That tradition impels us to consider three points:

- How our new cathedral church can make us more aware of God's presence in our everyday lives;
- How hearing God's transforming Word might truly change our lives and send us forth to live out that Word;
- What it means for us as a people to be built up, stone by stone, into that spiritual house, the living temple of the Lord.

In today's first reading, Nehemiah and the people finish restoring the city's devastated ancient walls and gates, destroyed by Israel's enemies. Once desolate and demoralized, they now realize once more God's presence with them, and allow that presence to be more deeply rooted in their lives. Nehemiah convokes them; invites them to listen afresh to God's Word; reminds them that God journeys alongside them in their city, in their daily treks, and in their lives.

For the Jewish people, the visible and eternal city of Jerusalem and its temple were the bedrock for their often fragile hopes, a gleaming reminder that God's tent was pitched in their land. These visible signs of God's dwelling among them— holy city and temple—gave direction to their own journey through life.

Luke's Gospel recounts how Jesus responds, first, to the desire of Zacchaeus to see Him from afar, from the safety of the

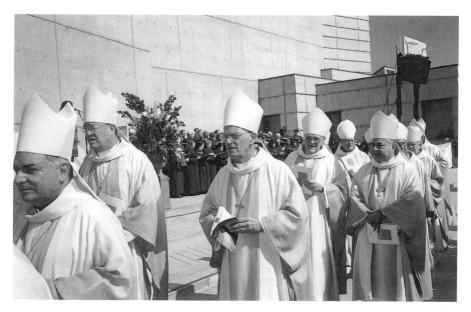

Cardinals, archbishops, bishops, priests and hundreds of laity attended the cathedral's dedication. *Source: The Tidings*

sycamore tree; then to Zacchaeus' hope that Jesus might enter his house, his life, and, indeed, transform him in ways he never would have dreamed. But this smallish Zacchaeus must first find a good vantage point—a place from which he could see Jesus–a sycamore tree.

Does not this longing in the heart of Zacchaeus evoke a similar yearning deep within our own hearts to see God, to know His gentle and enduring presence? Like the Jewish people of Nehemiah's time, like those living in the time of Jesus, and like the pioneer evangelizers who traversed the length of California, we, too, yearn to have some visible anchor of God's presence within our midst. Our new Cathedral is that anchor for the ages.

Today, the Cathedral of Our Lady of the Angels joins the storied ranks of the early missions, the first permanent structures built across the California landscape. It sinks its foundations in the very heart of the City of Los Angeles, astride *El Camino Real*—today's less colorfully named Hollywood Freeway—where it will stand and soar for many centuries as a sign of God's enduring presence in our lives and community.

The Cathedral of Our Lady of the Angels was the site of an inter-faith prayer service on September 11, 2002.

Millions of people travel the 101 Freeway each year. I expect that many will have their lives brushed by God—some profoundly changed—as they glance at the great cross on the east side, or the grand campanile on the west side. The road which leads to this spot becomes a different kind of *camino real,* closer to the route the friars first imagined, a road to Christ our King. Many motorists may exit the freeway allured by this towering icon of God's dwelling with us. Within every human heart stirs some, often unnamed, thirst for its creator. No substitute can ever quench that deep-seated thirst. In the shadow of his outpost cathedral, the Bishop of Hippo, St. Augustine, wrote: "You have made us for yourself, Lord, and our hearts are restless until they rest in you."

Like Zacchaeus, we, too, long to see Jesus. Unlike Zacchaeus, however, we need not search out a fragile bough on a sycamore tree. The cathedral is our perch. From here we glimpse our great city of many cities, the home of peoples of many races, lands, and languages. As people cast their eyes upon this perch, from their many perches in downtown office skyscrapers, or from one of the vistas along Temple or Grand, or from one of the many major freeways converging near here, hearts will catch up with where eyes have set their gaze. At long last, there is a noble great church at the heart of Los Angeles, radiating out toward the civic and governmental hub, the commercial, residential, and cultural focal points of our city— all astride the historic and history-laden *El Camino Real.*

But this cathedral must be much more than an optical delight for those who chance upon its beauty in the shifting shadows of the day. We might ask, with the poet John Dunne, for whom this cathedral bell doth toll? For those who lie ill in the USC—County Hospital and other nearby hospitals and rest homes, the peal of the great bells in the campanile will ring a sound of solace. For the elderly and lonely, dwelling within the circle of these bells' sway, its tolling might become, in time, a familiar echo, evoking remembered joys. For those, in the too-many and over-populated jails downtown, we pray that the ringing of these cathedral bells soften their fettered burdens and instill some sense of inner peace that no one can snatch away. For our Catholic sensibilities, the sounding of church bells ring out a clarion message of good news: we are redeemed, even us sinners, and summoned by the bells to a close intimacy with God.

Is all this splendor and architectural artistry enough for us? Can we rest content with the beauty arising from this spot? We must answer, an emphatic "NO"! Not as a kind of cultural treasure was the cathedral built. As a vibrant symbol of God's habitat in our city, this outer form must find an echo in the inner graces of a people who listen intently to God's Word as it comes to us as challenge and consolation.

Nehemiah and Ezra not only read God's Word but broke it open so that the people could savor its meaning and put it into practice. The people who received that Scripture with open hearts wept, as it dawned on them how frequently they had been unfaithful to that Word. But the ministers in the restored temple convinced them not to mourn. Rather, they stirred the people on to find unutterable joy in the Word which embraced them: "This day is holy to the Lord your God . . . the joy of the Lord is your strength."

The Word of God is fruitful when it truly transforms us. In today's Gospel, Zacchaeus embodies this transforming faith. Like few others, he came into a direct personal contact with Jesus the very Word—the Son of God. This encounter remarkably shook up Zacchaeus. He welcomes Jesus into his home, despite the mocking ridicule of the self-righteous who scorned him as an outsider. Zacchaeus realizes that his past life stands in sharp contradiction to the person of Jesus toward whom he is now so urgently drawn. With spontaneous gratitude, he volunteers: "Behold, half of my possessions, Lord, I shall give to the poor, and if I have extorted anything from anyone I shall repay it four times over."

This cathedral exists to effect in us an extraordinary transformation like that of Zacchaeus. Only a deep personal encounter with God's Word can bring this about. It is not enough that we merely hear the Word of God here, or take note of it as "interesting." Rather, just as Zacchaeus, who had not set out that morning with any inkling of welcoming Jesus into his home that day, so, we too, must welcome the Word and allow ourselves to be transformed by it.

Only when that occurs will this majestic cathedral begin to fulfill the dream and meet the expectations which have been ours from its beginnings; only when that happens will it be worth all the effort, struggles and resources poured out to make this cathedral a reality. Only when that happens does this structure merit the name, "cathedral."

When the transforming Word of God takes root in our lives, the light of God can light up our hearts. As the psalmist so ardently prays: " In your light, we see light." One of the most conspicuously beautiful features of this building stands forth when the sun's beams are at play across the interior of the cathedral, highlighting nuanced colors and patterns, refracted through the alabaster that laces this space. This evokes an awareness of the brilliant light of God's love soaking into us and bathing us with its warmth and healing.

No one should leave this spot untouched by God's reshaping Word. A traveling family, tourists, truck drivers or a carpool of co-workers on the Hollywood Freeway; an isolated person or small group coming for prayer; people in the neighborhood for whom this will be their regular place of worship—as much their local church as a great cathedral—each will feel God's own touch and presence and be opened to the light of God touching their own deepest places, the geography of their own hearts.

God's Word always calls us to move beyond our fears and limitations, to take risks that will fashion us more and more into God's image. Anyone who comes here should continue on their journey with a replenished spirit of respect for all other peoples—in a special way, rendering thanks for the gift of ethnic diversity in this great urban center. No traces of discrimination or racism are to be found in this space. God's temple is a house for all peoples. All are invited to the banquet. No one is excluded because of race, color, gender or national origins. Nor, as Zacchaeus shows us, is this a place only for those who manage to keep each and every detail of the law.

Be assured that the fullness of the Gospel of Life will be proclaimed here, and each human life, from its earliest moments to its eldest years, will find in this place nurture and respect. We will work together here to heal differences, be they among family members, co-workers, or sectors in the city. The great cathedrals have been shaped by the craft and loving skills of countless artisans, many anonymous. Here we will strive to become different kinds of artisans, of peace and good-will, forging links among diverse groups.

Touched by God's Word, we sense that we are inter-dependent, one people, one community. All must profit from our bounty and be empowered to share in the good things for which Los Angeles is known across the globe. God's Word calls us to nothing less: no one can be excluded; one neighborhood must not be walled off from another. The gifts received within these walls must overflow as we leave this space.

A cathedral achieves its destiny when the mystery of the Church is fully lived out: in the gathering of God's People; in

Both supporters and protestors took an active part in the cathedral's dedication. *Source: The Tidings*

the celebration of the Eucharist and the sacramental life of the Church. Every Eucharist is both a gathering and a sending, and both are only possible by the prior action of God.

The reading from the First Letter of Peter reminds us that Jesus, the corner stone, was sent by the Father to renew all creation. Peter then urges us to allow ourselves, like living stones, to "be built into a spiritual house to be a holy priesthood to offer spiritual sacrifices acceptable to God through Jesus Christ." God surely dwells within His people, "a temple built of living stones, founded on the apostles with Jesus Christ its corner stone."

God continues to build up the Church, the Body of Christ, as a holy city, "enlivened by the Spirit, and cemented together by love." The 135 men, women, and children visible along the walls of the nave serve as our models. The saints and blesseds call us to be ever more faithful in our discipleship with the Lord Jesus, as we move forward with them to the fullness of the kingdom. The power to become a new spiritual house of the Lord flows from the Word of God, but just as potently, that grace emanates from the celebration of the Eucharist. The power of the Eucharist is expressed symbolically and spiritually through the concentric stone floor circles that begin at the base of the altar and eventually envelop everyone in the cathedral.

As we journey out from the cathedral, we encounter the plaza or Cathedral Square, a vitally important part of this hallowed ground. St. Thomas More, we recall, situated his *Utopia,* his conversation about a more humane and just city, in the Cathedral Square before the towering cathedral in Antwerp. In our Cathedral Square, the dreams of cooperative living—even with those who never darken a cathedral's door—will drift across the plaza stones. Linked to Cathedral Squares throughout the ages, and throughout the world, it is from our plaza that we go forth—forging links to commerce, in the fairs and selling booths; links to politics, in the concerned voices for a more just society. The plaza is a venue for outdoor dialogue about the greatness that we, together, might achieve as a city.

Links across social classes are also strengthened. The great bishop, Saint John Chrysostom, insisted that the poor and rich mingle in the square, expressing the unity celebrated in the Eucharist. We are linked, too, in those celebrations which remind us that God is glorified when the human family is fully, even playfully, alive: in the fiestas and religious dramas outside the Cathedral steps. Here in Los Angeles we have built a capacious plaza which demonstrates the relationship of the

One of the largest gatherings of hierarchy in the state's history attended the cathedral dedication.

cathedral to the longings of our larger city. Hearing the words "The Mass is ended, Go in peace," we are sent forth to be a leaven and a light at the heart of this city, every city. It is the Spirit of God, Spirit of Christ, impelling us, doing more in and through us than we could ever ask or imagine.

It is the one and same Spirit who led the 18th century Franciscans to evangelize California, carrying the Gospel message as they trod the *Camino Real*. It is the Spirit of God, Spirit of Christ, who has challenged and consoled generation after generation of Catholics throughout Southern California, and today has gathered us here for the dedication liturgy of the Cathedral of Our Lady of the Angels.

It is the same Spirit who is stirring now in our hearts as we are ready to make the Profession of Faith for the first time in the cathedral, our voices rising in proclamation of a living faith from the time of the apostolic church until now, at this time and in this place. Let our proclamation echo to the ends of the earth: We believe in one, holy, catholic and apostolic Church. We stand amidst that blessed communion of saints, women and men, young and old, heroic and humble, sung and unsung, as we prepare to invoke their names in litany. Hallowing the altar with the relics of saints and blesseds we are unceasingly reminded of the faith of those who have gone before us, leading us onward, interceding for us and strengthening us in our call to holiness.

And as we lift up our hearts in the prayer of dedication of the cathedral altar, we enter more fully into the mystery of Christ's Church, a Church fruitful, holy, favored, and exalted. For the Church is the very Body of Christ—member for member—a living sacrifice of praise to the glory of God the Father. Transformed by the Word, strengthened by the celebration of the sacraments, we, the Body, become a spiritual house, a living temple of the Lord, more radiant still than the hallowed ground on which we stand, and even more resplendent than the grandeur which today we behold.

From this day forward, the stones of this building will sing, echoes rolling down the ages, telling of love and justice through the lives of all who come and go from this "house of prayer for all peoples." [8]

There were other related religious and cultural activities in the days that followed, none of which was more symbolic and prayerful as the one for the city's non-Catholics. The cardinal wanted the cathedral to be a house of prayer for everyone, for peoples of all faiths. To encourage that sense of inclusiveness, approximately seventy local religious leaders representing diverse faiths–including Hindu, Buddhist, Muslim, Sikh, Baha', Jewish, numerous Christian denominations along with the major artisans were invited to a prayer service and reception on September 4, 2002. Father Alexei Smith, director of the archdiocesan Office of Ecumenical and Interreligious Affairs, said "The archdiocese is opening up the cathedral to these different faith groups on these special days, and it's certainly the beginning of the many things we hope to do."[9]

Rabbi Lawrence Goldmark spoke for others when he said that

Over the years I've had a wonderful relationship with the archdiocese in many ways. Highlights have included being invited to meet Pope John Paul II during his 1987 trip to Los Angeles, participating on a religious radio program with local Catholic priests, and having Cardinal Mahony accept our invitation to address a group of 250 rabbis at a meeting of the

---

[8]AALA, "Dedicatory Address," September 2, 2002.
[9]*The Tidings,* August 2, 2002.

Cathedral Recorded in Rome

The Cathedral of Our Lady of the Angels has joined a prestigious group on the floor of Saint Peter's Basilica in Rome. The Los Angeles' new cathedral is now inscribed on Saint. Peter's floor alongside other major cathedrals of the world–between Saint John Lateran Basilica in Rome, the pope's actual cathedral, and the Cathedral Church of La Plata in Sucre, Bolivia, and adjacent to the Cathedral of Mexico City.

The story behind the inscription is simple. "Given the very large size of the interior of Saint Peter's Basilica, they have placed inscriptions in the floor as if your own cathedral or basilica were placed inside St. Peter's," Cardinal Mahony observed. "It shows you how far back your own church is in comparison to Saint Peter's. The dimensions are done in meters, and outside wall to outside wall."

The actual inscription reads: *Ecclesia Cathedralis B.V.M. Angelorum in California, M. 120.62,*" indicating meters (or 395,735 feet in length).

The only cathedrals in the United States represented on the floor are Saint Patrick's (New York); the Cathedral of the Holy Cross (Boston); and the National Shrine of the Immaculate Conception (Washington, D.C).

Board of Rabbis of Southern California where he spoke about the importance of interfaith dialogue.

It was the first time in anyone's memory that an archbishop of Los Angeles had taken time to address our board members; it was special for me. I think it serves a purpose to gain understanding between our two faiths, and I expect that collaboration to continue with the new cathedral[10]

The Cathedral of Our Lady of the Angels will be observed and written about for many years to come. It would seem premature at this juncture to make any definitive statements beyond the obvious. The architectural writer for the Los Angeles *Times* spoke for his colleagues by simply observing "The grandeur of its interior will instantly make it the city's most glorious public space."[11]

There were other reactions worth recalling. David Littlejohn of the *Wall Street Journal* called the structure "the most impressive large interior space ever built in Los Angeles," a building that has "nothing to do with the entertainment industry and very little to do with the wealthy Anglo businessmen and politicians who have decided since the 1920s what this sprawl of a city would look like." The architect created an exterior that is "intentionally blank and introspective" encouraging people to penetrate the enclosure to discover the "wondrous, light-filled world inside."[12]

John King of the San Francisco *Chronicle* observed that the structure is "a triumph that conveys the essence of both religious faith and great architecture." He called the new Cathedral of Our Lady of the Angels "the most significant building to open in the United States this year."[13]

Time magazine's Richard Lacayo labeled the dedication a "signal event . . . with roots simultaneously in the here and now and in the sunlit antiquity of the Mediterranean rim."[14] Alan Hess of the San Jose *Mercury* wrote that Moneo had designed a "landmark building" distinguished by "clean, sharp edged abstraction."[15]

Finally Paul Goldberger of *The New Yorker* suggested that the plaza "manages to be a true public place–the poor man's Getty Center, which is not an insignificant achievement." Liking the interior, which is a "sumptuous modern space," he concluded that the architect had made a "valiant

---

[10]*Ibid.*
[11]September 2, 2002.
[12]September 3, 2002
[13]September 13, 2002.
[14]"To the Lighthouse," September 2, 2002.
[15]September 3, 2002.

effort to render sacred space on a large scale, and he has done it without tricks or gimmicks."[16]

There were even more plaudits on the local level. Placido Domingo said that Moneo "had created a grand opera, but one out of stone." Eli Broad said that the cathedral is "not designed to be a piece of contemporary architecture, like Disney Hall. The cathedral is making a different kind of statement–it's a statement of permanence." Rabbi Uri D. Herscher of the Skirball Cultural Center remarked that the cathedral was "very different from any European cathedral that I've ever seen. Moneo's architecture provides a more intense relationship between the worshipper and what the cathedral means; the size is not so grandiose that the worshipper feels diminished." Finally, author Richard Rodriguez noted that "it recalls rather dramatically, by engaging a Spanish architect, Los Angeles to its Spanish Catholic roots, which the city has deliberately tried to ignore, in its purposeful blonde way, for the past 150 years."[17]

Imagine Paris without Notre Dame, Mexico City without its Metropolitan Cathedral, New York with out St. Patrick's. More than a public monument, "a great cathedral serves as a spiritual beacon that draws the faithful with the curious, the bored with the desperate, the sainted with the pickpockets, as if all of them were looking for the same thing."[18]

How can anyone in the future describe or remember Los Angeles without mentioning the Cathedral of Our Lady of the Angels?

---

[16]September 23, 2002.
[17]Quoted by Los Angeles *Times,* September 2, 2002.
[18]Mary Rourke in Los Angeles *Times,* September 18, 1997.

Appendix 1

Nomenclature—Our Lady of the Angels

The selection of Our Lady of the Angels as the patroness for the southland's magnificent new cathedral has an historically long and richly significant precedent which dates back to 1769 and the beginnings of Christianity in Alta California.

The provenance of the title itself can be traced to Fray Juan Crespi (1721–1782), the Mallorcan-born friar who accompanied the Gaspár de Portolá expedition of 1769–1770 as diarist. All subsequent writers accepted his generic terminology, though not a few were guilty of textual corruption.

Crespi recorded that late in the afternoon of July 31, 1769, the explorers crossed an *arroyo* of muddy water and stopped a little further on in a wide clearing. He had stated that the next day was one of rest "for the purpose of exploring, and especially to celebrate the jubilee of Our Lady of Los Angeles de Porciúncula," a liturgical commemoration observed only in the Franciscan calendar.

The following morning on the vigil of the feast, the expeditionary force continued its journey and came through a pass between two hills into a broad valley abounding in poplar and alder trees. A beautiful brook crossed the valley and later turned around a hill to the south. After traveling three more leagues, the Spaniards camped along a river which they appropriately named "in honor of *Nuestra Señora de los Angeles de Porciúncula,*" a title derived from the day's sanctoral cycle.

Authorities are in general agreement that the name of the town established adjacent to the *Río Porciúncula* in the fall of 1781, was taken from the title of the nearby river. Fray Francisco Palóu (1723–1789), a contemporary observer, related that "work was begun with a few families in founding the projected town of *Nuestra Señora de los Angeles* on the banks of the river named *Porciúncula.*"

When Felipe de Neve decided to set up the town, he incorporated the religious title of the river and the popular appellation of Assisi's chapel in the name and the result was *El Pueblo de Nuestra Señora de los Angeles de Porciúncula.* The initial church in the *pueblo* was erected as

This statue of Our Lady of the Angels, the work of Professor E. Pattarino, was enshrined in the old cathedral before being moved to the new Mother-church of the archdiocese.

an *asistencia* of Mission San Gabriel. Its name was taken from that of the town in much the same way as the *pueblo* received its title after that of the river, a fact confirmed by the first entry in the baptismal register of the church, written in the hand of Fray Gerónimo Boscana (1775–1831), which read: "*Dia 4 Marzo de 1823, en la Iglesia de este Pueblo de Ntra. Sra. de los Angeles. . . .*"

By the time that Bishop Thaddeus Amat moved the seat for the Diocese of Monterey-Los Angeles to the southland in 1859, the official patroness of the jurisdiction was Saint Vibiana and it was under her patronage that Amat's cathedral was erected in 1876.

In 1943 Archbishop John J. Cantwell revealed his intention of building a new cathedral for the Archdiocese of Los Angeles which would be placed under the patronage of Our Lady of the Angels. On July 11, 1945, Cantwell issued a pastoral letter about the proposed new cathedral which he planned to locate atop a block long site on Wilshire Boulevard at Hudson Avenue.

With Cantwell's demise and the installation of a new archbishop in 1948, priorities changed and plans for a new Mother Church were put aside in favor of educational facilities.

Several times during the ensuing years the existing Cathedral of Saint Vibiana was renovated and otherwise restructured until the venerable edifice suffered irreparable damage during the Northridge earthquake of 1994.

As early as 1962, Roman officials hinted at the desirability of changing the patronage of Saint Vibiana Cathedral to that of Our Lady of Angels. Subsequently, the remains of Vibiana were removed from their place of prominence and replaced by a life-size porcelain statue of Our Lady of the Angels by the renown artist, Eugenio Pattarino

Meanwhile in 1981, Timothy Cardinal Manning thought it would be appropriate to seek Roman authorization for changing the traditional feast day of Our Lady of the Angels from August 2nd to September 4th, the day on which the City of Los Angeles was founded in 1781. For the last twenty years, Los Angeles has been among the five American jurisdictions identifying title and patron.

It was shortly after the Northridge earthquake that Sir Daniel Donohue proposed the building of a wholly new cathedral for which he volunteered that the Dan Murphy Foundation would be the major contributor.

About the time that the initial plans to erect the cathedral on the site of the earlier edifice were put aside in favor of a new location alongside the Hollywood Freeway, Roger Cardinal Mahony decided to invoke the earlier Cantwell patronage of Our Lady of the Angels. Fittingly, the first great cathedral in all the world erected in the third millennium of the Christian era will be named for Mary, the Mother of the Savior.

Statue of Our Lady of the Angels as it was enthroned at Saint Vibiana Cathedral.

Foundation Mural

A short dedication ceremony was held at the cathedral on September 29, 2003 for the unveiling of the first in a series of contemplated murals depicting the establishment of the Catholic Church in Alta California.

Located in the wall near the south ambulatory or main entrance, the colorful mural is the work of Frank Alonzo Martinez. The Blessed Mother is portrayed as looking down on Blessed Junípero Serra while his Franciscan confreres, soldiers on horseback and settlers arrive in what would become the "Golden State."

Sponsored by the William H. Hannon Foundation, the mural expresses, in the words of its artist, what Fray Junipero Serra and his contemporaries must have felt as they confronted the obstacles and challenges of a new frontier for Christianity.

Appendix 2

History of the Cathedral Site

No evidence has been unearthed to substantiate the claim that the area now occupied by the Cathedral of Our Lady of the Angels was ever a Native American village or a cemetery. But the site does have an interesting history as was reported in an interview with a colorful local pioneer, Ralph Truglio, who lived for some years on a portion of the site when his family owned the Alpha Hotel.

For over three decades, the Alpha Hotel was an unassuming but well-kept men's residence until it was taken over by the city to be used as office space. Ralph recalled that his grandfather, Adamo Roberto, came to the United States from Southern Italy early in the 1900s to work for the railroad. He saved his money until be was able to buy a lease on a hotel near Temple and Main streets. Later he purchased a second hotel at 304 North Grand Avenue which he fixed up and named "Alpha". By 1925, Adamo had paid for the hotel which originally cost $12,000.

Ralph recalled that "on the ground floor, in addition to the owner's flat, was a barber shop and a dry cleaner. Across the street was another hotel, a creamery and a high Victorian house; to the north was California Street (where the Hollywood Freeway is located) and a few blocks away was the Red Top Can Company. There were palm trees all around" the site.

The Alpha Hotel was located on what was known as the Eichoiz tract. There were sixteen rooms at the Alpha Hotel and most were rented on a long-term basis and only to working bachelors.[1]

A portion of the sloping downtown parcel of land was inherited by Morris Levine from his mother in the 1930s. In 1947, the Los Angeles County Board of Supervisors condemned the land to put up a courthouse, paying Levine and the co-owner about $60,000 each.

When the county decided to locate the courthouse a few blocks away, Levine sued to force the county to abide by its original intentions. He lost but then launched a subsequent suit charging officials with conspiracy, fraud, misrepresentation, gross negligence and wasting $2.2 million in condemning the property and needlessly evicting tenants from the aging Victorian houses on the land. Levine pursued the case to the state Supreme Court —and lost again. Levine lived on until 1982, calling him-

---

[1]Mike Nelson, Interview in *The Tidings,* June 19, 1997.

Looking west on Temple Street. Spring Street is in the foreground and the Temple Block on the extreme left. The site of the Cathedral of Our Lady of the Angels would be at the top of the hill on the right. The photograph was probably taken sometime before 1900. *Source: Photo Collection/Los Angeles Public Library*

self "the attorney for the damned." He had succeeded Jerry Giesler as President of the local Criminal Courts Bar Association in 1956.[2]

In 1940, the State of California began purchasing property for what was then called the Hollywood Parkway. The envisioned 16.1-mile stretch would connect the San Fernando Valley with downtown Los Angeles. Controversial from the outset, the Hollywood Freeway plunged through crowded neighborhoods and necessitated the destruction of at least 2,000 buildings, including the Alpha Hotel. The last link of the freeway, completed in 1948, had longer on-ramps, wider lanes, paved shoulders and functional and banked curves to accommodate the speeding vehicles on what Bob Hope called the "biggest parking lot in the world." The area just south of the freeway as it approached the downtown interchange, called the "stack", was thereafter used as a parking lot.

---

[2]Cecilia Rasmussen, "L.A. Scene," Los Angeles *Times,* December 2, 1996.

The Alpha Hotel, located on the northeast corner of Temple Street and Grand Avenue, about 1923. In the 1930s, Temple was widened thereby cutting off about eight or ten feet of the buildings. In the early 1950s, the city purchased the hotel itself and converted it into an office for court reporters. Eventually the entire block was razed and became a parking lot. *Source: Archives of the Cathedral of Our Lady of the Angels*

Appendix 3

Patronage of Saint Vibiana

At the very time when California's soil was yielding up its richest deposits of gold to anxious prospectors, a treasure of quite another kind was unearthed in a subterranean canyon of far-away Rome.

Early in 1851, Pope Pius IX had purchased a vineyard on the outskirts of Rome directly above an extensive network of catacombs that had gone unexplored for almost a thousand years. Excavation of the area was entrusted by the Holy Father to the Pontifical Commission for Sacred Archeology which, at that time, was under the direction of the famous Giovanni Battista de Rossi.

Late in 1853, excavations were made in the vast necropolis of *Pretextatus,* to the left of the Appian Way, in that portion of the catacombs known as *San Sisto.* In the locality of *Bonfiglioli,* about a mile from *Porta di San Sebastiano,* workmen discovered an ancient entrance to the cemetery, in almost complete ruin. On December 9, a vault was unearthed containing a number of vials filled with aromatic spices, along with quite a few marble tablets with discernible epitaphs. Among the unbroken sepulchers was that of a certain "Vibiana." To the left and adjoining her tomb was a rose-colored crystal vase purportedly containing dried blood.

An inscribed marble tablet, seventy centimeters long and thirty wide, sealed the sepulcher. The plaque was unbroken, although cracked in several places. When workmen attempted to remove the tablet, the arch, weakened by the excavations, collapsed and partially buried the tomb. After the debris had been cleared away, they uncovered the skeleton of a young woman, apparently put to death in a violent fashion. The date of the maiden's demise, as well as other information about her person, could not be determined. However, from surrounding epitaphs archeologists conjectured that the youthful person had lived in the third century. The inscription read: "*Animae innocenti adque pudicae Vibiane in pace D. Pr. K. St*" (To the soul of the innocent and pure Vibiana, laid away the day before the kalends of September [August 31]. At the end of the inscription was a wreath of laurel, a character similar to the letter "Q" with foliate ornaments, an emblem commonly used by early Christians as a code symbolizing martyrdom.

After the relics had been carefully removed from the catacombs, Pope Pius IX ordered a hurried investigation to ascertain whether the designation "virgin and martyr" could be ascribed to Vibiana. Within a

Another depiction of Saint Vibiana is the one executed by Isabel Piczek for the rectory chapel at the old cathedral. It is now in Roger Cardinal Mahony's chapel in the new residence.

View of Saint Vibiana inside the shrine at the new cathedral. *Source: Archives of the Archdiocese of Los Angeles*

few weeks, a favorable decision was reached and "equivalent canonization" was bestowed on the third-century witness to the Faith.

In February 1854, shortly after their authentic character had been officially established, "the precious relics of the illustrious Virgin and glorious Martyr" were exposed for public veneration. As John J. Clifford of *The Tidings* put it in September 9, 1904:

> The process of her canonization may have been quick, in accordance with the discipline of the ancient Church, yet her name and fame were blotted out of the memory of men until God's own time for revealing her existence had appeared. There is no record of her life and martyrdom in the books in which such records are kept. The book of the *Acts of the Martyrs* is silent about her. The tablet which lay near her resting place, and the phial of blood are the mute witnesses of her existence and sanctity.

Public enthusiasm for the recently "proclaimed" virgin and martyr was manifested not only in the Eternal City, but in adjacent areas as well. A number of prominent ecclesiastics unsuccessfully petitioned the pope for custody of the relics. It remained for the newly- consecrated Bishop of Monterey to win the privilege, almost without asking. When Thaddeus

Amat was received by the Holy Father, on March 18, 1854, the pontiff conferred the precious relics of Saint Vibiana on Monterey's new ordinary with the express stipulation that a cathedral be erected in her honor.

The authentic document by which the Holy Father's Vicar General entrusted the relics to the prelate noted that the pope was giving to "The Most Illustrious Bishop of Monterey, Thaddeus Amat, the body of the maiden, Saint Vibiana, unearthed by mandate of Pius IX on December 9, 1853, from the Cemetery of Pretestato (San Sisto) along with a vial of her blood and also a marble slab bearing the inscription 'to the soul of the innocent and pure Vibiana, laid away the day before the Kalends of September.' We hereby affix to the wooden container our engraved testimonial, a chaplet of red colored silk to which is attached our seal."

After securely packing the relics in wooden crates, Bishop Amat and his traveling companions left for the United States. He sailed from Le Havre on May 19, and, after a routine three week crossing, arrived safely in New York. In mid-October, the prelate sailed aboard the *Aspinwall for* Colon City, on Limon Bay, in north central Panama. The voyage to the isthmus was remarkably calm and there was "not even a white cap on the waters." Transferring to the Pacific Mail Company's steamship, *John C. Stephens,* the party left Panama on November 1st and, two weeks later, reached San Francisco.

Following a short stay in the Bay City, Bishop Amat set out for Monterey. He then continued south on the coastwise schooner, *Powhattan.* According to one account, barely had the ship "reached the high seas when it seemed as though all the furies of the lower world had conspired to prevent the sacred relic from entering the diocese in which it was destined to be enshrined." Violent gales tossed the little vessel constantly, but in spite of the angry waters, the *Powhattan* arrived safely at Santa Barbara on December 2. The following Tuesday, the Feast of Santa Barbara, the relics, encased in their artistically-designed reliquary with a golden crown, were borne in solemn procession to the Church of Our Lady of Sorrows where a special shrine had been prepared to the right of the main altar. The local newspaper, taking note of the ceremonies, hoped that the relics might "possess a miraculous influence, in which case that town will become a resort."[1]

On March 28, 1856, Pope Pius IX granted the privilege of a special feast for Saint Vibiana in the Diocese of Monterey and declared the "virgin and martyr" principal patroness of the southland's ecclesiastical jurisdiction. Two years later, when Bishop Amat asked for and received papal approbation for the Association of Saint Vibiana. Pius IX prefaced his remarks about the new society with these words:

---

[1]Santa Barbara *Gazette,* December 6, 1855.

Since a pious society of the faithful of both sexes has been canonically erected in the Diocese of Monterey, under the title of Saint Vibiana, patroness of the diocese, and will be attached to the cathedral which Our venerable brother, the present Bishop of Monterey, has informed Us will be built in honor of this saint and martyr, We grant the following indulgences in order that this society may grow in influence and numbers:

(1) A plenary indulgence to those who join the society now and in the future, on the day of their entry if they have confessed and received Holy Communion;

(2) A plenary indulgence to those at the point of death who receive the sacraments, or if this is impossible, at least invoke the name of Jesus or say it in their hearts;

(3) A plenary indulgence to all members of the society on the feast day of the saint, provided that they receive the sacraments, either in the church of Saint Vibiana or in their own parish church, and that they pray for the peace of Christian peoples, the extirpation of heresy, and the exaltation of Holy Mother the Church;

(4) A plenary indulgence may be gained under the same conditions on any day of the octave of the saint, and also once a month on a day of one's own choosing;

(5) A partial indulgence of 100 days for any good work performed with a contrite heart

Bishop Amat had several aims in mind when he set up the society, among which were raising funds to help defray the building of the cathedral and the enrolling of all members in memorial books for which monthly Masses would be said at the shrine itself. Further interest and approval came on August 17, 1862, when Rome granted permission to transfer the solemnity of Saint Vibiana to the Sunday immediately following her feast day. In December of the following year, authorization was obtained to insert into the diocesan breviary supplement an historical account of Vibiana's discovery in the catacombs of the Eternal City.

On the afternoon of August 23, 1863, the Church of Our Lady of Sorrows was totally destroyed by fire. The tiny shrine housing the earthly remains of Vibiana was also consumed, but the relics of the saint, reposing in a glass and metal case, escaped unharmed. Although the reliquary was badly singed and the glass broken, no part of the relics, encased in a wax figure and clothed in silk garments, exhibited any effect of the conflagration. This seemingly miraculous event created wide commotion and did much to increase popular devotion to the diocesan patroness.

No provisions were made in the new church for a permanent shrine and, in 1868, the relics were brought to Los Angeles and placed in the Old

Plaza Church of *Nuestra Señora de los Angeles,* where they remained for the next eight years. The penultimate disposition of the relics occurred in 1876, when the cathedral dedicated to Vibiana's honor was solemnly consecrated by Archbishop Joseph Sadoc Alemany of San Francisco.

A solemn procession of translating the remains of Saint Vibiana from Our Lady of the Angels Church to the cathedral started from the Plaza at six o'clock in the evening, headed by the Mexican brass band. Several of the city's societies joined in the procession, followed by more than 200 children, all dressed in white. Father John Basso carried the metropolitan cross, followed by sixteen priests chanting the Litany of the Saints. The shrine itself was borne by four priests, vested in albs and red stoles. Archbishop Alemany and Bishop Francis Mora came behind the shrine and the aging Bishop Amat, exhausted by the long and tiring ceremonials, rode in a carriage. As soon as the procession reached the cathedral, the relics were deposited in the middle of the sanctuary and "a most eloquent and impressive sermon in Spanish" was delivered by the archbishop. At the end of his remarks, the clergy sang the *Te Deum,* after which Father Joachim Adam delivered a short homily in English. The ceremony ended with Benediction of the Blessed Sacrament. Early the next morning, the crystal and gilt casket containing the relics of Saint Vibiana was raised to a place in a niche above the high altar, in the tower,

Over the ensuing decades, Catholics in California's southland have regarded "the tablet which lay near her resting place, and the phial of blood" as "mute witness of her existence and sanctity." While attributing the same equivalent canonization to Vibiana as have the Roman decrees issued at different times, the various panegyrics delivered on her person have traditionally acknowledged that historically "there is no formal definition of her saintship. . . . " Rather, "the Church of the nineteenth century accepted the verdict of the Church of the third century in assigning to the pure and chaste Vibiana a place on the roll of canonized saints.

Appendix 4

Shanahan Carillon

Carillons are fairly uncommon in the United States. Only 129 true carillons and thirty-six electric-action carillons are known to experts in the field. San Fernando Mission was one of the nine places in California with such an instrument and its thirty-five electrically operated bells were known to the 35,000 tourists who annually visit the seventeenth of the Golden State's missionary outposts.

According to the Guild of Carillonneurs in North America, a carillon is a musical instrument consisting of at least two octaves of bells arranged in chromatic series. A carillon is a cast, bronze, cup-shaped bell whose partial tones are in such harmonious relationship to each other as to permit many such bells to be sounded together, in various chords with a concordant effect.

The first carillon consisted of four to eight bells, operated by hand levers. About the sixteenth century, Belgian, Dutch and northern French carillons began to be built of about thirty-five bells. The historical background of the Shanahan carillon at San Fernando Mission, the only such instrument in a Catholic Church west of the Rockies, can be traced back almost eighty years.

Shortly after Msgr. Nicholas Connelly announced plans to build Saint Monica Church in 1925, he was approached by Johanna Shanahan, an elderly Irish-born parishioner who had spent most of her life in the employ of Senator John P. Jones, founder of Santa Monica. Miss Shanahan offered to give her life savings of $11,000 if the pastor would allow a carillon to be built and installed in the bell tower of the envisioned church.

It did not take Connelly long to recognize that such a gift would impart a unique feature to his already fanciful designs. He immediately instructed his architect to make whatever modifications would be necessary to accommodate the carillon. (Generally Carillon bells do not swing; they are mounted in a stationary position and provided with clappers inside and a hammer outside if there is an automatic player).

Connelly then did some research and decided on the type of carillon then being manufactured by Felix Van Aerschodt of Louvain. In mid 1927, Connelly contacted Father Thomas K. Gorman, a student priest attached to the Diocese of Monterey-Los Angeles then studying in Rome, and asked him to explore the possibilities of engaging Van Aerschodt for the project.

The Shanahan Carillon while still located at San Fernando Mission.

It was an ideal choice. The Van Aerschodt family name had been associated with bells for centuries. Felix had been at the helm of the business since 1898. Like his father, he was a metallic sculptor, having been educated in the studios of the famed Jef Lambeaux. His reputation was widespread enough to bring invitations to exhibit at the Universal Expositions in Paris (1898), Antwerp (1894), Brussels (1910), and Ghent (1913).

Felix was among the many outstanding residents at Louvain taken captive by the invading German forces in World War I. He later escaped and went to England, where the government entrusted him with the management of a munitions factory at Spitalfields (London). Unhappily, during Felix's absence from Louvain, his foundry was sacked and mostly destroyed. His ancient models and mortars, plans and mechanisms, mountings and bas-relief ornaments, inventories and archives were forever lost. Mr. Van Aerschodt returned to Louvain after the hostilities were ended and, by 1920 was again busily at work. Despite several economic mishaps, the foundry continued in operation. Felix had recently entered into a partnership with Marcel Michiels of Tournai and it was that latter gentleman who was deputized to draft the specifications for the Santa Monica carillon.

The casting of the thirty-five bells took several years. It was decided to use a combination of 78% copper and 22% tin. They were tuned to the chromatic scale, thus allowing music to be played in all keys. The biggest of the bells weighed in at half a ton, the smallest a mere twenty-two pounds.

Miss Shanahan insisted that Michiels accompany the instrument to the United States and personally supervise its installation. Unhappily, she died on October 14, 1931 and was unable to see the carillon operational.

Michiels and Gabriel Castelain spent several agonizing months uncrating and then hoisting the thirty-five bells into place. A five-tiered iron frame was designed for that purpose inside the picturesque tower.

The bourdon-bell, weighing half a ton, was the largest of the group and was engineered to strike the hours, while a second large bell counted off the half hours. From the smallest bells on the top tier to the largest on the grand tier, they were designed to be tone perfect in their three-octave range. The largest ones were made of iron and the smaller ones of soft metal. The tiniest were fashioned from hard steel, all of which imparted evenness of tone to the ensemble.

Aside from the clock driver, the bells were played by a mechanical baton in the loft with a wire leading to each bell. Directly under the bells, Michiels provided a huge iron drum which contained numerous perforations. Pegs were placed in the holes to correspond with the notes to be sounded. When the drum revolved, the bells would strike in succession against a mechanism which activated the bells in the proper sequence.

The carillon, which one newspaper account said was "unrivalled on the west coast," was solemnly dedicated by Bishop John J. Cantwell on

Shanahan Carillon. *Source: Tom Bonner*

December *22,* 1931. Each of the bells had a sponsor for the ceremony and names were bestowed for each unit. While the bishop read the prayers, a priest climbed a ladder into the tower and sprinkled the bells with holy water. Marcel Michiels then gave a short concert. Three days later, Michiels also played carols at the Christmas Masses offered in the church.

Since so few carillonneurs were available on the west coast, Msgr. Connelly investigated the possibility, in the mid 1930s, of engineering an electronic system whereby the bells could be operated from the keyboard of the church's pipe organ. Designed by L.M. Davis and installed by John Clevenger, the automatic device operated with solenoids which activated the bell clappers. It was a crude arrangement which, surprisingly, worked quite well.

In 1956, the whole system was dismantled; its metallic frame sand-blasted and then repainted and placed back in service. During the following decade, however, the carillon was used only rarely, mostly because of its operational complexity. On at least one occasion, it went off accidentally during the night and upset the entire neighborhood before being shut off.

From the very outset, Michiels was concerned that the carillon would never achieve its maximum effect because the bells were sixty feet from the keyboard and thus not easily controlled by the over-extended wiring. And, partly due to the poor tuning and the repetitious melodies, the carillon became controversial among neighbors and others who outspokenly disliked its "noise." Connelly's dream became "Connelly's folly," and before long the irritated priest and his successors turned off the switch.

During the devastating earthquake of February 9, 1971, the bell tower at Saint Monica Church suffered structural damage and was judged unsafe to support the massive weight of the carillon. The bells were taken down and placed in storage.

When plans were announced to rebuild the church at San Fernando Mission, mortally jolted during the same 1971 tremblor, it was suggested that the carillon be installed in the newly constructed bell tower. The instrument was crated and carefully moved the twenty-four miles to Mission Hills. Installation and rewiring of the massive system was supervised by Justin Kramer. After several months of diligent work, the carillon was ready for the re-dedication ceremonies which took place on December 4,1974.

The carillon was programmed to play the *Cantica del Alba,* an ancient melody sung by the Fernandino Indians at the Old Mission. Once again the historic carillon pealed forth its beautiful tones for the glory of God.

Appendix 5

Ezcaray Altar Furnishing

The main chapel at Queen of Angels Seminary (Mission Hills, California) reflects an harmonious combination of artistic embellishments found in few public or private oratories. The seventeenth century reredos, against which the simple marble altar stands out so starkly, is carved from solid blocks of black walnut, surfaced with minutely hammered gold-leaf. It "represents a skill of workmanship, a beauty of design, and a lavishness of ornamentation that has passed from the modern scene."

The ornately executed, baroque woodwork can be traced to 1687, when Domingo Angel, a wealthy Burgos silk-manufacturer, had it installed in the chapel attached to the Congregation of Saint Philip Neri, at Ezcaray, Spain. In 1925, the chapel was dismantled and placed in storage. Some years later, the main reredos, two smaller backdrops, three wooden confessionals, a dozen carved statues, an organ and pulpit, several paintings and two bronze bells were acquired by the late Raymond Gould of Pasadena.

Shortly after its new owner's death, a group of public-minded people responded to Edward T. Foley's appeal to acquire the chapel furnishings for the southland's envisioned Cathedral of Our Lady of the Angels. On January 21, 1944, the sanctuary appurtenances were transported to San Fernando Mission, where they were partially displayed in several rooms of the *convento* building by James A. Tierney.

When sketches for the new cathedral were definitively shelved, in 1948, there were some weighty overtures made about installing the portions of the reredos in the mission church, at San Fernando. Those proposals, however, were ultimately vetoed for reasons of artistic conformity.

Shortly before the completion, in 1954, of Queen of Angels Seminary, adjacent to the mission, plans were drafted for installing the largest panels of the Ezcaray furnishings in the chapel. The extensive alternations were entrusted to Judy Serbaroli, a well-known southland artist.

The restructured reredos, resting atop a black and gold marble base, lacks much of its original embellishments. The glass reliquary of Saint Philip Neri and its statue of *Nuestra Señora del Pilar,* for example, were replaced by a simple crucifix mounted against the central panel.

To the immediate right is a statue of Saint Andrew, holding in his right hand the crossbar of the cross on which he was crucified. In the

Ezcaray reredos while it was still located at Queen of Angels Minor Seminary (now Bishop Alemany High School) in Mission Hills. *Source: Archives of the Archdiocese of Los Angeles*

opposite niche is a wooden replica of Saint Peter, with an outstretched hand which once held a chain binding the image of Satan at his feet.

Four twisted columns, each carved from a single walnut trunk, now support the upper part of the central reredos. The clusters of grapes surrounding the graceful columns are symbolic of the Precious Blood. The gold leaf on the vines is accentuated by traces of red and green polychrome.

At the left of the pinnacle is a statue of Saint James, Patron of Spain, bearing the triple crown. On the right approach is an image of Saint Teresa, one of the Iberian Peninsula's outstanding religious figures. The depiction of Saint Philip Neri, which originally occupied the central panel at the top of the reredos, was replaced by an equally attractive painting of the Madonna of the Chair.

Directly behind the white marble altar is a bas-relief bearing the seal of James Francis Cardinal McIntyre, during whose archiepiscopate the reredos was refurbished. The corresponding Gospel panel portrays Saint Francis of Assisi receiving the stigmata, while the matching side depicts the Christ Child appearing to Saint Anthony.

Further alterations were made, in 1969, when the *mensa* and its four stipes were separated from the reredos to allow for implementation of new liturgical directives. The tabernacle was moved from the altar table to an elevated platform anchored midway to the central panel of the reredos. The crucifix now has an additional prominence in the niche formerly encasing the painting of the Madonna of the Chair. The artistic, life-size candelabra and the specially designed sanctuary lamp, though not part of the original altarpieces, are a worthy complement to the overall scene.

The presence, at Mission Hills, of the centuries-old Ezcaray furnishings serves only to sustain the view that "California shines with renewed luster to the world as the home and haunt of beauty—a region where abides the creative spirit of art, and where there remains for the American world to cherish and make use of one of the most precious possessions any people may have, namely, visible symbols and links of tradition, joining the present with the past and supplying a glorious perspective for the future.'

THE RETABLO TABERNACLE

The handsomely carved tabernacle, restored by the late Hector Serbaroli, can be certainly dated from the Jubilee Year, 1672, in the pontificate of Clement X. Purchased from the Raymond Gould estate by then Auxiliary Bishop Timothy Manning, it was presented to Saint John's Seminary, where it served for many years as the Holy Thursday repository. It was moved to San Fernando and reunited with the other Ezcaray altarpieces, at Queen of Angels Seminary, on October 24, 1970. An inscription on the rear of the tabernacle reads. *"Thomas Faustius Rector ex parte fecit Scipio, Paris Matefice Aude. de ligno statuit. Antonius Maria de Brunis de Saxoferrato ex Aui. Regnante Clemente X Pont Opt. Anno Jubilei MDCLXXII."* (taken from a brochure written by the author in 1964)

Appendix 6

Whatever Happened to the Old Cathedral?

When plans for relocating the new Cathedral of Our Lady of the Angels were announced, the fate of its historic and beloved predecessor became a widely discussed topic. In November of 1996, the Los Angeles Conservancy announced the selection of a group of architects and urban experts to study the abandoned downtown cathedral. Headed by a member of the University of Southern California's School of Architecture, the panel was given three months to see if the 120 year old edifice could be converted into offices, housing, a community center, school or arts complex. Linda Dishman, the Conservancy's executive director, said her group would fund the $25,000 study because "it is incumbent on everyone to find a positive solution." For its part, the Archdiocese of Los Angeles was willing to sell the church and its property for about $5 million.[1]

An editorial later proclaimed that the Conservancy's action "offers the Civic Center's ragged northeastern edge a bit of hope." And it envisioned that efforts would "not be just a paper exercise; decaying churches here and in other cities have come back to life as performing arts centers and museums." The writer felt that "St. Vibiana's—and its dreary surroundings—deserved this last chance for a reprieve."[2]

The architectural critic for the Los Angeles Times, Nicolai Ouroussoff, wrote a few days later that the old cathedral had become "a dilapidated embarrassment unsuited to be the glorious seat of a powerful church . . . But by abandoning an admittedly dysfunctional structure, the archdiocese is also erasing much of the cathedral's historic meaning forever. Looking at the battered cathedral today, it is hard to defend it as a major architectural work. Awkwardly proportioned, the church's architecture has neither the inspiring simplicity of a New England meeting house nor the refined complexity of its European models." Nevertheless, it was "one of maybe a dozen nineteenth century structures still surviving downtown. Finding a new role for the cathedral will only add to the

---

[1]Los Angeles *Times,* November 21, 1996.
[2]Los Angeles *Times,* November 23, 1996.

structure's richness and complexity. What seems fragile now will gain a strong presence in a context of urban renewal."[3]

An exhibit was staged on the USC campus along with proposals of how best to convert the cathedral into new uses—including a facility for Immigration and Naturalization Services, a hotel for nearby Little Tokyo, senior housing, a faith center, a Latino Cultural Center, a concert hall, and a Japanese trade center. The public relations officer for the archdiocese said that "our basic attitude is that if the right buyer comes along and wants to buy the cathedral, and as long as that purpose is not a profane one, we would not object to selling."[4] All nine plans on display at USC "would save the Spanish Baroque style church and construct new buildings on the two acre property at Second and Main streets.[5]

It was then that Ira Yellin, a developer who had already restored such historic landmarks as the Bradbury Building and the Grand Central Market announced that he had been given "an exclusive option to buy the beleaguered edifice."[6]

Politicians got into the act. Mayoral candidate, Tom Hayden, introduced a bill in the state legislature to provide $1 million in matching funds to help preservationists save the structure. He said that "Los Angeles is a city that has too few memories and this is one that should not be demolished with a wrecking ball."[7]

The question of value came up. One expert felt that it was "worth about $250,000 in the non-profit world." But there were no prospective buyers. The National Trust for Historic Preservation announced that the old cathedral had made its list of America's eleven most endangered places, joining the Flathead Indian reservation in Montana and the Ellis Island National Monument in New York.[8]

Early in November the sale of Saint Vibiana Cathedral was announced in downtown Los Angeles for $4.65 million. The developer who bought the earth-quake damaged structure was Tom Gilmore, a man described by the New York *Times* as "the loudest, most ebullient true believer in the unconventional wisdom that Los Angeles has a soul—it's beautiful but down-at-the heels historic downtown, which the middle class has forgotten for years except as a movie location."[9] Gilmore said that he planned to convert the cathedral, its rectory and school building into a "trendy residential loft district." His plans for the cathedral and its adjacent

---

[3]Los Angeles *Times,* November 30, 1996.
[4]Los Angeles *Daily News,* March 22, 1997.
[5]Los Angeles *Times,* March 24, 1997.
[6]Los Angeles *Times,* October 28, 1997.
[7]Los Angeles *Daily News,* March 25, 1997.
[8]Los Angeles *Times,* June 17, 1997.
[9]New York *Times,* January 25, 2001.

buildings included classroom space for Cal State Los Angeles, a charter school, a small hotel, a new apartment building and a restaurant. Gilmore estimated that the whole complex would cost about $40 million.[10] According to Mayor Richard Riordan, "the project will not only preserve this beautiful cathedral and turn it into an important performing arts institution, but it will also play a catalytic role in downtown economic development."[11]

Monsignor Terrance Fleming, Vicar General for the Archdiocese of Los Angeles, said "we've been trying to market it for a number of years and we are very happy that someone of Mr. Gilmore's stature and experience is willing to make the investment."[12] An editorial in the city's leading newspaper proclaimed that "Tom Gilmore is either a genius or a madman. Or perhaps he is a bit of both. The developer has a gutsy new vision for the crumbling Saint Vibiana Cathedral in a gritty part of downtown." The editorial went on to say that "it's good to see that even one of the saddest parts of downtown can spark dreams."[13]

The cardinal was also pleased. He told Gilmore that "your vision and planning are very exciting and your commitment to downtown Los Angeles is a genuine blessing for us all."[14]

However, he reminded Gilmore that he would not be permitted to use the word "cathedral" or the words "St. Vibiana" in the formal name of the site or the project.[15] Later the cardinal did approve the term "Vibiana Place" to designate the old site at Second and Main streets.[16]

In early June of 2002, the former cathedral sanctuary was put to "remarkably effective use as the home of 'Crossings,' a refreshing, emotionally direct production from the Cornerstone Theater Company, using updated Bible stories to explore the journeys of Catholic immigrants to Southern California." Part of Cornerstone's Faith-Based Cycle project, the six plays' content represented Cambodia, Mexico, and Arab and African nations. Most of the cast members were from local parishes. A newspaper reviewer, Diane Haithman, said that " while these dramas may resonate more strongly for Catholics, or Catholic immigrants, the universality of experience presented in 'Crossings' provides a general audience with just enough separation between church and stage."[17]

---

[10]Los Angeles *Times,* November 2, 1999.

[11]*Daily News,* November 2, 1999.

[12]Los Angeles *Times,* November 2, 1999.

[13]Los Angeles *Times,* November 3, 1999.

[14]AALA, Roger Cardinal Mahony to Thomas Gilmore, Los Angeles, December 15, 1999.

[15]AALA, Roger Cardinal Mahony to Thomas Gilmore, Los Angeles, June 26, 2000.

[16]AALA, Roger Cardinal Mahony to Thomas Gilmore, Los Angels, February 7, 2001.

[17]Los Angeles *Times,* June 26, 2002.

Appendix 7

Tilma *of San Juan Diego*

Early in 2003, Roger Cardinal Mahony gave the Apostolate of Holy Relics permission to take the piece of Juan Diego's tilma, for many years housed in the Archival Center for the Archdiocese of Los Angeles, on a nationwide tour of twenty-one American cities. The precious relic was returned to the Cathedral of Our Lady of the Angels for the feast of San Juan Diego where it will remain permanently. The following description of the relic and how it came to be in Los Angeles is taken from a chapter in *California's Catholic Treasury* (1984).

In mid 1941, the Apostolic Delegate to Mexico invited Archbishop John J. Cantwell to make a pilgrimage to the National Shrine of Our Lady of Guadalupe. The southland prelate was anxious to comply for many reasons, mostly because "a visit by our people to the City of Mexico would be a gracious compliment to the hierarchy and Catholics of a country that has sent so many of its children to California."

A Solemn Pontifical Mass was celebrated at the Shrine on October 12th. It was a gala event, attended by a military delegation representing the president of Mexico. The entire diplomatic corps turned out to welcome the archbishop and his party.

Speaking over the National Broadcasting System from Mexico, Cantwell observed that "the missions built in California are our title deeds to show newcomers that we of the Church are in California by right of inheritance." He concluded by praying that "the traditions that made Mexico distinguished and honorable in the past may be perpetuated in a fuller measure in years to come and that the glory of days gone by may be surpassed" by the pledge of the future.

The visit marked a thawing in the delicate relations then existing between the Catholic Church and the Republic of Mexico. From all indications, the event was favorably received in all quarters. Following Cantwell's return to Los Angeles, Archbishop Luis Maria Martinez of Mexico City proposed to the Canons of the National Basilica that a most appropriate way of commemorating the visit would be to present a relic of Juan Diego's tilma to the Archbishop of Los Angeles. He pointed out that, even then, Los Angeles boasted a larger Mexican population than any city in the world outside the *Distrito Federal*.

The Canons agreed with the proposal and delegated a "Father Gomez" to personally bring a small rectangular piece of the famed tilma,

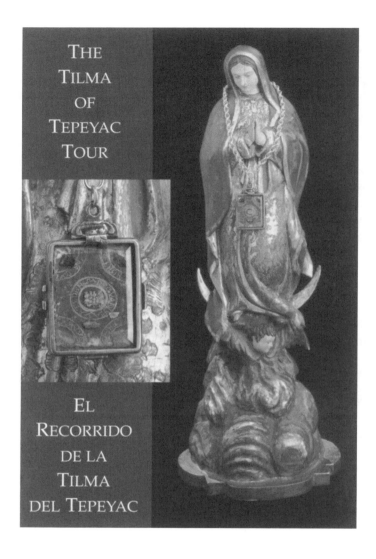

THE
TILMA
OF
TEPEYAC
TOUR

EL
RECORRIDO
DE LA
TILMA
DEL TEPEYAC

encased in a silver reliquary, to Los Angeles. Cantwell was understand-ably pleased with the gesture and received the relic with great devotion. Very likely it marked the first (and last) time a piece of the tilma had ever left Mexican soil. The archbishop entrusted the relic to Father Fidencio Esparza, a Mexican-born priest from Guadalajara, who had long been active among the southland's Hispanic community.

Late in 1981, forty years after the historic trek to Mexico by Cantwell, Timothy Cardinal Manning headed another pilgrimage to the National Shrine. Upon his return to Los Angeles, Esparza confided the relic to His Eminence for final disposal. It was then placed on display in the Historical Museum attached to the Archival Center.

The relic, the only known segment ever detached from the original tilma, is draped over an artistic 17th century statue of Our Lady of Guadalupe. And it is highly significant that it be preserved in such surroundings for beneath the tilma of Our Lady, Fray Francisco Garcia Diego y Moreno received episcopal ordination as the proto bishop of *Ambas Californias,* on October 4, 1840.[1]

---

[1]Interestingly, the titular Diocese of *Ambas Californias* was re-activated as a title for retired bishops. It is now borne by the Most Reverend John J. Ward, retired auxiliary of Los Angeles.

Appendix 8

"Triumph of David"

When Saint John Seminary College closed in 2003, it was suggested that its most treasured art object, the "Triumph of David," be removed to Los Angeles and exhibited in the Cathedral of Our Lady of the Angels. The following historical sketch and artistic description is taken from *The Tidings* for October 8, 1982.

The magnificent wool and silk tapestry known to the artistic world as the "Triumph of David" was presented to the Archdiocese of Los Angeles in 1974 by Daniel J. Donohue. Measuring twenty feet four inches wide by twelve feet nine and one half inches high, the historic work of art was subsequently hung in the Carrie Estelle Doheny Memorial Library at Camarillo.

From the initials B. B. at the lower right hand corner and the symbol of a warrior's hatchet on the opposite extreme, the tapestry can be identified as the work of Bernard Van Orley. That distinctive signature dates the tapestry as existing prior to the edict of King Charles V in 1528 which directed artists to incorporate into the galoon band at the lower right hand side of the tapestry the coat-of-arms for the city in which it was woven.

The "Triumph of David" was initially owned by Eleanor, the grandaughter of Maximillian, who married Francis I of France. Two of her aunts, Margaret of Parma and Mary of Hungary, had been among Van Orley's principal patrons. The exquisite tapestry remained in the French royal family until Louis XIII presented it to Francesco Cardinal Barberini, who sent it to his uncle, Pope Urban VIII, at the court of France.

In 1889, the Van Orley masterpiece was among the 135 tapestries acquired from the Barberini family by Charles M. Ffoulke of Washington. In 1905 the tapestry was displayed at Brussels, in a famous exhibition of old and treasured masterpieces. The catalogue for that event described and illustrated the famous Van Orley tapestry with information from a manuscript by Luco Holstenio, written on October 25, 1695. The "Triumph of David" was purchased form the Ffoulke estate by the late Earle C. Anthony in the 1930s.

The picturesque tapestry graphically illustrates the incidents related in I Samuel 18, 6-7. In the right foreground, the youthful David, with no apparent effort, carries the head of Goliath atop the decapitated giant's own sword. He is followed by King Saul, astride a richly caparisoned horse. The king, wearing a wide-brimmed hat ornamented

the Triumph of David

with tassels, holds a scepter in his left hand and gestures approval with his right one.

Included in the royal escort is Jonathan, carrying the baton of a commander. Numerous lesser armored officials follow, along with civilians wearing caps. Two helmeted soldiers and two bare-headed pages dressed in breeches and close coats with puffing sleeves, are also portrayed. The shoulder belts of the pages bear the imprint of a double eagle, symbolic for the House of Hapsburg, which ruled the Netherlands at the time the tapestry was woven.

Passing through the town gates, the crowd greets Saul and the victorious David. Young maidens are playing the harp, the hurdy-gurdy, the bagpipe and the tambourine. A youthful man manipulates the triangle, another the gongs and a third the ovular bells sewed into his clothing. While one of the musicians plays the maring trumpet, others play the flute, hautbois and drum.

In a panel, at the upper left, Saul is shown in front of his mountain tent as Abner, the captain of the hosts, introduces David, who has brought him the head of Goliath. The other side depicts a turret in the foreground and, at a distance, the walls and towers of the Elkron Temple.

The rich and decorative border is enhanced by colorful flowers, fruit and vegetables, among which can be seen carnations, iris, lilies, apples, peaches, grapes, pumpkins and the like. The two gold shields in the upper border, with the silver *fleur-de-lis* in three horizontal rows, probably reproduces the coat of arms of the patron.

Index

Page numbers appearing in italic type refer to pages that contain photos